MW00711636

Especially for:

_____

From:

_____

Date:

_____

Daily
Wisdom
for
Women

2018 Devotional Collection

BARBOUR BOOKS
An Imprint of Barbour Publishing, Inc.

© 2017 by Barbour Publishing, Inc.

Print ISBN 978-1-68322-211-8
Special edition ISBN: 978-1-944836-14-6

eBook Editions:
Adobe Digital Edition (.epub) 978-1-68322-521-8
Kindle and MobiPocket Edition (.prc) 978-1-68322-522-5

Published by Barbour Books, an imprint of Barbour Publishing, Inc., P.O. Box 719, Uhrichsville, Ohio 44683, www.barbourbooks.com

Our mission is to publish and distribute inspirational products offering exceptional value and biblical encouragement to the masses.

 Member of the
Evangelical Christian
Publishers Association

Printed in China.

Jesus first tells you, His follower, to "Come to Me" (Matthew 11:28 NKJV). Later He says, "Abide in Me" (John 15:4 NKJV). Yet you may think you must have your *behavior* fixed (read your Bible, go to church every Sunday, pray, have the perfect attitude, family, and relationships—spiritually and otherwise) before you can come to and deeply abide in Jesus. But the truth is, when you yield yourself up totally to Him, when you stop trying to live right by your own efforts, His power will come through you, allowing you to become a picture—and extension—of who He is, which will affect not only *your* life but the lives of those around you.

To aid you in coming to, abiding in, and going deeper into God's Word, the *Daily Wisdom for Women 2018 Devotional Collection* contains readings about living a life abiding in Christ (see John 15:1-12), being rooted as a branch in the Vine, having your identity seated in the eternal instead of the temporal, and doing so with the help of the Holy Spirit—the life-giving sap between the Vine (Christ) and the branch (you).

Every devotion corresponds to a particular day's reading based on Barbour's "Read Thru the Bible in a Year" plan found at the back of this book. As you read each day's devotion and focus verse, allow them to pull you into Christ's presence. Then pray around them, and walk on, making God's Word a part of your daily abiding life.

Delight in His Word

*Blessed is the man that walketh not in the counsel of the
ungodly, nor standeth in the way of sinners, nor sitteth in the
seat of the scornful. But his delight is in the law of the LORD;
and in his law doth he meditate day and night.*

PSALM 1:1-2 KJV

"That week between Christmas and New Year's Day is always so exciting for me," Meredith said to her friend, Jan, as she poured herself a second cup of coffee. "I wake up on New Year's Day with so much anticipation for the coming year."

"Really?" Jan asked, "Do you feel that way every year?"

"Yes." Meredith smiled. "And I especially love how, as I start fresh with my Bible reading plan each year, I discover how the Word of God speaks something new to me. I have notes in my Bible from years past, but lots of times, I see something new and different."

"Wow, you read your Bible every day? I don't," Jan admitted, "though I know I should."

"Well, there are days I miss. When it happens too often, I start to feel detached. I need that connection with God every day. That time really empowers me and gives me a sense of His presence. I know I've come to know Him—and myself—better through reading His Word."

---

*Lord, I make a fresh commitment to truly abide in Your Word this year.
Help me read, discover, delight, and live in Your truth.*

A Daily Walk with God

*And they heard the sound of the Lord God walking in the garden
in the cool of the day, and Adam and his wife hid themselves from the
presence of the Lord God among the trees of the garden. But the
Lord God called to Adam and said to him, Where are you?*

GENESIS 3:8-9 AMPC

Are you an on-time person or are you constantly running late? Does the tardiness of others or your own put a strain your friendships? Imagine what it would be like to have an appointment with God every day. Time allotted not to do anything in particular, but simply to spend time with Him, sharing your heart in conversation and companionship.

That must have been what it was like in those early days of Eden. How did Adam and Eve feel knowing God would come down from heaven just to spend time with them? Were they excited to see Him or did they take His presence for granted?

You can experience God each day. He desires to spend time with you. He wants you, His child, to share your heart with Him. Are you there, waiting to hear His voice? Take the time now to walk, to abide with Him today, though prayer.

*God, forgive me for allowing the busyness of life to consume me.
Remind me there is nothing more important than abiding in You.*

"The Delight of My Life"

*The moment Jesus came up out of the baptismal waters, the skies o
pened up and he saw God's Spirit—it looked like a dove—descending
and landing on him. And along with the Spirit, a voice: "This is
my Son, chosen and marked by my love, delight of my life."*
MATTHEW 3:16-17 MSG

If you're a parent, no doubt you've experienced much delight in your
children. From the moment they were born, you took pleasure in being
a part of their life, experiencing a relationship with them as you watched
them grow.

God the Father wanted a family. After Adam, the first son, who
God created from the earth, fell to sin, there was a chasm between God
and His family. Jesus came to restore that breach.

In Matthew 3:16-17, God declared Jesus to be the "delight" of His
life. Through Jesus, God is the loving Father of many sons and daughters
today—including you (see Romans 8:29).

Just as God delights in Jesus, He also delights in you. He does so
the same way you delight in your own children.

Rejoice that "the LORD takes delight in his people; he crowns the
humble with victory" (Psalm 149:4 NIV).

---

*Father, thank You for delighting in who I am and who You created
me to be. It gives me great pleasure to know I belong to You.*

Peace

In peace I will lie down and sleep,
for you alone, O LORD, will keep me safe.
PSALM 4:8 NLT

"Mommy," Christian called out as Ellen turned to leave her preschooler's bedroom, "I can't go to sleep without Bear in my bed." The family's five-year-old cocker spaniel, scheduled for minor surgery the next morning, was spending the night at the vet.

"Oh, honey," Ellen whispered, trying to soothe her son's fears. "Bear will be just fine. He'll come home from the vet tomorrow."

"But, I can't go to sleep. He always lays here by me. I don't want to be alone. Will you sleep with me tonight?" he asked.

"I'll lay down with you until you fall asleep," Ellen said. That seemed to appease Christian. She felt his tiny fingers in her hair. *It's probably what he does to Bear,* she thought.

As she lay there waiting for her son to doze off, she thought about her own need to feel safe. She remembered the many nights she laid awake, feeling alone while her husband was deployed for nine months overseas. Just a month into his deployment she discovered God's incredible promise to never leave her. Knowing He kept her safe throughout the night, she felt amazing comfort in His peaceful presence.

Thank You, Lord, for Your promise of peace.
You are always with me. You will never leave me alone.

Just Following God

*"I will make your descendants as the dust of the earth;
so that if a man could number the dust of the earth, then your
descendants also could be numbered. Arise, walk in the land
through its length and its width, for I give it to you."*
GENESIS 13:16-17 NKJV

Sarai's family worshipped other gods (see Genesis 20:12; Joshua 24:2),
yet the Lord Almighty asked her husband to leave everything they'd
ever known for a land they had never seen, saying, "Abram, pack up and
start walking. I'll show you where to go."

The Bible doesn't say if Sarai struggled with the grief of leaving
everything familiar or if she embraced it with excitement and expectation.
Whatever her attitude, Sarai followed Abram as he followed God.

Sarai and Abram, just ordinary people, trusted God for something
bigger than they could have ever imagined. They just stepped out,
confident God would deliver all He promised.

Although Sarai at some later crossroads had her moments of doubt,
struggled to believe God's promises included her, and battled her earthly
circumstances and thoughts, she continued to follow the Lord.

Like Sarai, God has called you to walk with Him. He has set *you*
apart to follow Him and live according to His way. Choose to do so today.

---

*God, I choose to walk with You. No matter what the earthly circumstances
are surrounding me, I trust You to lead me on the right path.*

Unity with the Father

*"Love your enemies and pray for those who persecute you,
that you may be children of your Father in heaven. . . .
Be perfect, therefore, as your heavenly Father is perfect."*
MATTHEW 5:44-45, 48 NIV

The biggest challenge facing you today is probably a person—what she said or did—or didn't say or do—to you or someone you love. Relationships are difficult on any level—from someone you've never met who takes *your* parking place, to your closest friend who makes a disparaging remark about you, to your perfect prince who acts like a frog.

It's easy to get caught up in the drama when someone pushes your buttons or you feel used, abandoned, mistreated, or hurt. Society is full of people looking for revenge and a way to make someone pay for wrongs done to them. As a child of God, you can choose another way—your heavenly Father's way.

He responds with grace and forgiveness to both good and evil people. He is the calm in the middle of the storm. He desires to put His love, poured out lavishly upon you, to work *in* you and let it operate *through* you. You can rest in His peace, knowing He chose a perfect way for you.

*Father, thank You for pouring Your love out on me.
I desire to walk in unity with You, allowing Your love
to flow through me and responding in peace to all.*

Consistent in Prayer

*"But when you pray, go into your room, close the door
and pray to your Father, who is unseen. Then your Father,
who sees what is done in secret, will reward you."*

MATTHEW 6:6 NIV

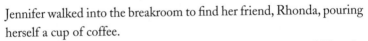

Jennifer walked into the breakroom to find her friend, Rhonda, pouring herself a cup of coffee.

"Good morning," Jennifer chirped, almost dancing toward Rhonda.

Rhonda smiled. "Look at you, all bursting with sunshine and happiness. Don't get me wrong; I'm glad to see you so cheerful, but this is three days in row. What's up?"

"I've had a hard time transitioning to my new position here, and my personal life has been a mess—as you well know. The truth is, I've not spent the time I really should in prayer, and I finally saw the movie, *War Room*, that you were telling me about. It really inspired me to take my time with God seriously. I'm making it a priority every day, and I can really tell there's a difference in my relationship with Him."

"Well, keep it up," Rhonda replied. "I'm sure your quality time with God is making a huge difference in your heart, if that glow on your face is any indication."

*Thank You, Father, for our time together. As I open my heart to You
in prayer, You pour into my spirit all I need for my day. Help me
be faithfully consistent in my prayer life. You are my priority.*

Lovingly Connected

*I look up at your macro-skies, dark and enormous, your
handmade sky-jewelry, moon and stars mounted in their settings.
Then I look at my micro-self and wonder, Why do you bother with us?
Why take a second look our way? Yet we've so narrowly missed
being gods, bright with Eden's dawn light. You put
us in charge of your handcrafted world.*
Psalm 8:3-6 msg

You have family and friends that you love. You think about them and visit them. You carry them in your heart. You feel their hurts and celebrate the good times in their lives. You desire to stay connected to them even when you're apart.

In today's verse, God is asked, "What is woman that You think about her? Not only that, but You visit her?" The writer takes notice that as God's creation, He thinks about you. He longs for a relationship with you. He wants to visit you and spend time with you. He is always with you, even when your thoughts are not on Him.

God holds you close. You are precious and valuable to Him. His relationship with you runs deeper than even the tie you share with friends and family. You are lovingly connected to the Lord of the world without end.

*God, I am Yours and You are mine. Thank You for
loving me unconditionally and desiring to have
a relationship with me. You astound me.*

Faithful Friend

The LORD kept his word and did for Sarah exactly what he had promised. She became pregnant, and she gave birth to a son for Abraham in his old age. This happened at just the time God had said it would.

GENESIS 21:1-2 NLT

God faithfully directed Abraham and Sarah as they left their friends and family to follow Him. Their journey was not without challenges and opportunities to doubt, and yet, in His own time, God proved to them His friendship and faithfulness.

God is your faithful companion as well. As you read and study God's Word, you come to know Him more and more. His Word describes His character, His nature, and His promises to you. Whatever He speaks to you through His Word, you can trust Him to do *what* He says He will—and *when* He will.

What promises has God made to you? Do you remember times when He proved Himself faithful?

Regardless of what you're going through today, God is your faithful friend. Remind yourself of His presence and His promise to walk with you—to never leave you or forsake you. Hold fast to Him and His promises!

Lord, You are my closest, most faithful friend. I trust You to keep every promise You've made to me. Because I know I can count on You, I'm holding tight to You as You walk with me through my life journey.

A Sure Foundation

*"These words I speak to you are not incidental additions to your
life, homeowner improvements to your standard of living. They are
foundational words, words to build a life on. If you work these words into
your life, you are like a smart carpenter who built his house on solid rock.
Rain poured down, the river flooded, a tornado hit—but nothing moved
that house. It was fixed to the rock."*

MATTHEW 7:24-25 MSG

Jennifer sat numbly in church. Her mind faded from the platform as
her pastor's words faded. She and her husband, Clark, were navigating
a hellish ordeal. Suffering silently, they had told no one but God.

Her heart lost, her mind continued to slip away. Her eyes fell on
a young mother sitting a few rows up from them, slowly rocking her
baby. Before Jennifer knew it, she herself was rocking, too.

As tears ran from her eyes, comforting and powerful promises
from God's Word broke into her mind. The healing scriptures she'd
read so many times, flooded her, and she began to feel alive again. As
her body moved back and forth in that same calming motion as that
mother rocking her child, Jennifer, in her heart, knew it was her Savior
gently rocking her back to life.

*When life hurts, I will run to You, God, my healer.
In Your presence I find just what I need. No matter what I'm
facing, Your healing words rock me gently back to life.*

Christlike Compassion

Suddenly, a man with leprosy approached him and knelt before him.
"Lord," the man said, "if you are willing, you can heal me and make
me clean." Jesus reached out and touched him. "I am willing," he said.
MATTHEW 8:2–3 NLT

What compels you to take the actions you take each day?

Jesus' heart of compassion compelled Him to help, to intervene, to take action. The love of God shed abroad in His heart moved Him to touch the untouchables, accept the rejected, dine with the unclean, and see those whom society preferred to remain invisible. Jesus couldn't help but reflect the heart of His heavenly Father among even the most unlovable people.

Sometimes it's difficult to see a homeless person on the street or someone who is being treated unjustly or taken advantage of. The Spirit of God living inside of you opens your eyes to see, gives you ears to hear, and softens your heart to understand in a way most people can't comprehend. Perhaps He's showing you something so you can pray for that person. Maybe He wants you to give someone a smile or say a kind word.

Allow God to speak to you about how He'd like you to respond with compassion as you walk with Him each day.

Lord, forgive me for closing my eyes to the pain others experience.
Show me how I can be Your hands and feet to those You bring
across my path, to listen and respond with a heart like Yours.

This Very Moment

LORD, You have heard the desire of the humble; You will prepare their heart; You will cause Your ear to hear, to do justice to the fatherless and the oppressed, that the man of the earth may oppress no more.
PSALM 10:17–18 NKJV

Nola climbed behind the wheel of her car and turned slowly down her street toward her son's elementary school. Although it was only a ten-minute drive, each day she was determined to experience the moments with God and her son. In those ten quiet minutes, she felt the Lord's presence as she began to pray, thanking Him for her blessings and then listening for what He might impart to her heart.

As she pulled into the pickup line and waited for her son, she smiled, knowing this was another moment in time she would never get back. As he climbed excitedly into the backseat and began to spill out the details of his day, she caught a glimpse of the sparkle in his eyes.

Determined to hold each moment close instead of wishing her life away, she drove back toward the house slowly, drinking in the experience, cataloging in her memory the things her son chose to share.

Lord, sometimes I'm filled with an urgency to look way ahead, making it difficult to live in the moment. Help me drink in the time I have with You and those I love. Help me be present in the now, this very moment.

His Promises Are True

"Behold, I am with you and will keep you wherever you go,
and will bring you back to this land; for I will not leave
you until I have done what I have spoken to you."
Genesis 28:15 nkjv

"Daddy, can we go to the fair this weekend?" ten-year-old Peyton asked. Olivia shot her husband, Richard, a knowing look, which Peyton caught instead. "I know. You have to talk about it, right?" Olivia smiled and nodded her head.

Richard and Olivia had had many conversations about promises before Peyton was ever born. Olivia's parents had failed to keep most of those they'd made to her and her siblings. As a result, trust was a big problem for her. She even once had trouble trusting God.

Richard and Olivia had agreed they'd keep their promises to their children, others, and each other. "If you promise, you deliver—even if it hurts," Olivia had told her husband on many occasions. And there'd been times when keeping a commitment had been a painful process, but they'd followed through.

Because of Richard's determination to carefully weigh commitments before making them, Olivia trusted him to deliver on his word. She and her children never doubted his promises—or God's faithfulness.

God, people have failed me, making it hard for me to trust.
But You are faithful. You have kept Your word to me. So I
know I can count on You, for You never fail to follow through.

His Hands and Feet

"Go and announce to them that the Kingdom of Heaven is near.
Heal the sick, raise the dead, cure those with leprosy,
and cast out demons. Give as freely as you have received!"
MATTHEW 10:7–8 NLT

The disciples knew Jesus. They spent years following Him around, watching everything He did and hearing everything He said. They knew intimately His character, nature, and teachings. Through His constant companionship, He prepared them for ministry. He furnished them with the resources only He could provide for their journey ahead.

As you spend time with Jesus in prayer and in the Word, you come to know the Father through Jesus, just as the disciples did. Jesus said, "If You've seen me, You've seen the Father" (see John 14:9). And as He ascended into heaven, He left them with a promise: "The Helper, the Holy Spirit, whom the Father will send in My name, He will teach you all things, and bring to your remembrance all things that I said to you" (v. 26 NKJV).

You, too, are prepared because God is with you; the Holy Spirit is your teacher. Allow Him to demonstrate His presence and His power through you. Be His hands and feet today.

God, I know You. You have made yourself real to me.
Your Holy Spirit resides in me, furnishing me with all the
wisdom, knowledge, and understanding I need for my journey.
I choose to be Your hands and feet. Work through me today.

Living the Truth

But I have trusted, leaned on, and been confident in Your mercy and loving-kindness; my heart shall rejoice and be in high spirits in Your salvation.

PSALM 13:5 AMPC

Martin Luther King Jr. said, "We must accept finite disappointment but never lose infinite hope." This statement is a good description of the biblical David's tenet.

David's life was a roller coaster ride of ups and downs. Just a few verses before the scripture shared above, David asked God, "How long must I wrestle with my thoughts and day after day have sorrow in my heart?" (Psalm 13:2 NIV).

Have you had days when God seemed distant and you were overcome with questions like these: *Has God forgotten? Did He leave me? Why can't I hear Him?*

When you abide in Christ, you are equipped to battle those negative thoughts. His Word comes alive within you, reminding you of His faithful promises.

Like David, you can hope again. You may not have the answers you think you need, but God is there—as He has always been.

David ends his prayer: "But I trust in your unfailing love; my heart rejoices in your salvation. I will sing the LORD's praise, for he has been good to me" (Psalm 13:5–6 NIV).

Lord, sometimes I struggle to see the truth. Hide me in You as I remember Your promises. You love me; You will not fail me. You are my hope and expectation.

His Miraculous Intervention

God is present in the company of the righteous. You evildoers
frustrate the plans of the poor, but the LORD is their refuge.
PSALM 14:5–6 NIV

Diane hadn't heard from her twenty-four-year-old daughter, Trena,
for months. Each attempted communication went unanswered. Diane
asked God daily to please let her hear from her daughter. Diane really
needed to know Trena was okay.

One Sunday morning Diane's heart ached to hear Trena's voice. Tears
streamed down her face as she drove a few miles to church. Emotion
washed over her and she could barely see the lines of her parking space
in the church parking lot.

She composed herself and went into the building. Unable to focus
on the message, deep in her heart she cried out to God, praying for her
daughter as she sat there.

After church she walked slowly out of the building. As she raised
her head to look toward her car, her heart leaped. Trena stood in front
of her—just outside the doors. *Oh, God, how You love me—and Trena.*
Thank You, she prayed.

Trena had had no idea Diane was in church that day. Miraculously
God had led Trena straight to her mother.

Thank You, Lord, for Your constant presence. You are at work,
perfecting those things that concern me, even when I don't see them.
I trust You for divine intervention in my situation today.

When He Calls Your Name

*Then God appeared to Jacob again, when he came from Padan Aram,
and blessed him. And God said to him, "Your name is Jacob; your name
shall not be called Jacob anymore, but Israel shall be your name."*
GENESIS 35:9–10 NKJV

Brendan called to his four-year-old daughter, "Sierra, it's time to go." He
watched her stop short in front of the swing set and turn toward him.
He could see her bottom lip begin to pout as she dropped her head and
crossed her arms. He walked closer to her and reached for her hand.

"Daddy," she said, looking up at him, "my name is not Sierra—I'm
Rain."

Here we go again, Brendan thought. For the past few days, his
daughter had refused her first name, insisting everyone call her by her
middle name, Rain. He'd told his wife, Carolyn, "I hate it when kids
go by their middle names."

"Well, maybe we should pray about it. So far she's not giving this
up," Carolyn replied. "Names are really important. Maybe there's a
reason she so strongly identifies with her middle name. After all, God
changed people's names in the Bible, remember?"

Brendan's voice softened. "Okay. Let's pray and see where God leads."

*Jesus, You know who I am. When You call my name, You have my
attention. When You speak to me, I'm reminded of all You have done.
Thanks for giving me Your name and the authority that comes with it.*

Sweet Surrender

*Come to Me, all you who labor and are heavy-laden and overburdened,
and I will cause you to rest. [I will ease and relieve and refresh your souls.]*
MATTHEW 11:28 AMPC

If you have ever stood under a powerful waterfall, the water—though it pummeled your body—offered a sense of fresh renewal. Jesus said if you come to Him, He will refresh your soul. He offers spiritual rest. Unlike physical rest, one definition of *spiritual rest* is "to cease from striving."

Spiritual rest offers a place of sweet surrender. In his book *The Saints' Everlasting Rest,* seventeenth-century English Puritan church leader, poet, hymn writer, and theologian Richard Baxter said, "They who seek this rest [to cease from striving] have an inward principle of spiritual life. God does not move men like stones, but He endows them with life, not to enable them to move without him, but in subordination to himself, the first mover."

Jesus is calling you to a higher place of rest. As you move in Him and with Him, you can let go of those things you are trying to control and can experience His sweet, easy rest.

Jesus, I want to experience the spiritual rest You have for me. I let go of my control and submit to Your direction. I stand under the waterfall of Your spiritual rest and will not move except to do so in step with You.

Whispers of Love

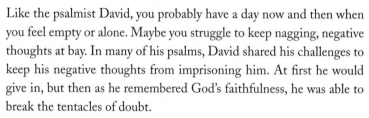

I am praying to you because I know you will answer, O God. Bend down and listen as I pray. Show me your unfailing love in wonderful ways.
PSALM 17:6–7 NLT

Like the psalmist David, you probably have a day now and then when you feel empty or alone. Maybe you struggle to keep nagging, negative thoughts at bay. In many of his psalms, David shared his challenges to keep his negative thoughts from imprisoning him. At first he would give in, but then as he remembered God's faithfulness, he was able to break the tentacles of doubt.

When those self-assaulting thoughts come to the forefront of your mind, refuse the lies and focus on the many times God has come through for you. He loves you with an everlasting love. He is faithful. He will never leave you. He is with you always. He has given you a future and a hope.

Remind yourself of God's Word, just as David did, and doing so will bring you back to your spiritual senses. As the light of God's truth makes its way in, you will begin to break free. His promises remove the prison bars of doubt so that you can hope again.

God is there—as He has always been. Listen quietly for the gentle whispers of His unfailing love.

Thank You, God, for Your whispers of love. When negative thoughts challenge me to give in and doubt, I will remember Your mercy, compassion, and faithfulness. Lord, hear my prayer.

Irrefutably His

Then Pharaoh said to his officials, "Isn't this the man we need? Are we going to find anyone else who has God's spirit in him like this?" So Pharaoh said to Joseph, "You're the man for us. God has given you the inside story—no one is as qualified as you in experience and wisdom."

GENESIS 41:38–39 MSG

After years of living far from where they'd grown up, high school sweethearts Rachel and Blake took the kids home to family and friends. They both found jobs in the city and bought a house in the small community they'd grown up in. Their children would finally have support from grandparents, aunts, uncles, and cousins.

One afternoon as their daughter, Abby, waited outside the middle school gym for her mother to pick her up, a woman around Abby's mother's age approached her.

"Hi," the stranger said, "I'm Pam. Could your mother's name possibly be Rachel?"

Abby was startled at first but relaxed when the woman continued, "I knew your mother when we were kids. You look exactly like her. I heard your family moved back to town." At that moment, Rachel arrived and the two former classmates were delighted to reconnect.

"She's undeniably your child," Pam said several times.

When you reflect God's character, do others recognize you as His child?

God, I belong to You. Help me make decisions that reflect Your character so others will recognize me as irrefutably Yours.

Lights On

For You cause my lamp to be lighted and to shine; the Lord my
God illumines my darkness. . . . As for God, His way is perfect!
Psalm 18:28, 30 AMPC

Often, as shadows fall and the night rolls in, some people fail to turn on their headlights while driving. Whether it's dusk or dawn, rain or fog, some drivers are forgetful or distracted or refuse to use their lights, a powerful personal safety feature that takes little effort to switch on and provides much safer conditions for everyone in their path.

Abiding in Christ keeps your spiritual lights on—no matter how much the enemy wants to distract you and make you forget that God is on your side. No matter what the "road" conditions, as you maintain a constant connection with Christ, your heart light remains bright.

God's presence is a constant, guiding light that brightens your path and assures your footing along the road He has set you on. No matter how dark it seems, whether fog or storms roll in, you can see where to go and the direction to take as He leads you.

Lord, You are always with me. As I abide in You, You illuminate the
darkness and light the path You have set before me. I will follow You today,
knowing that in the light of Your presence, I'll find my way perfectly.

Secrets of the Kingdom

He replied, "You are permitted to understand the secrets of the Kingdom of Heaven, but others are not. To those who listen to my teaching, more understanding will be given, and they will have an abundance of knowledge. But for those who are not listening, even what little understanding they have will be taken away from them."

MATTHEW 13:11–12 NLT

"Mom, how do you know me so well?" Cameron asked. "Others don't get me, but somehow you see me in a way no one else does."

Katelyn paused the TV show they were watching and looked at her son. "Well, I've learned the secrets of the kingdom," she said. "I understand you on a deeper level because I've been given insight and discernment into who you are. I've asked God to give me understanding so I can help you become the man He created you to be."

Jesus told stories to crowds, but His disciples, who were also listening, were given more knowledge than those who saw Jesus only on the surface. When you live in Christ and walk closely with Him, when you go deep with Him, you, too, will see and experience more than those who know Him superficially.

Lord, I want to know the secrets of the kingdom. Give me ears to hear, eyes to see, and a heart that understands You on a deeper level. Help me live my life in accordance with the purpose You destined me for each day.

Let Your Soul Return

*The law of the LORD is perfect, converting the soul; the testimony
of the LORD is sure, making wise the simple; the statutes of the
LORD are right, rejoicing the heart; the commandment
of the LORD is pure, enlightening the eyes.*
PSALM 19:7–8 NKJV

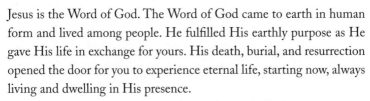

Jesus is the Word of God. The Word of God came to earth in human form and lived among people. He fulfilled His earthly purpose as He gave His life in exchange for yours. His death, burial, and resurrection opened the door for you to experience eternal life, starting now, always living and dwelling in His presence.

You grow in relationship with your heavenly Father as you come to understand Him and His ways through the Bible. Psalm 19:7 says, "The law of the LORD is perfect, converting the soul." The law—or the scriptures from God's Word—renews your soul. As you live and breathe in the wisdom and knowledge God has revealed to you through His words, your soul is made new in Him.

Just as the sun restores a darkened earth's light, the word of God restores your entire person, bringing your mind, will, and emotions back to that divine connection for which you were created—a relationship with Him.

*Jesus, I desire Your truth found in the Holy Scriptures
as much as I desire sunlight. Let Your Word renew my
soul and bring me into a closer relationship with You.*

The Strength That Does Not Fail

But [Joseph's] bow remained strong and steady and rested in the
Strength that does not fail him, for the arms of his hands were
made strong and active by the hands of the Mighty God of Jacob,
by the name of the Shepherd, the Rock of Israel.
GENESIS 49:24 AMPC

It's often easy to fight the battle on your own or try to fix things yourself, failing to remember that God stands ready to supply you with His strength. Whether the fight you face is physical or spiritual in nature, your rescue depends on your willingness to invite God to step in.

Joseph endured great adversity, starting with his older brothers selling him into slavery as a young boy. Each battle Joseph faced required courage and faith in God to rescue him and provide him with strength. Joseph's bow remained strong because he relied on God's strength. God's hands supported Joseph as he used his weapon against his enemies.

As you endure difficulties, burdens, and persecution, remember that you don't have to fight alone. God is with you and has provided you with the strength that does not fail.

God, remind me that I don't have to do things on my own. Please give
me the strength I need to face hardships. I believe that as I follow You,
I cannot fail. You will fight for me. All I have to do is invite You in.

No More Sinking Feeling

Peter, suddenly bold, said, "Master, if it's really you, call me to come to you on the water." He said, "Come ahead." Jumping out of the boat, Peter walked on the water to Jesus. But when he looked down at the waves churning beneath his feet, he lost his nerve and started to sink. He cried, "Master, save me!"

MATTHEW 14:28–30 MSG

Have you ever been hopeful about something—like getting a position you have applied for or the house you have put an offer on—but then couldn't seem to shake that sinking feeling?

Perhaps you were simply overthinking the situation, running dozens of what-ifs over in your mind. Or perhaps, even though you may have believed God had given you an opportunity and you were semiconfident it would all work out, you just didn't want to be disappointed.

No matter what the cause, when you do get that sinking feeling, remember that God will not disappoint. He opened the door and you walked through. So trust Him and ask Him to help you let go of that sinking feeling.

Pray about it. And exchange your what-ifs for His Word.

Lord, when that sinking feeling tries to attach itself to me, I will remember I don't have to fight it on my own. Instead, I will come to You in prayer, hold on to Your Word, and be buoyed by Your promises.

Let Go and Let God

And Moses said to God, Who am I, that I should go to Pharaoh and bring
the Israelites out of Egypt? God said, I will surely be with you; and this
shall be the sign to you that I have sent you: when you have brought the
people out of Egypt, you shall serve God on this mountain [Horeb, or Sinai].
EXODUS 3:11–12 AMPC

When the Jews were slaves in Egypt, Pharaoh ordered all their male children to be murdered. As Moses was just three months old, his mother Jochebed knew she couldn't hide him anymore, so she did only what she knew to do—she gave him to God, trusting Him to take care of her son (see Exodus 2:3). In her hands, Moses could be found out; but in God's hands, he became the deliverer of his people.

As Jochebed released the basket that held her baby boy, she didn't know what would happen. She didn't know God's plan, but she trusted God to go with, protect, and keep her baby.

What has God asked you to entrust to Him? He can do a greater work than you can ever imagine, but you have to be willing to let go and let God.

God, I've held tightly to some things. You know what they are.
Today I release them to you, trusting You to do a
greater work than I can ever imagine.

Revelation Just for You

Jesus replied, "Blessed are you, Simon son of Jonah, for this was not revealed to you by flesh and blood, but by my Father in heaven."
MATTHEW 16:17 NIV

Do you ever just have a sort of knowing in your heart about something? Perhaps there have been times in your life when you have had a prompting to do something, like go a different route to work, and after you did so, you discovered you'd avoided an accident. Or you were prompted to call someone immediately, only to find out she needed your prayers or encouragement at that moment.

Or sometimes the Lord may give you an idea or a question to ask one of your children, and you end up learning about something that's going on in their lives or the occasion becomes an opportunity to instruct or teach them—or yourself. Other times, it's a knowing in your heart that, when you follow it, keeps you from danger or positions you for promotion.

God often gives you insight and revelation to walk out your journey with Him. He is always there, ready to show you the path to take, the word to say, or the move to make. His job is to speak into your life. Your job is to listen and obey.

Heavenly Father, I want to hear Your voice. I will listen quietly to what You are revealing to me today. Give me insight into Your plan and help me follow Your instructions.

Quiet Moments

*The LORD is my shepherd; I shall not want. He makes me to
lie down in green pastures; He leads me beside the still waters.
He restores my soul. . . . Yea, though I walk through the valley
of the shadow of death, I will fear no evil; for You are with me.*
PSALM 23:1–4 NKJV

You live in a loud world. From the busy rush hour traffic to the constant
noise from technology, it's easy to fill every moment to capacity with the
sounds and activities of life. E-mails, social media, texts, and phone calls
constantly interrupt the tasks you have to do for yourself and others. It's
easy to become distracted and perhaps too busy for the Lord.

If you are not intentional about spending time with God, before
you know it, you have become distant or have detoured away from Him.
You find your soul is hungry for His presence and peace.

God is calling you to reconnect. No matter where you are, when you
recognize your need for Him, stop whatever you are doing and step away
from others. Once you are alone with Him, establish a reconnection.
Allow His presence to wash over you and restore your soul.

*Lord, my peace comes from You. Forgive me when I become too busy.
When life begins to consume me, speak to my heart and draw me to You.
Help me disconnect from the busyness of this world and reconnect with Yours.*

In the Middle of It All

Six days later Jesus took Peter and the two brothers, James and John, and led them up a high mountain to be alone. . . . Peter exclaimed, "Lord, it's wonderful for us to be here!" . . . But even as he spoke, a bright cloud overshadowed them, and a voice from the cloud said, "This is my dearly loved Son, who brings me great joy. Listen to him."

MATTHEW 17:1, 4, 5 NLT

You may have experienced some rough patches in your life, a time when you were discouraged, praying and standing in faith day after day yet getting no tangible results. And then, *wham!* God showed up in an amazingly big way.

That's when you realized that God was at work the whole time; you just couldn't see all that He was doing. And then there was good news and answered prayers all around.

Times like those should encourage you. For answered prayer will give you the courage to trust God more in the times when it seems like He's silent. In future challenges, you will find yourself even more confident that He will be at work in the middle of it all—even as you speak.

God, You are in the middle of it all. Thank You for being so faithful, always at work, providing Your very best for me! Thanks for giving me the confidence to trust You more every day.

Right in Step with Your Guide

*The secret [of the sweet, satisfying companionship] of the Lord
have they who fear (revere and worship) Him, and He will show
them His covenant and reveal to them its [deep, inner] meaning.*
PSALM 25:14 AMPC

In times of doubt, you may think your ship sailed without you, and you may be tempted to sink into a sea of regret. Instead, consider that perhaps it wasn't your ship that sailed after all.

How many times has someone literally missed a boat or plane and it saved his or her life? People missed the Titanic and lived to tell about it. What about those who didn't go in to work at the Twin Towers or missed their flight on one of the planes that crashed on 9/11?

When you find yourself in a place where you think you have "missed it," take a moment to look at it from a different perspective. You don't have to lose your peace over it. You can embrace the moment with a fresh perspective. With the Holy Spirit as your guide, you can rest in God's promise to reveal His purpose and plan. "In all things God works for the good of those who love him, who have been called according to his purpose" (Romans 8:28 NIV).

*Holy Spirit, lead me in the way I should go. I want to
fulfill my purpose. Thank You for revealing Your plans to me.*

Press in a Little More

For where two or three are gathered together in my name,
there am I in the midst of them.
MATTHEW 18:20 KJV

Just a few days into the chaotic workweek and Angie's head and heart hurt. The merger had taken everything out of her as she watched people she'd known for years get moved around to other departments, receive assignments to other states, or lose their jobs completely. She just wanted to go home and sleep, but she'd committed to attend the women's meeting tonight at her church.

She knew she needed to be there. She hadn't spent much time with the Lord with her long work days. She downed a protein shake and drove to the church. The worship music soothed her and she was able to relax a little.

Lord, I need a fresh drink of your love. I'm tired. I don't know how much more I can take. Suddenly a hush fell over the sanctuary as the music slowed to an unhurried and peaceful song. Women all over the sanctuary began to move toward the altar without anyone asking them to do so.

Angie sensed the Lord calling her. He was there, just as He'd promised, in the midst of them. She walked forward and He met her there.

Lord, I don't want to miss an opportunity to experience You.
Your presence fills and refreshes me. Help me recognize when
I need to press into Your love just a little more.

One Graceful Step

Wait patiently for the LORD. Be brave and courageous.
Yes, wait patiently for the LORD.
PSALM 27:14 NLT

The first month of 2018 is over. You'd hoped and prayed this year would bring a fresh start with the potential for. . .near *perfection*?

Yet the laundry is still piles high. You are still several pounds away from your goal weight. You have chosen to forgive a loved one, but the process feels daunting, messy, and uncomfortable. So today, when you read Matthew 18:21–35, it may seem challenging to continue to forgive and love others as Jesus has commanded.

But maybe a new year isn't about fighting or toiling to have everything under control. One of the most important steps is the one you are taking right now. As you abide in God's Word, you are already patiently putting one foot in front of the other with Jesus by your side. Today you can lean in, and find wisdom in these Old Testament words, "The Lord will fight for you, and you shall hold your peace and remain at rest" (Exodus 14:14 AMPC).

Wherever you are at in your faith walk, just remember, one month down and eleven more to go this year! That's one grace-filled step toward progress.

Lord, before I put away the laundry, head to the gym, or reach out to a friend, I desire to have the right priorities. Today, please show me one step I can take toward abiding in You. Fill me, Jesus.

Spring Eventually Comes

*The LORD is my strength and my song; he has given me victory. This is my
God, and I will praise him—my father's God, and I will exalt him!*
Exodus 15:2 NLT

Back in 1887, a groundhog in Punxsutawney, Pennsylvania, began
predicting the weather on Groundhog Day, February 2. If this highly
acclaimed meteorologist comes out from his hole and sees his shadow,
that means six more weeks of winter weather. But if Punxsutawney
Phil doesn't see his shadow, spring will come early. The bottom line?
Spring eventually comes, regardless of whether or not the groundhog
sees his shadow.

Wouldn't it be nice if something or someone would predict *your*
future? Will the figurative storms in your life continue to rage or cease?
How long will a season of hardship and suffering continue? Regardless
of today's shadow, spring will inevitability come in your own life. The
cold, dark, bitter challenges you might be facing will eventually end.
As you cling to the promises found in Scripture, you will find hope.
Blossoms will bloom!

David, who understood these complexities, said, "The LORD is my
strength and shield. I trust him with all my heart. He helps me, and
my heart is filled with joy. I burst out in songs of thanksgiving" (Psalm
28:7 NLT).

*Father, whether I'm walking through heavy snowdrifts or
dancing in a field of lilies, I'll praise You because I believe
that spring is on its way or has already come!*

Not by Works

Jesus looked at them and said, "With man this is impossible,
but with God all things are possible."
MATTHEW 19:26 NIV

The disciples seemed perplexed. They'd been engaging in a conversation with Jesus, asking Him who could enter the kingdom of heaven. Jesus' response didn't make a lot of sense to them; maybe that's because it wasn't what they'd expected or wanted to hear.

Living under God's authority is often counterintuitive but always what you need. David said, "The LORD rules over the floodwaters. The LORD reigns as king forever. The LORD gives his people strength. The LORD blesses them with peace" (Psalm 29:10–11 NLT).

The disciples continued their conversation, asking Jesus who could be saved if a rich, commandment-obeying man could not. Jesus said that entering the kingdom of God was impossible for anyone to do on his or her own strength.

Why did Jesus say this? Because often you might try to be justified by your good works. Yet your accomplishments, or good deeds, aren't what pave the way to the promised land. It's the grace of God that sustains you and allows you to enter into communion with Him here on earth and in heaven.

Lord, You are my daily portion. Help me not to live a life that is
about measuring up or checking things off of my to-do list.
I come to You, longing for Your hope, mercy, and grace.

Grace Given

So the last shall be first, and the first last:
for many be called, but few chosen.
MATTHEW 20:16 KJV

Is receiving grace a hard concept for you to accept from God? Often it may be easier to extend grace to another person as opposed to extending it to yourself or receiving grace from another.

You might follow all of the commandments (see Exodus 20:3–17) or sing praises to the Lord (see Psalm 30), but you still feel like something isn't right between you and God. Could it be that something is holding you captive? Enslaving you to the point where there is a figurative barricade between you and God?

The parable of the workers in the vineyard, found in Matthew 20:1–16, is about God's grace in your life. Sometimes it doesn't feel fair when grace is given to others. You might want justice. Yet when the tables are turned, it may be hard for you to receive unmerited favor.

Why some people are given their fair share, others less, and some more doesn't always seem to make sense. What is clear is that God loves you no matter what! Even when circumstances in your life don't make sense, abide in Him. As you do, watch the barricade in your life come tumbling down because you are open to the grace He gives.

Lord Jesus, I come to You with the desire to place You first in my life.
I choose to receive Your grace and extend it to others.

To Serve or Not to Serve?

"You must serve only the LORD your God."
EXODUS 23:25 NLT

Jesus responded to a question asked by James and John regarding service and leadership:

"You know that the rulers in this world lord it over their people, and officials flaunt their authority over those under them. But among you it will be different. Whoever wants to be a leader among you must be your servant, and whoever wants to be first among you must become your slave. For even the Son of Man came not to be served but to serve others and to give his life as a ransom for many."
MATTHEW 20:25–28 NLT

Jesus must have understood David's heart when he said, "Love the LORD, all you godly ones! For the Lord protects those who are loyal to him, but he harshly punishes the arrogant" (Psalm 31:23 NLT).

As you go about the day, be mindful of who you are serving—Jesus Christ—and how you can serve others out of the love you have for Him. Focus on serving God and leading by His example. Doing so will be more fruitful and satisfying than anything this world has to offer.

Jesus, I need to remain connected to You by serving and leading in the ways that glorify You. May my life be an instrument—a reflection—of You.

Fixed and Focused

I trusted in, relied on, and was confident in You,
O Lord; I said, You are my God.
PSALM 31:14 AMPC

Trusting God might sometimes seem attainable. Other times, not so much. Factoring in things like your background, upbringing, childhood, and the relationships you have experienced throughout life, trust might be a very difficult thing to do.

If trusting God seems like it's nearly impossible, you might be tempted to put your faith and hope into things and people. This is because they might seem to be able to provide a quick fix or instant gratification. Yet the paradox is that as you abide in Jesus, all you need is to trust *Him* with things and people.

In Psalm 31 David petitions for God to shower His grace and mercy on him, for help and protection in regard to his enemies. He cries out to God in desperation for the challenges in this life, looking for—and expecting—God to fight for him.

Can you relate to David's pleas when you consider the stories and struggles both you and your fellow brothers and sisters face? No matter what's happening, know that God is able. Have mustard seed faith to trust in, rely on, and be confident in His faithfulness, and He will lead you to victory.

Jesus, I trust You in the good and hard times. Holy Spirit,
please fill me with the ability to stay fixed and focused on You.

Expectant Faith

Be strong and let your heart take courage,
all you who wait for and hope for and expect the Lord!
PSALM 31:24 AMPC

When was the last time you clung to scripture in the same way a little child, with a white-knuckled grip, held on to her daddy's pant leg? How long has it been since you had the kind of childlike faith that believed, with expectancy, that God would grant you victory, bring about deliverance, or provide a miraculous breakthrough in your life?

If you have been a bit detached in your faith walk, today is your day to turn things around! To reconnect with expectant faith, find a Bible promise and mark it with a highlighter, pen, pencil, or child's crayon. Or write on a note card whatever stands out to you in a chapter, passage, or verse. Then hang that card up where you will see it regularly, such as on a bathroom mirror, the refrigerator, or the dashboard of your car. Pray the words you'd like to memorize over whatever area in your life you need God's help.

Above all, take courage and find strength in the Lord. His words are sovereign and faithful.

Jesus, I want to cling to Your truth and abide in You.
Thank You for providing Your Word and Your promises.
You are all I want. You are all I need. You are my expectation!

First Things First

*"'Love the Lord your God with all your heart and with all your soul
and with all your mind.' This is the first and greatest commandment.
And the second is like it: 'Love your neighbor as yourself.'"*
MATTHEW 22:37–40 NIV

A Pharisee who was considered an expert in the law tested Jesus by asking Him, "What is the greatest commandment?"

Jesus told the man that first, above all things, he must love God with all his being. Second, he must love others as he loved himself.

Jesus' reason for His answer is twofold. First, Jesus knows you may struggle sometimes with keeping Him first in your life. Second, Jesus knows it's sometimes not very easy to love and forgive someone who has hurt or sinned against you, even if that someone is yourself.

Take a moment now to love God with your whole being. Then do some self-reflecting. See if there's something for which you need to forgive yourself—and do so. Then extend that same love and forgiveness toward others. Ah, how freeing! Like David, you can now say to God, "You are my hiding place; you will protect me from trouble and surround me with songs of deliverance" (Psalm 32:7 NIV).

*Jesus, You are the greatest thing in my life! I revel in the love You have
for me, the love I have for others and myself, and the love I have for You.
Thank You for helping me set my priorities straight.*

I Am

I will dwell among the children of Israel and will be their God.
And they shall know that I am the LORD their God, who brought
them up out of the land of Egypt, that I may dwell among them.
I am the LORD their God.

EXODUS 29:45–46 NKJV

The Bible gives many names for God: Yahweh, Abba, Elohim, El-Shaddai, Jehovah, and Adonai, to name a few. The Bible also speaks of many attributes that can remind you of who God is in your life: faithful, provider, advocate, vindicator, liberator, the great I AM, and friend. Often it is during the darkest hours of life that you find yourself crying out to God, perhaps praying and referring to Him with these names and attributes.

As you read this devotion, where are you at? Take inventory of your thought and prayer life. Recall the times God has been faithful to you, when He figuratively brought you out of the land of Egypt and provided supernatural breakthroughs. Reflect on "who" He is being in your life right now. Then, whatever name or attribute best fits Him, take the psalmist's advice and "Sing to him a new song; play skillfully, and shout for joy" (Psalm 33:3 NIV).

Lord, here I am. I have a lot on my plate today, but You are
bigger than my circumstances. I choose to recite Your names,
recount Your attributes, and sing to You a new song!

Wait and Watch

Our soul waits for the LORD; He is our help and our shield. For our heart shall rejoice in Him, because we have trusted in His holy name. Let Your mercy, O LORD, be upon us, just as we hope in You.
PSALM 33:20–22 NKJV

About six months after moving into her new apartment, Janice was still looking for a church to join. She continued to attend some of the local churches and read the Bible regularly but was getting restless to settle into a community of believers.

One day while Janice was walking home from the bus stop, a woman she had regularly seen on the same route started chatting with her. Her name was Amy. She had seen Janice reading a Bible on the bus. Over the next several days, Janice and Amy talked about their faith. Amy invited Janice to check out the church she attended. That Sunday the two of them went, and Janice felt right at home.

At times Janice had been frustrated about finding a new church. But now she knew God had heard her prayers and had put someone in her life to help her find her way. She was thankful she hadn't rushed the process but had waited and watched for God to move.

Lord, reveal Yourself to me as I hold tightly to You and Your Word. Give me Your wisdom and patience as I wait on You. Help me be open and receptive to Your divine appointments.

Resting during Delays

*The LORD replied, "I will personally go with you, Moses,
and I will give you rest—everything will be fine for you."*
EXODUS 33:14 NLT

Home on furlough, Beth watched as the snow gently fell onto her family's back porch. She admired how the fresh flakes glazed the New England scenery. It was breathtaking to witness the still-falling snow topping the snow that had fallen overnight, making for a grand total of fifteen inches within twenty-four hours!

Beth had hoped to get out of the house to meet some friends, run a few errands, and take in the sights and sounds she'd missed while being away on mission. But the snow forced her to stay inside and rest.

Beth was a bit worried about having to reschedule her appointments. She had only one more week left before traveling back to Haiti. But for now she handed over her concerns, her desire to meet with others, and her schedule to God.

Whatever rescheduling you might be facing today, take a deep breath. Delays can be an opportunity for rest.

---

*God, help me place every detail about my schedule into Your hands.
It takes faith to let go and rest, because then I have to trust Your hands
are at work even when mine aren't. Thank You for the assurance of
knowing that everything will be fine for me and help me accept
your divine delays with a peaceful heart and mind.*

Playdate

*"So you, too, must keep watch! For you do
not know the day or hour of my return."*
MATTHEW 25:13 NLT

Jessica took her kids to the park where she met Jennifer, who was new in the neighborhood and desperate to connect with other moms. Through their initial conversation, Jessica learned that her daughter and Jennifer's had been born within a few days of each other.

Jessica said, "Our girls are the same age. I know we don't know each other well, but would you be up for a playdate sometime?"

"Sure!" said Jennifer, smiling.

A week later the two moms and their girls had a playdate. While their little girls ran around the playground giggling, Jessica and Jennifer got to know each other better. Jessica shared how several years earlier she had walked through a challenging season that really changed her perspective on faith and family. She told Jennifer, "After what my husband and I walked through, I couldn't help but ask myself, 'Am I really serious about what I believe in? Do I really know where I'm going when I die?'"

When was the last time you got together with a young mom or neighbor? Pray for her and ask God to open a door so that you can have a grown-up "playdate."

Lord, I don't know when You will return—and that's okay. Until then, help me watch for women with whom I can share Your good news.

A Standing Ovation

"His master replied, 'Well done, good and faithful servant!
You have been faithful with a few things; I will put you in charge
of many things. Come and share your master's happiness!'"
MATTHEW 25:23 NIV

As the Olympic figure skater nears the end of her performance, she nails all her landings. While the music fades, she comes to a graceful halt. Her eyes gaze into the crowd of people as they give her a standing ovation.

With a smile that beams from ear to ear, she skates her way over to her coaches. They embrace her as they wait to receive the judges' remarks. Several minutes later, to her surprise, the figure skater is rewarded with what she had trained so hard for: Olympic gold.

As the 2018 Winter Olympics in PyeongChang, South Korea, are well under way, scriptures tell us that the most important training you can commit to is faithfully serving and abiding in God's Word. Like an Olympic athlete that can be so intensely focused on winning the prize, focus on being faithful to Jesus Christ, Father God, and His Word, because in God's eyes there is—and will be—a standing ovation waiting for you!

Lord, here I am. Speak to me through Your Word. I want to receive all the rewards You have in store for me. I desire to one day hear you say, "Well done good and faithful servant!"—which will be the best reward of all.

Remember You Are Loved

My soul shall be joyful in the LORD; it shall rejoice in His salvation.
PSALM 35:9 NKJV

According to History.com's article, "History of Valentine's Day," "approximately 150 million Valentine's Day cards are exchanged annually, making Valentine's Day the second most popular card-sending holiday after Christmas"!

So today you might find yourself consumed with sharing in the message of love and affection toward others. Maybe you remembered to get your loved ones Valentine's Day cards or you will be commemorating your affection for them in some other way.

As you rejoice over others, also rejoice in the Lord whose love saved you from the penalties of sin and death. As you share in the joy of showering others with cards, gifts, or flowers, remember that the joy of the Lord resides in you. And whether or not you receive a Valentine's Day card, remember that in His eyes you are enough.

On this day, which is also Ash Wednesday, the beginning of Lent, remember you are loved, cherished, and redeemed. You were saved and celebrated in a way far more valuable than the receipt of any greeting card! "God in your midst, The Mighty One, will save. . .quiet you with His love. . .rejoice over you with singing" (Zephaniah 3:17 NKJV).

Jesus, thank You for loving me and for dying on the
cross for my sins. Help me love others the way You do.
And be Your vessel for sharing the joy of salvation.

An Assignment

Moses proceeded to do everything
just as the LORD had commanded him.
EXODUS 40:16 NLT

On this second day of Lent, today's verse might remind you of how important it is to obey the Lord. Is God calling you to fast from something during this Lenten season? Is He prompting you to take a step of faith in a certain area of your life?

You read today in Exodus 40 that Moses was appointed by the Lord to build the tabernacle. This was no small task. It was a very detailed, time-consuming assignment. But after Moses finished this major effort, the glory of the Lord filled the tabernacle (see Exodus 40:33–35).

And in today's reading of Matthew 26:1–35, you were given insight into the final days of Jesus on earth. Jesus' work was to save us from our sins, an assignment for which He endured the pain of the cross. Yet on the other side of this earthly appointment was the glory of the Lord.

Perhaps God has called you to do something bold for Him. It could be sharing the Good News with a friend, coworker, neighbor, or family member. It could be going on a mission trip. Whatever it may be, ask the Lord to prepare you and show you the next step toward your assignment.

Jesus, show me the next step of faith in all areas of my life,
including the ones I've been hesitant to embark on.

Paid in Full

*Going a little farther, he fell with his face to the ground
and prayed, "My Father, if it is possible, may this cup
be taken from me. Yet not as I will, but as you will."*

MATTHEW 26:39 NIV

Knowing what was ahead of Him, what God wanted Him to do in obedience to the calling on His life, Jesus walked through the pain that led to promise.

You may never fully know or understand the suffering Jesus went through to endure the cross on your behalf. But it's reassuring that when Jesus was on earth, He understood what it meant to endure challenging circumstances like the ones you face. How many times have you prayed for God to take away something, heal something, or change the situation in an instant? That's probably how Jesus felt when He prayed in Matthew 26:39.

During Lent, as you reflect on the cross, think back on those times you prayed, "Jesus, take this away." Or "Jesus, please change my situation." How did God pull you through? What was on the other side of the trial that you couldn't see at the time? How did God make His will, not yours, a blessing at the end?

*Jesus, thank You for enduring the cross on my behalf, for paying all
my debt in full! Thank You for proving that in my life, my true joy is
found in You and Your will—not in my circumstances or my will.*

Poured Out

*Then the LORD said to Moses, "Give the following instructions
to the people of Israel. This is how you are to deal with those who
sin unintentionally by doing anything that violates
one of the LORD's commands."*
LEVITICUS 4:1–2 NLT

The words to describe the book of Leviticus present an oxymoron, for it is both mundane and marvelous. It's a book about worship, obedience, and being set apart by God as holy. It's also a firsthand glimpse of what life was like for sinful people who had to adhere to very strict laws.

But in today's New Testament scripture, Matthew 26:69–27:26, you read how Jesus is betrayed and then goes before Pilate. How He's sentenced to crucifixion, a punishment He didn't deserve but endured on your behalf anyway so that your sins would be forgiven and you could be reconciled to God. What Jesus did on the cross finished what was required in Leviticus. The strict law ended as grace, love, mercy, and forgiveness poured out.

Abiding in Jesus this Lenten season allows for reflection on what was and now is in your life. How strict are you being with yourself and others? Where do you wish you were more gracious, loving, merciful, and forgiving? Ask God to help you take inventory today.

---

*Jesus, I need Your grace to be kind, loving, and compassionate
toward myself and others. Thank You for the freedom to walk
in Your love and grace because of Your love and mercy.*

Resurrection

Commit everything you do to the LORD. Trust him, and he
will help you. He will make your innocence radiate like the dawn,
and the justice of your cause will shine like the noonday sun.
PSALM 37:5–6 NLT

Commitment is hard to come by these days. With a fast-paced, give-it-to-me-now culture, it's hard to slow down and settle. Instead, the temptation is to jump from one thing to the next. This is particularly true in regard to technology and social media.

When it comes to measuring church membership, taking a count of members per household (or unit) is not a good representation of the number of people who actually go to church. It appears some attendees are just not committed enough to say, "I'm in this for the long haul."

When it comes to personal relationships, many people live together before they commit to getting married. First they want to see if things "will work."

All in all, it can seem like people are trying to bypass what David was saying in Psalm 37:5. Imagine if you did commit *everything* to God, trusting Him, like Jesus did when He humbled Himself on the cross (see Matthew 27:27–50).

When you commit and trust like Jesus, God will raise up your life to experience your own figurative resurrection.

Jesus, help me trust You and humble myself by
committing everything to You. I want to shine for You.

An Appointed Time

Be still in the presence of the LORD, and wait patiently
for him to act. . . . Put your hope in the LORD.
Travel steadily along his path. He will honor you.
PSALM 37:7, 34 NLT

At the end of the day, in whom do you trust?

Sometimes you might find yourself putting your faith, hope, and trust in your local, state, or national leaders more than you do your God. Perhaps you sometimes consider what they have to say is more important than what God has to say. If so, it's time to turn things around by looking into God's Word for the truth of the matter.

God wants you to be still in His presence. To put your faith and hope in Him, to wait for Him to act in your life. He wants you to keep walking steadily on the path He has placed before you. When you do, He will honor you more than any president or other world leader could.

Today while you are waiting patiently for government officials to make decisions and create change, remember that change begins with you, and it is ultimately God who is in control over all.

Jesus, You are the one in whom I put my ultimate faith, hope,
and trust. For You are in control of all things—including those
who make decisions. Give my leaders the grace and wisdom
necessary to carry out their appointed calling.

Glimpses of Goodness

Jesus came and told his disciples, "I have been given all authority in heaven and on earth. Therefore, go and make disciples of all the nations, baptizing them in the name of the Father and the Son and the Holy Spirit. Teach these new disciples to obey all the commands I have given you. And be sure of this: I am with you always."
MATTHEW 28:18–20 NLT

Jesus' disciples saw the bloodshed and the pain. They witnessed the resurrected body. How could it be? Is this what Jesus meant when He said He'd come back?

Have you ever thought about how you would have responded if you had witnessed Jesus in His resurrected state? Would you have had the faith to believe it was Him, or not? And if you had still been skeptical after seeing His scarred hands and feet, would you have been willing to accept His Great Commission?

Fortunately, none of those "ifs" really matter. Because Jesus said, "Blessed are those who believe without seeing" (John 20:29 NLT). That's how the Christian faith is. You come to believe you are saved by grace and forgiven of your sins. You put your faith, hope, and trust in an eternal Father who has an eternal plan for you. And although you don't get to see Jesus on this side of heaven, you do get to see glimpses of His goodness.

Thank You, Lord, for Your provision of blessing me and my life regardless of what-ifs!

Baptized

John announced: "Someone is coming soon who is greater than I am—
so much greater that I'm not even worthy to stoop down like a slave
and untie the straps of his sandals. I baptize you with water,
but he will baptize you with the Holy Spirit!"
MARK 1:7–8 NLT

Think back to when you were baptized. Perhaps you were really little, so you may not remember all of the details from that day. However, you may be able to reflect by looking at pictures or a baptismal gown, or by talking to a family member to remind you of the important milestone in your faith journey.

Perhaps you were baptized as an adult. Through a series of situations and circumstances, you came to an all-consuming relationship with Jesus Christ later in life. Eventually you decided to publicly declare your faith.

Or perhaps your baptism happened somewhere in between these two scenarios.

In Mark 1:7–8, John was willing to baptize others, but he also recognized that someone else was coming who would do more than he ever could: a Savior who could baptize your body with water and purify your soul through forgiveness. John recognized that he could only take people so far, and that Jesus would offer the next steps.

Jesus, use me to point people in Your direction. Then give me the wisdom to leave them in Your hands, knowing You will offer them the next steps.

Where You Go

But He said to them, "Let us go into the next towns, that I may preach there also, because for this purpose I have come forth."
MARK 1:38 NKJV

Imagine what it must have been like to witness Jesus performing all those miracles on that Sabbath sunset (see Mark 1:32–34). Imagine you got to see Jesus heal many who were ill and cast out many demons. Imagine that He healed you, too! And then, the next morning, you wanted to see Jesus again!

Mark 1:38 says Jesus wasn't going to stay. For Him to continue His ministry, He had to move on, keep going. What He did on the Sabbath sunset was something He was called to do throughout all of Galilee.

Have you ever wondered what it must have been like to hear Jesus say that they had to go to the next town? Would you have said, "Jesus, they need us here. We need You to stay here!" Yet Jesus said He must go.

The same holds true for you. You can't hold on too tightly to people or places. You need to go where God tells you to go, especially if it's a part of your calling.

Lord, help me avoid holding too tightly to this world and instead be obedient to Your call and go wherever You want me to go.

Sing a New Song

*He has given me a new song to sing, a hymn of praise to
our God. Many will see what he has done and be amazed.
They will put their trust in the L*ORD.

PSALM 40:3 NLT

In Mark 1:40–2:12, Jesus cleansed a leper and healed a paralytic. Imagine what it must have been like to witness—or better yet, receive—those healings from Jesus.

Jesus came so people could receive full healing and not have to live under the penalty of the law anymore or follow all of the religious rituals, such as those for cleansing a healed leper (see Leviticus 14). In essence, Jesus has freed all people from spiritual legality and allows them to sing a new song.

Sing a song of praise for what Jesus has done in *your* life, how He heals and restores you! David wrote, "O LORD my God, you have performed many wonders for us. Your plans for us are too numerous to list. You have no equal. If I tried to recite all your wonderful deeds, I would never come to the end of them" (Psalm 40:5 NLT).

How wonderful to sing a never-ending song about all the amazing things Jesus has done in your life, how He turns all your sorrow into joy!

*Lord, whatever physical condition I might struggle with, help me
have an endless supply of praise for You. Your never-ending
wonders give me hope. To You I sing a new song!*

Bending the Knee

When Jesus heard [the criticism of His eating with tax collectors and sinners],
He said to them, "Those who are well have no need of a physician, but those
who are sick. I did not come to call the righteous, but sinners, to repentance."
MARK 2:17 NKJV

Andrea didn't know what to do. The cancer diagnosis was not what she'd expected. As a young child, she had watched several family members go in and out of remission, even pass away, as a result of the dreaded C word.

"What are the next steps in this process?" she asked her physician.

Almost as if from a distance, she heard her doctor tell her about the surgery and months of therapy she would need to endure. Her chances were good; in fact, the cancer had been detected in its early stages. But those words didn't comfort her. If anything, they only magnified the situation, leaving her feeling traumatized and isolated.

Although Andrea had put her faith in Jesus Christ as a young girl, she was still scared and found herself on her knees crying out to God.

No matter when you put your faith in Jesus, you, or a loved one, may be walking through a challenging situation. Lean in with patient endurance and watch as God sends the Divine Physician to meet all your needs!

Jesus, I humbly admit my brokenness and daily need for You. Be my strength
in all circumstances, out of which I know something good will result.

Lesson Learned

And He said to them, "To you it has been given to know the mystery of the kingdom of God; but to those who are outside, all things come in parables."
MARK 4:11 NKJV

Parables often have a little edge to them. A twist at the end of the lesson that maybe the disciples didn't want, or expect, to hear. The same may be true for you, too. But the amazing and mysterious thing about parables is that the lessons they teach will always lead you back to your primary focus: Jesus Christ.

Mark 4:33–34 says, "And with many such parables He spoke the word to them as they were able to hear it. But without a parable He did not speak to them. And when they were alone, He explained all things to His disciples" (NKJV). How wonderful that Jesus is still teaching and explaining all things to each of His disciples—including you—today.

As you seek God's Word in these moments, endeavor to absorb all God has for you in the richness of His Word, filled with some of the best lessons this life has to offer! As it permeates your very being, it will become a lamp to your feet and a light on your path (see Psalm 119:105).

Lord, speak to me. I come to You, receptive
to Your Word and ready to abide in it.

By His Grace

*Praise the LORD, the God of Israel, who lives from
everlasting to everlasting. Amen and amen!*
PSALM 41:13 NLT

Praising God in all seasons is a tough thing to do. When circumstances aren't good, you might be tempted to blame God more than praise Him. And when circumstances are great, you might be tempted to believe you did something right to deserve all of the blessings and favor being showered on you.

What is the truth? God wants you to praise Him in good times and in bad. It's when you praise Him during the hard times that He increases your faith and helps you to see His goodness in all situations. When you praise Him in the good times, you fully appreciate all that He has done in and through you, only by His grace.

As you focus on abiding in Christ, think of five things you are grateful for today. Write them down in your journal or on a sticky note. Throughout the day, look at your list and praise Him for those things. If you can think of more than five—great! Remember the Giver of grace, and how it's only *by* His grace that you have been saved and freed up to praise Him.

*Jesus, thank You for everything You have done and given me!
Thank You that this life isn't about my works. It's all about
Your grace. Thank You for Your endless supply of blessings.*

A Dash of Faith

But Jesus overheard them and said to Jairus,
"Don't be afraid. Just have faith."
MARK 5:36 NLT

"Don't be afraid and just have faith"—wouldn't it be nice if your faith walk seemed that easy?

At times, it's easier said than done, right? Yet as Jesus was healing people, it appeared that the primary ingredient, perhaps the *only* ingredient, those individuals needed was a dash of faith. That dash was enough to heal, redeem, and restore the lives of individuals who had been suffering for *years*.

Perhaps all you need today is fearless faith. Not fix-it-yourself, find the strength and faith from within. Just fearless faith in who God is, and says He is, in your life. A fearless, expectant faith that He will heal, redeem, and restore you. Perhaps adopt the psalmist's attitude: "Hope in God and wait expectantly for Him, for I shall yet praise Him, Who is the help of my countenance, and my God" (PSALM 42:11 AMPC).

Today, as you reflect on these passages, ask God to give you a dash of faith where you need it the most and expect Him to work wonders in your life.

Lord, I want faith that is childlike but can also move mountains!
Help me avoid mustering up enough willpower or gumption within myself
and instead have faith that is filled with Your divine strength and courage.

Compassionate Prayers

Jesus told [the crowd gathered in the synagogue], "A prophet is honored everywhere except in his own hometown and among his relatives and his own family."

MARK 6:4 NLT

Lisa tried to explain the Good News to her cousin Meredith. But Meredith thought Lisa was going against what she and Lisa were taught at a young age.

As a young girl, Lisa was brought up to believe in God but in a different way, a different religion, and under a different set of traditions. Now Lisa stood out like a sore thumb among her family members because she had just put her faith in Jesus Christ.

Meredith wondered, *Who was this Jesus Lisa was so excited about? Had she been brainwashed?*

Lisa felt disheartened as she explained her newfound faith to her family members, some of whom rejected her words and beliefs. But she knew that although she might be rejected by family, she was accepted unconditionally by her heavenly Father.

Today you might be reminded of times when you have tried to share your faith with a family member and felt rejected. Remember that Jesus understands because He had the same experience—but that didn't stop Him from proclaiming the Good News. As you continue to share your faith, counter any rejections you receive with compassionate prayers for those you love.

Lord, help me pray for my family members who are far from You. Please help me look past their rejection and onto our Father.

Stop, Look, and Listen

"Work six days. The seventh day is a Sabbath, a day of total and complete rest, a sacred assembly. Don't do any work. Wherever you live, it is a Sabbath to GOD."
LEVITICUS 23:3 MSG

You may be one of those women for whom nothing is more satisfying than checking things off on a to-do list. Groceries, check. Dinner plans, check. Kids' homework, check. Lunches packed, check. Project deadline met, check. Date night, check. Bible reading, check. Prayer, check.

Yet amid this breakneck pace, you may be losing sight of something that is very important to God: a day of no to-dos. A day when you take a respite from the hectic. A day when you gather with those of like mind to stop, look, and listen to what God would have you be, see, and hear. A day to get in touch with your spiritual Root—the Vine, Christ—who on at least one occasion told His stressed-out disciples, "'Come off by yourselves; let's take a break and get a little rest.' For there was constant coming and going. They didn't even have time to eat" (Mark 6:31 MSG).

So stop: take a day to sit and sup in Christ. Look for what the Holy Spirit is ready to teach you. Listen to what God has to say.

Here I am, Lord. Quiet. Still. Sitting before You. Be with me. Reveal Yourself to me. Speak to me as I melt into Your presence. Amen.

Calmer of Souls and Storms

*[Jesus' disciples in the boat] all saw Him and were agitated (troubled
and filled with fear and dread). But immediately He talked with
them and said, Take heart! I AM! Stop being alarmed and afraid.*
MARK 6:50 AMPC

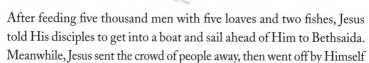

After feeding five thousand men with five loaves and two fishes, Jesus
told His disciples to get into a boat and sail ahead of Him to Bethsaida.
Meanwhile, Jesus sent the crowd of people away, then went off by Himself
to pray. When evening came, a storm rose up on the sea.

With the wind against them, the disciples had trouble rowing.
Jesus, seeing their futile efforts, walked on the turbulent sea toward
them, then acted as if He were going to pass them by. The frightened
disciples thought they were seeing a ghost! To ease their fear, Jesus
spoke, knowing His followers would recognize His voice. He identified
Himself and encouraged them to stop being afraid. Once He got into
their boat, the wind ceased.

Remember who Jesus is and the amazing things He has done for
you. Never think He's overlooking you. Take courage that you will
recognize His voice, His presence, and His power when He is near.
Be assured He's looking out for you. He will never pass you by. He has
words to calm your spirit. He's ready to get into your boat and still your
storms. Simply allow Him into your vessel.

Lord, come to me now. Speak to me. Calm my inner and outer storms.

Be Opened!

Looking up to heaven, He sighed as He said, Ephphatha, which means,
Be opened! And his ears were opened, his tongue was loosed,
and he began to speak distinctly and as he should.
Mark 7:34–35 AMPC

The people bring to Jesus a man who is deaf and has trouble speaking, then ask Jesus to put His healing hand on him.

Jesus takes the man away from the crowd, to a private place. Once there, He doesn't just lay His hand on him but pushes His fingers into the man's ears, spits, then touches his tongue. Looking up to God, Jesus yells, "Be opened!" And the deaf man could hear and speak normally!

What proof that Jesus is the Messiah! That He is the one on whose arrival, "the eyes of the blind shall be opened, and the ears of the deaf shall be unstopped. Then shall the lame man leap like a hart, and the tongue of the dumb shall sing for joy. For waters shall break forth in the wilderness and streams in the desert" (Isaiah 35:5–6 AMPC)!

As you spend time in the restful yet rejuvenating presence of Jesus, be open! Allow His presence to sweep into your eyes, ears—and heart. Doing so will fill you with joy, prompting you to break out in prayer, praise, and song!

Jesus, I come to You in this private place, opening up my heart, soul, body, mind, and spirit to Your healing presence. Ah! What deep abiding joy!

Be Still—and Know!

God is our refuge and strength, always ready to
help in times of trouble. So we will not fear.
Psalm 46:1–2 nlt

At times, you may hear about war or see devastation wrought by earthquakes, fires, hurricanes, famine, tornadoes, and tsunamis. There is only one place you can go to escape all the chaos.

God is your refuge, high tower, fortress, stronghold, strength. He is there at the first sign of trouble in every area of your life—within and without. He is your go-to God.

He commands you: "Be still, and know that I am God!" (Psalm 46:10 nlt). He will diminish your fears, realign your thoughts with His, settle an overwhelming peace on you, and give you a new vision.

A blind man was brought to Jesus. He took him by the hand, away from the crowd. After His first touch, the blind man saw people but they looked like trees walking. Then when Jesus touched his eyes again, the man's sight was fully restored. "He could see everything clearly" (Mark 8:25 nlt).

Allow God to lead you away to a place where you and He can be alone. Allow Him to give you new sight and knowledge in the stillness of His presence.

Here I am, Lord. Still before You. . . . Open my eyes to Your strength,
give me a new vision, as I abide quietly in Your presence.

God Dwelling Within

*"Appoint the Levites to be in charge of The Dwelling of The
Testimony. . . . Their job is to carry The Dwelling and all its
furnishings, maintain it, and camp around it. . . . The Levites are
responsible for the security of The Dwelling of The Testimony."*
Numbers 1:50, 53 MSG

Over three thousand years ago, The Dwelling of The Testimony was
a symbol of God's throne, His presence and power, among the tribes
of Israel. The Levites were in charge of maintaining its furnishings,
carrying it, *and* keeping it safe from intruders.

Today God's throne is in heaven, Jesus sits at His right hand, and
God's Spirit abides in you! Yet at times you may become unmindful of
all the power, knowledge, and resources you have dwelling within. In
this moment, consider taking stock and seeing where you may be falling
short in your God maintenance. Are you increasingly conscious of His
presence within, conferring with Him when needed via prayer and
scripture? Are you securing your relationship with Him by being vigilant
of any strange thoughts that threaten to creep in and dislodge Him?

Remember, "The mystery in a nutshell is just this: Christ is in
you" (Colossians 1:27 MSG). Your job? Abiding in Him in every step
of your journey.

*Lord, make me more conscious of You dwelling within my heart, mind,
body, and soul! Your presence within is the awesome mystery I embrace!*

Constant Help

Lord, I believe! [Constantly] help my weakness of faith!
MARK 9:24 AMPC

A man's young son had issues. He would go into convulsions, foam at the mouth, grind his teeth, and then fall into a stupor. The danger was that the boy would be thrown into fire and water. The loving yet desperate father said to Jesus, "If You can do anything, do have pity on us and help us" (Mark 9:22 AMPC).

Jesus replied, "[You say to Me], If You can do anything? [Why,] all things can be (are possible) to him who believes!" (Mark 9:23 AMPC). That's when the father asked Jesus to constantly help him with his weakness of faith. Moments later, Jesus healed the boy of his affliction.

Jesus has one request when you ask for help with your own issues: Take the if out of the equation when it comes to believing in His power. Have faith that *He can do* anything in your life, that for Him *nothing is impossible*.

But when (and if) you do fall short in faith, know that the Lord will constantly help you, pouring on you more than a sufficient amount of grace, enabling Him to work even through your weakness.

No matter what your level of faith, constantly call on Jesus. He will come, grip your hand, and lift you up into a life of seemingly impossible miracles.

Jesus, everything is possible with You in my heart.
Help me believe this more and more each day.

Your Forever God

We pondered your love-in-action, God. . .Your name,
God, evokes a train of Hallelujahs wherever it is spoken,
near and far; your arms are heaped with goodness-in-action. . . .
Our God forever, who guides us till the end of time.
PSALM 48:9–10, 14 MSG

When spending time in God's presence, you can feel His love and light reaching out and enfolding you. In response, you cannot help but praise Him for all He has done for you, in you, with you, and by you.

It seems almost impossible to imagine that God is with you now, surrounding you with His protection and strength. That He will be with you when it's time for you to cross over to heaven, giving you all the peace and comfort you need before being with Him in an entirely new way. And that He will be with you for all eternity, when there will be no more sorrow, pain, war, or death itself.

Although this constant presence of a living Lord may seem impossible, Jesus assures you that "all things are possible with God" (Mark 10:27 AMPC). So rest easy every moment of every day, knowing you will be forever guided by the One who loves you with all of His being.

Just thinking of Your constant presence, Lord, fills me with such awe
and comfort, peace and strength. I feel Your arms surrounding
me even now and am filled with eternal praise!

A Free and Faith-Filled Follower

Bartimaeus threw aside his coat, jumped up, and came to Jesus.
MARK 10:50 NLT

The blind Bartimaeus, sitting by the road begging, heard Jesus was nearby. He shouted for mercy. When others told Bartimaeus to be quiet, he yelled even louder.

Jesus heard his cries and stopped, instructing His disciples: "Tell him to come here."

Bartimaeus threw off his coat—the one thing that might cause him to stumble—and ran to Jesus. The Lord asked, "What do you want me to do for you?" (Mark 10:51 NLT).

Bartimaeus said, "I want to see!" (v. 51 NLT).

Jesus said, "Go, for your faith has healed you" (v. 52 NLT). That very instant, Bartimaeus received his sight. No longer having to be led, he willingly began following the One who had healed him.

Have you spoken to Jesus lately or allowed others to silence your cries? Have you thrown off anything that might trip you up—your sense of self-sufficiency or entangling sin—and run to Him, clearly telling Him what you want?

Search your heart. Call out to the Master. When He stops, waiting for you to catch up to Him, throw off any hindrances and run to His side. Tell Jesus your heart's desire. And watch your faith, combined with His power, work a miracle. Then follow Him.

I'm throwing off all my self-reliance, Lord, and running to You!
Take my desire, add Your power, and work a miracle in my life.

Constant and Continual

Jesus, replying, said to them, Have faith in God [constantly].
MARK 11:22 AMPC

This faith thing isn't a once-and-done deal, nor is it something to be thrown away at the first sign of trouble or forgotten when all is well. It's a persistent, dogged, determined belief in God.

This faith is the constant belief that a beneficent force, one that sustains and propels everything around you—from the tiniest of ant colonies to the farthest of planets—is blessing, guarding, watching, and keeping you; smiling down, bursting to favor you with gifts galore; looking you in the face and giving "you peace (tranquility of heart and life *continually*)" (Numbers 6:26 AMPC, emphasis added).

Your only part is to be constant in your faith. And the only way to do that is to spend lots of time with God. When you do, His part is to be continually giving you peace—within and without—no matter what is going on in your life.

God has created you to be with Him, so abide in Him. He has given you His Son Jesus to guide you in all things, so follow Him. He has left behind His Spirit to comfort you, so cling to Him. This faith is fed and fueled by your actively spending time with the greatest of beings—Father, Son, and Spirit. Do your part (He is already doing His) and you will have a constant, living faith and a continual, abiding peace.

Here I am, God. Let's talk.

In God's Mind

*I know and am acquainted with all the birds of the mountains, and the
wild animals of the field are Mine and are with Me, in My mind.*
PSALM 50:11 AMPC

So many things that may be out of your reach are at God's command.
Look at birds. They are not only in His sight and in His company—they
are in His mind. He has knowledge of their position, their power, their
prowess, their prey. He knows every feather and feature of every fowl.

And He is more than acquainted with all the wild animals in the
field. They, too, reside in His mind and are at His command. He knows
their movement, color, conquest, and conflict.

In the same way that God knows His birds and animals, He knows
you. He sees your struggles, has memorized your features, and knows
the number of hairs on your head.

No matter where you go or what you do, you are with Him. You
are in God's mind. There is nothing you can hide from your Master,
your Creator.

Allow His Word, His voice, to speak to you. Meld your mind with
His. Seek the wisdom He is bursting to share. Know Him as He knows
you. Love Him as He loves you.

For when you become one with the great I AM, nothing He has
will ever be out of your reach.

*I want to know You, Lord, as You know me. I come to You now,
opening myself to You. Enter into my heart and mind.*

The Path before You

On the day the Tabernacle was set up, the cloud covered it. But from
evening until morning the cloud over the Tabernacle looked like a pillar of
fire. This was the regular pattern. . . . Whenever the cloud lifted from over
the sacred tent, the people of Israel would break camp and follow it. And
wherever the cloud settled, the people of Israel would set up camp.
NUMBERS 9:15–17 NLT

Back in the days of wilderness wanderings, God's presence resided in or
hovered above the tabernacle. The Israelites followed the cloud when
it rose above the tent, then stopped to rest when it settled back down.

Today you can follow this pattern by staying near God both night
and day. Although you may not have the tabernacle, you *do* have God's
divine will, His Word, and His Spirit to direct and guide your soul in
every area of your life.

Seek this path, the guidance of God's will, Word, and Spirit, and
you will find your way through the wilderness, as, at their command,
you allow your heart to move or find its rest.

Lord, where You lead, I will follow. When You rest, I will rest.
Seeking Your will, focused on Your Word, and led by Your Spirit,
I no longer see the wilderness around me. Only Your path before me.

Your Inmost Heart

Behold, You desire truth in the inner being;
make me therefore to know wisdom in my inmost heart.

PSALM 51:6 AMPC

Psalm 51 was written by David after his adultery with Bathsheba and the murder of her husband Uriah. What had begun for David as a nice view of a woman bathing on a rooftop, later ended in death, family tragedy, and his separation from God.

Sin is not just in your actions but begins in your heart, a place from which anyone can stray from the Way if she is not honest with herself and God.

Proverbs 4:23–27 from *The Message* gives some ideas of how to keep our hearts in check: "Keep vigilant watch over your heart; that's where life starts. Don't talk out of both sides of your mouth; avoid careless banter, white lies, and gossip. Keep your eyes straight ahead; ignore all sideshow distractions. Watch your step, and the road will stretch out smooth before you. Look neither right nor left; leave evil in the dust."

When you are honest with yourself and God, true in your innermost heart of hearts, you will not stumble. But if or when you do, go to God. Let Him know you know He knows. Ask His forgiveness and ask Him to make you a wiser woman.

Lord, help me keep my eyes on You. Deep within I long
for Your truth. Make me "heart smart" as I walk in Your way.

God's Perspective

*Caleb quieted the people before Moses, and said, "Let us go up
at once and take possession, for we are well able to overcome it."*
NUMBERS 13:30 NKJV

When the twelve spies returned from checking out the Promised Land,
their report to Moses started out sounding good. They told him the
land really was flowing with milk and honey. They even brought back
fruit samples. But then the spies told Moses of the giants who lived in
Canaan and how fortified their cities were.

When the crowd began murmuring in fear, Caleb calmed them,
saying, "Let's go right now and take this land for our own. We can do
it for sure!"

But the other ten spies (all but Caleb and Joshua) said, "We saw
the giants. . .and we were like grasshoppers in our own sight, so we were
in their sight" (NUMBERS 13:33 NKJV).

What eyes do you use when issues arise? Is your perspective one
of faith or of fear? Do you side with the crowd of impossibility or with
the God of all things possible? Do you see, with your own limited
perceptions, giants that are so big you feel like a grasshopper, or do you
see a God who is bigger than anything you might face?

Spy out your land with God's unlimited perspective, knowing that
with Him you are well able to overcome anything!

*Give me Your vision for my life, Lord,
as I seek to see things with Your eyes.*

A Passionate Follower

"But my servant Caleb—this is a different story. He has a different spirit; he follows me passionately. I'll bring him into the land that he scouted and his children will inherit it."
NUMBERS 14:24 MSG

Almost all the Israelites were devastated by the report of giants in the land God had promised His people. That night they cried and grumbled and complained and wailed, ready to pick a new leader to take them back to their slavery in Egypt.

Finally, Joshua, one of the twelve scouts and the only other man who'd agreed with Caleb, told them, "Don't rebel against GOD! And don't be afraid of those people. . . . They have no protection and GOD is on our side" (NUMBERS 14:8–9 MSG).

But the Israelites had forgotten all about the miracles God had already performed—the plagues, parting of the sea, and so much more. Their hearts were not into following God into the unknown. They wanted to go back to the misery they had always known.

The only two spies that survived the next forty years of wilderness wanderings were Joshua and Caleb. Caleb's name means "whole heart." And that's how He followed God.

Are you a courageous and passionate God-follower, giving Him your all? If so, your wilderness-wandering days are over. God is bringing you into your promised land. Lord, I want to be a persistent and passionate follower of You. Give me a spirit that embraces You with a whole heart.

Women on the Fringe

*"When you see the tassels, you will remember and obey all
the commands of the LORD instead of following your
own desires and defiling yourselves, as you are prone to do."*
Numbers 15:39 NLT

Getting distracted, following your own desires instead of what God would have you do, is all too easy. You, like the Israelites, might need a reminder to keep your eyes on Jesus and follow His will and way. Perhaps you could use a cross necklace, a card with a Bible verse, or angel earrings.

Our spiritual foremothers wore tassels on their clothing as a reminder to follow God. About these women on the fringe, Matthew Henry wrote, "They must look upon these ornaments to awaken their consciences to a sense of their duty."

Jesus wore such tassels on the hem of His garment. In the Garden of Gethsemane, He knew His duty to God, praying: "Please, not what I want—what do *you* want?" (Mark 14:36 MSG), a stark contrast to His nearby disciples who'd fallen asleep on the job. Jesus admonished Simon, "Part of you is eager, ready for anything in God; but another part is as lazy as an old dog sleeping by the fire" (v. 38 MSG).

In which camp do you fall? Are you awake or asleep? Are you looking to fulfill your godly duty or distracted by the world?

*Wake me up, Lord! I want to be aware of Your presence,
remembering You and the task You have given me to do!*

Your Rock of Escape

Behold, God is my helper and ally; the Lord is my upholder. . . .
For He has delivered me out of every trouble.
PSALM 54:4, 7 AMPC

David was in big trouble. The Ziphites, among whom David had been hiding, had promised to deliver David into Saul's hands (see 1 Samuel 23:19–20). Yet instead of wallowing in worry, David *expected* God to save him. Assured that God was with Him, David called Him his helper and ally. He had no doubt God would avenge those who had betrayed his position to the king.

Later in Psalm 54, David promised to praise God for what He was about to do. In fact, David, who was running from His enemy, talked as if God had already rescued him: "He has delivered me out of every trouble"!

And the result of such expectant faith? Just when Saul and his men were closing in on David, a messenger came to Saul, saying, "Make haste and come, for the Philistines have made a raid on the land" (1 Samuel 23:27 AMPC). So Saul left David's Rock of Escape (see 1 Samuel 23:28 AMPC) to pursue the Philistines.

There is tremendous power in expectant prayer. Pray as if God has already answered yours—even if you are still on the run. Know that God, your Rock, has already planned your escape.

You, Lord, my Rock and Refuge, You have delivered
me out of every trouble. I sing praises to Your name!

Taking Root

*You shall write Aaron's name on the rod of Levi [his great-grandfather]. . . .
And the rod of the man whom I choose shall bud, and I will make to cease
from Me the murmurings of the Israelites, which they murmur against you.*
NUMBERS 17:3, 5 AMPC

Legend has it that Saint Patrick not only banished snakes from Ireland
but that the ash walking stick he carried once grew into a living tree. It's
said he took so long to explain his message in one Irish town that his
stick, which he'd thrust into the ground in front of him at the outset,
took root!

Whether or not these stories are fact, one thing is sure: God chose
Saint Patrick to bring the faith to Ireland, where more than three
hundred churches were formed and a hunded thousand Irish people were baptized.

As God chose Saint Patrick, He also chose Aaron. He made it
clear that Aaron was His designated priest by causing only Aaron's
rod—one among twelve—to not only bud and blossom but to produce
almonds as well!

You, too, have been chosen for a specific task, one that only you,
in the power of the Spirit, can accomplish. Go to God today. Ask Him
where He wants you to work, to blossom, bud, and bear fruit, as you
live in Him.

*God, here I am. For what have You called me? Show me. Lead me.
Guide me. My faith is ready to bear fruit as I take root in You!*

God's Way

GOD said to Moses and Aaron, "Because you didn't trust me, didn't treat me with holy reverence in front of the People of Israel, you two aren't going to lead this company into the land that I am giving them."
NUMBERS 20:12 MSG

Moses, Aaron, and the Israelites were in Kadesh without water. So, of course, the people started complaining to Moses.

In response, Moses and Aaron went to God. The Lord, patient as always, told them to take Moses' staff, *speak* to the rock, and it would bring out water. But when the brothers went before the people, an irritated Moses said to them, "Do we have to bring water out of this rock for you?" (Numbers 20:10 MSG)—as if this was something to be done in his own power—and then *struck* the rock! And not just once, but twice! The water did gush, so the people got what they wanted. But not in the way God wanted it to happen.

God says Moses didn't trust Him. If he had, he wouldn't have distorted God's directions, turned prideful, or let his irritation with the people get the best of him.

Has God ever told you to do a specific thing and, instead of following His directions exactly, you did it your own way—and perhaps even justified your doing so? If so, ask God to help you not strike out again.

Lord, help me trust You every day, making Your way my way.

Focused on Jesus

And Moses made a serpent of bronze and put it on a pole, and if a serpent had bitten any man, when he looked to the serpent of bronze [attentively, expectantly, with a steady and absorbing gaze], he lived.
Numbers 21:9 AMPC

After a victorious battle, God's people once again became tired of walking, eating manna, and being thirsty. So they spoke out against God and Moses.

In response, God sent some poisonous snakes to bite the ingrates, many of whom died. That's when they wised up, apologized to Moses, and begged for him to pray for them.

So God instructed Moses to make a snake of bronze and put it on a pole. Anyone who looked—really steadily looked—at it, would live.

"Just as Moses lifted up the serpent in the desert" (John 3:14 AMPC), so was Jesus lifted up to save you. So look away from all that distracts to Jesus, the author and finisher of your faith (see Hebrews 12:2). And not just with a casual glance, a once-in-awhile glimpse, a just-in-case peek but with an all-consuming, all-absorbing gaze.

Take some time today to really "see" your Savior. Step away from the world and put your spiritual eyes on the prize of your life. Cling to Him. See Him. And He will save you.

Lord, I'm here, seeking Your face, ready to melt in
Your presence, as I lift my eyes to Your saving grace!

An Impressive Precept

*Mary said, Behold, I am the handmaiden of the Lord; let it be done
to me according to what you have said. And the angel left her.*
LUKE 1:38 AMPC

Mary, a young girl visited by the angel Gabriel, is confused when he calls
her "Blessed." So he tells her she has found favor in God's eyes and is to
become pregnant and give birth to God's Son! Uncertain as to how this
may happen, Mary asks the angel to explain. Gabriel not only does so
but also tells Mary that her barren, elderly cousin Elizabeth is pregnant!
Because "with God nothing is ever impossible and no word from God
shall be without power or impossible of fulfillment" (Luke 1:37 AMPC).

These words make such an impression on Mary that she immediately
acquiesces to the plan, saying, "I'm God's servant. May it happen to me
just as you say."

Amazingly enough, thirty-three years later, Jesus, the son Mary
raises, remembers the precept His mother had impressed on Him, the
precept that resulted in His being born on earth: God's will be done.
While praying in the Garden of Gethsemane, Jesus says, "Father, if You
are willing, remove this cup from Me; yet not My will, but [always]
Yours be done" (Luke 22:42 AMPC).

Are you just as impressed?

*Lord, You are amazing. I know that with You nothing is impossible.
So I'm leaving all of myself and my circumstances in Your care.
May Your will alone always be done!*

Do Not Fear

"Blessed is she who believed, for there will be a fulfillment
of those things which were told her from the Lord."
LUKE 1:45 NKJV

Upon seeing the angel Gabriel in the temple, Zachariah was gripped by fear. But Gabriel told him, "Don't fear, Zachariah. Your prayer has been heard. Elizabeth, your wife, will bear a son by you" (Luke 1:13 MSG). Later, Zachariah couldn't help but sing praises to the Lord when his son John was born.

When Mary saw Gabriel, she was troubled. Gabriel told her not to be afraid. God favored her, and she would give birth to God's Son (see Luke 1:30–33). Later Mary burst into song, praising God, already giving Him credit for what He was going to do: "For He who is mighty has done great things for me" (v. 49 NKJV).

When Jesus was born, an angel visited shepherds to announce the event, telling them, "Do not be afraid, for behold, I bring you tidings of great joy" (Luke 2:10 NKJV). Then an entire heavenly host appeared, singing and praising God.

The point? Don't fear. God has heard your prayer. Don't be troubled. God is looking upon you with favor and has great things in store for you. Don't be afraid. Jesus is the source of your greatest joy.

Your job? Pray with expectation, believe the best, and spread the Good News.

Thank You, Jesus, for replacing my fear with Your joy!
My heart sings with love for You!

Promptings of the Spirit

Now there was a man in Jerusalem whose name was Simeon. . . .
And prompted by the [Holy] Spirit, he came into the temple [enclosure].
Luke 2:25, 27 AMPC

The Holy Spirit had shown Simeon, a good and devout man, that he would see his people's Messiah before he died. Then one day, a day that had seemed like any other, Simeon followed the prompting of the Holy Spirit and went into the temple. There he saw Mary and Joseph bringing in Jesus.

Imagine if Simeon had not followed the nudge of the Holy Spirit to enter the temple at the exact time of Jesus' arrival. Simeon would have missed what he had been waiting for his entire life: the hope and salvation of his people.

When you are close to God, you, too, are in tune with the Holy Spirit. You, too, can feel His nudges and promptings. You, too, can hear His leadings.

Take some time today to draw close to God. "Seek the LORD while He may be found, call upon Him while He is near" (Isaiah 55:6–7 NKJV). Be open to His Spirit's leadings. Follow His promptings. If you don't, you will always be wondering what God had no intention of your missing.

Lord, keep me open to Your Spirit's nudges. I don't want to miss anything You may have in store for me. I want to see Jesus and His power in my life! In His name I pray, amen.

Heart Guard

His mother kept and closely and persistently
guarded all these things in her heart.
LUKE 2:50–51 AMPC

Jesus and His parents had gone down to Jerusalem for the Passover Feast. On the ride back home, His mom and dad realized they'd left without their son. They finally found Him in the temple, hanging out with teachers whom He'd impressed. But Joseph and Mary were upset. So Mary asked Jesus why He'd stayed behind; after all, they'd been frantically looking for Him for the past few days. Why had He put them through that?

Jesus answered, "Why were you looking for me? Didn't you know that I had to be here, dealing with the things of my Father?" (Luke 2:49 MSG).

His parents had no clue what He was telling them. But Mary held those precious words deep within her heart.

When reading God's Word or examining His promises, you may not totally understand what He is trying to tell you. And He doesn't expect you to. After all, His thoughts are so much higher than any human's. But what you can do is follow Mary's example. Seek out God's wisdom, ask for clarity, relish His every word, and treasure it in your heart, knowing that someday you will understand it all.

Jesus, I treasure Your Word. Help me hold it deep within my heart, whether or not I understand it, for I know it will determine the course of my life.

God Power

*Jesus was baptized. As he was praying, the sky opened up and
the Holy Spirit, like a dove descending, came down on him.
And along with the Spirit, a voice: "You are my Son,
chosen and marked by my love, pride of my life."*
Luke 3:21–22 msg

Jesus' baptism. What a wondrous example of the power of prayer—and
of the Three-in-One God in action.

Jesus, the one who opens doors that no one can shut, is an amazingly
powerful prayer, for, as He's praying, the sky actually opens up! Then
the Holy Spirit, like a dove alighting from the heavens, descends on
Him. At the same time, God's voice booms out, "You are My Son, My
Beloved! In You I am well pleased and find delight!" (Luke 3:21 ampc).

What a great example of the power you have access to in your
life! Just as Jesus' prayers could open up the sky, your prayers can move
mountains. You also have a three-man team on your side. Like Jesus,
you have a Father God who loved you—before you ever loved Him (see
Romans 5:8). Because of this great love, this Father God sent His Son
not only to seek you—but to save you (see Luke 19:10). And then He
left behind the Spirit to draw you to Him (see John 16:13–14).

What more could a woman want—or need?

In You alone do I have power, Lord. May I use it for Your good.

A Word on God's Word

*Jesus replied to him, It is written, Man shall not live and be sustained
by (on) bread alone but by every word and expression of God.*
Luke 4:4 AMPC

There is nothing more powerful or soul-sustaining than the Word of
God. It is your sword. And your *faith* in it is your shield.

Can you imagine a world without 24/7 access to the Bible you
have at your fingertips? How colorless, mundane, and heartbreaking
life would be.

Jesus used the Word of God to subdue the devil, aka the father
of lies, the twister of words. Jesus also used God's Word to heal, bless,
rescue, save, love, encourage, and minister to His people, to instruct His
disciples, to tell what was to come.

On this Palm Sunday, as you celebrate Jesus' triumphal entry into
Jerusalem, take a moment to thank God for His Word and its triumphant entry into your heart, mind, spirit, and soul. Know that as you
speak, learn, study, and apply it, amazing things unfold, for as God has
said about His words, "They'll do the work I sent them to do, they'll
complete the assignment I gave them" (Isaiah 55:10–11 MSG).

*Lord, I thank and praise You for the power of Your Word. Help me learn it,
study it, apply it, and speak it into my life. In Jesus' name I pray, amen.*

Grounded in Christ's Word

Master, we toiled all night [exhaustingly] and caught nothing [in our nets]. But on the ground of Your word, I will lower the nets [again].
LUKE 5:5 AMPC

You have been working hard all day but nothing has gone right. In fact, you feel as if you wasted an entire eight hours just going through the motions. Fatigued in body, soul, and mind, you start closing up shop. And then you hear Jesus begin to speak, to whisper in your ear. He tells you to go deeper into your task and see what comes up.

At this point, you may tell Him, "Lord, I've been working hard all day." And that's fine. Jesus wants to know how you are feeling. But the choice you make next is what really counts. Are you going to ignore His request or obey it?

If you choose to ignore His prompting, chances are you are going to miss out on something big. But if you respond as the exhausted fisherman Peter did when he said, "On the ground of Your Word, I will lower the nets [again]" (Luke 5:5 AMPC), you will find success beyond your imagination.

No matter how weary you may be, if you don't give up, you will find success in whatever God tells you to put your hand to. Just do your duty and leave the results to Him.

Lord, with You directing my moves and me grounded in Your Word, I know I'll meet with success—in Your time.

Your Mission

Let all that I am wait quietly before God, for my hope is in him. He alone is my rock and my salvation, my fortress where I will not be shaken.
PSALM 62:5–6 NLT

Your cell phone's alarm clock goes off. You sit bolt upright in bed, yawn, stretch, check the messages on your cell phone, then put your feet on the floor. Your favorite radio station playing, you head into the shower. While dressing, then eating breakfast, you watch TV for the traffic and weather reports. Once in your car, you put in a CD and head to the office where more gadgets and even some real-live humanoids will proclaim their presence via your auditory senses.

Amid all this hubbub, how can you wait silently before the Lord? In fact, how can you even sit still for one minute?

It takes commitment to make sitting silently before the Lord a priority. But only when you do so will you be able to, at all other times, step into the fortress where you cannot be shaken.

Make it your mission to seek the Lord in silence. Expect Him to be there and refill and refuel you. Make your motto the words "I wait quietly before God, for my victory comes from him" (Psalm 62:1 NLT).

Lord, all I need can be found in You. So here I am, Lord,
seeking Your presence, hoping in You alone, my Rock and my Refuge.

Moving On in Faith

"When we were at Mount Sinai, the LORD our God said to us, 'You have stayed at this mountain long enough. It is time to break camp and move on.'"
DEUTERONOMY 1:6–7 NLT

What should have been an eleven-day journey to the Promised Land turned into a forty-year wandering in the wilderness for the Israelites. Why? Because they didn't believe God would do what He said He would. Instead of seeing how the God who parted the sea would give them victory over all their obstacles, they saw only the obstacles.

The only two men who took God at His word, Joshua and Caleb, were also the only two of the original refugees alive at the end of the wilderness wanderings. Why? Because they believed God—in spite of what they saw or heard around them.

Is there some mountain you have stayed at long enough? Is it time for you to break camp and move on to something else?

Believe that God will see you through. Take Him at His word. Focus on what He can do. See His victory over your obstacles, not just the obstacles themselves.

"Trust the LORD your God, who goes before you looking for the best places to camp" (Deuteronomy 1:32 NLT), and you will reach your promised land.

*Lord, I believe that You are with me, going before me,
and defending me from behind. I'm ready to move on in faith!*

On the Run—with God

*O God, You are my God, earnestly will I seek You; my inner
self thirsts for You, my flesh longs and is faint for You,
in a dry and weary land where no water is.*

PSALM 63:1 AMPC

Absalom, King David's son, was attempting to overthrow his father.
So David fled his palace, his comforts, his people. Cursed, then pelted
with stones and dirt, this weary and beleaguered king wrote Psalm 63
in the wilderness of Judah.

There David remembered God's power and glory. He recalled His
loving-kindness, knowing that is more precious than life itself. And in
spite of all that was happening in his life, David told God, "So will I
bless You while I live; I will lift up my hands in Your name" (v. 4 AMPC).

Even though David was on the run once again, even though he
was out of his comfort zone, he hadn't forgotten the most important
thing: his love, worship, and pursuit of God.

When all seems lost in your life, when those who once loved you
now curse you, when you are relegated to a barren wasteland, remember
Psalm 63. Know that the most important thing you have—faith in
God—is there for you to cling to and rejoice in. He is all the comfort
you need, no matter where you are.

*You, Lord, are my all in all. You alone
are my comfort zone. You are all I need.*

A Good Day

Because He loved your fathers, He chose their descendants after them, and
brought you out from Egypt with His own Presence, by His mighty power.
DEUTERONOMY 4:37 AMPC

Before going over God's law again, Moses reminded the people of how God had rescued them. That He did so because of His great love. That He didn't send a surrogate to lead them out of captivity and danger, but had brought them out with His own Presence, by His great power.

In light of all God had done for His people, Moses once again emphasized why they were to keep God's rules: for their own good and for the good of the generations to follow (see Deuteronomy 4:40). God's laws were not restrictions but a framework in which His people would realize all the blessings God had in store for them.

As a Christian, you, too, are to keep God's laws. But because of Christ's sacrifice on Good Friday, you are given a different avenue to take. Rather than get all bogged down by sacrifices, regulations, and a myriad of specific dos and don'ts, you merely need to walk in love and, as you do so, fulfill God's rules in the power of the Holy Spirit. Living like this will make every day a good day.

For all You have done for me, Jesus, I thank You. Spirit,
lead me into all truth so I can love all, as Christ loved me.

Jesus Does the Unexpected

*When the Lord saw her, his heart overflowed
with compassion. "Don't cry!" he said.*
LUKE 7:13 NLT

A crowd followed Jesus and His disciples when they reached the village of Nain. There He noticed the funeral procession of a young man, a widow's only son.

When Jesus saw her, He couldn't help but be deeply touched by her grief and her dire situation. Without her asking anything of Him, He first told her not to cry and then, amazingly, brought her dead son back to life! After the boy sat up and began to talk, "Jesus gave him back to his mother" (Luke 7:15 NLT).

When you are at your wits end, when it looks like there's no hope for you, when you find yourself walking in a daze, struck with sadness, remember this story.

Know that Jesus sees what you are going through. That His heart overflows with compassion for you.

So don't cry. Don't be discouraged. Don't despair. Don't grieve. Only believe. At the last minute, Jesus just may surprise you beyond anything you ever imagined or expected and turn your entire life around by doing the impossible.

Jesus, You never cease to amaze me. Thank You for the reminder that I need never despair. For You see what is happening in my life. I feel Your love and compassion surround me! I will not grieve—only believe.

Reminder Sunday

"Are you the one who is to come,
or should we expect someone else?"
LUKE 7:19 NIV

He was sitting in a dark prison cell. And no one was coming. No rescuer bursting through the doors. No army taking over the city and wresting control out of the hands of corrupt rulers. Perhaps, sitting there alone, away from the crowds, and pondering his life, John the Baptist wondered if anything had really changed at all.

If John could have looked forward in time, he would have seen this day—the day of resurrection. The day Jesus silenced His critics and fulfilled the words of the prophets. The day He proved to those who stood there, watching His body be lifted limp and lifeless from the cross, that death indeed had lost its sting and there was no power on heaven or earth that could keep the Son of God in the tomb.

But John was blinded by the walls that surrounded him. And he just wanted to know for sure. "Are you the one?"

On this day, soak in the light of the resurrection. Sing songs of praise and power. Marvel at the miracle of Jesus, at the gift of His grace. And when your day of doubting comes, when you are blinded by the walls you keep hitting, remember that yes, He is the one. There is no one else.

Lord, open my eyes to see the constant reminders
of who You are, not just today, but every day. Amen.

Tell Them

Fix these words of mine in your hearts and minds. . . . Teach them to your children, talking about them when you sit at home and when you walk along the road, when you lie down and when you get up.
DEUTERONOMY 11:18–19 NIV

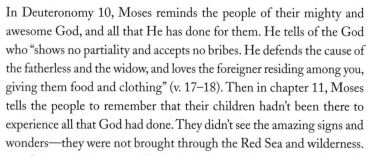

In Deuteronomy 10, Moses reminds the people of their mighty and awesome God, and all that He has done for them. He tells of the God who "shows no partiality and accepts no bribes. He defends the cause of the fatherless and the widow, and loves the foreigner residing among you, giving them food and clothing" (v. 17–18). Then in chapter 11, Moses tells the people to remember that their children hadn't been there to experience all that God had done. They didn't see the amazing signs and wonders—they were not brought through the Red Sea and wilderness.

So it was the responsibility of that generation to pass on what they knew about God's wonders to the next generation. Likewise, it is the responsibility of today's generation to pass on what it has seen and heard.

Tell the children in your life about what God has done for you. Teach them the stories that have been written down for you. Through the hearing you learn, and through the telling you claim it as your own. You become part of the story God has been writing since the beginning.

*God of wonders, help me take Your stories wherever I go.
Help me teach the children to know You. Amen.*

Soft Showers

You care for the land and water it;
you enrich it abundantly.
PSALM 65:9 NIV

Big, warm drops splash onto the ground, sliding down the blades of grass, forming puddles in the shallow indentations. The drops draw patterns in the dust and begin to join together in flowing arteries, taking life out to the parched earth.

You, just like all other women, experience dry spells in your life—times when the creative juices will not come, when productivity hits an all-time low, when no one wants what you have to offer. You most likely hit spiritual dry spells as well—when God's voice is hard to hear, when your prayers seem to go nowhere and your faith feels so small.

All you have to do in those times is hold out your empty, dry hands to God. Even if the only word you can manage to speak is "Help," it is enough. Even if you cannot speak at all. God will answer your silent cries with living water—water that leads to eternal life. Water that leaves you wanting more of Him.

Lord, water my dry land and enrich my life. Amen.

Changed

"What do you want with me, Jesus,
Son of the Most High God?"
LUKE 8:28 NIV

The transformation must have been truly astounding. A man went from naked, presumably insane, afraid, most likely speaking gibberish, and living among the dead, to clothed, in his right mind, able and willing to give his eyewitness account of Jesus, and sitting at the feet of the Lord of life. What kind of power can make that happen in the space of several minutes?

It's the same power that can stop a storm. Make demons beg. Drive a herd of demon-possessed pigs to their death.

Everyone else who had met that man had just given him up for dead. They left him to rot among the tombs. They could not contain him or tame him, and it was easier to let him wander as a stranger than to love him as a brother. But Jesus saw the man he once was, and He loved him.

Jesus sees you, too. If you have let some demon—an addiction, a toxic relationship, a sin you just can't shake—strip you of your humanity, turn to Jesus. Let Him look at you and love you. Ask Him what He wants to do with you. You may not get back all that you have lost, but you will gain more than you ever had.

God, give me the courage to let You make
me into who You designed me to be. Amen.

Tested

Praise our God, all peoples, let the sound of his praise be heard;
he has preserved our lives and kept our feet from slipping.
PSALM 66:8–9 NIV

This is one of those psalms that sounds lovely—until you read a little bit further. The verses begin by rejoicing in the God who has "preserved our lives and kept our feet from slipping" (Psalm 66:9). But how did God do this? By testing His people: "You brought us into prison and laid burdens on our backs. You let people ride over our heads; we went through fire and water" (vv. 11–12).

Doesn't sound like much fun, right? And surely those actions would not be on anyone's list of Top 10 Ways to Prevent Slips and Falls. But God works in mysterious ways indeed. Sometimes He carries you. But other times He pushes you to grow the strength you need to carry yourself. He's the ultimate trainer—seeing all your weaknesses and knowing exactly which muscles must be stretched to get you to your goal. Yet He pushes you even past that—past the small dreams you have into a place of abundance you could never imagine.

As you walk with Him today, consider the many times He has kept you from falling. Praise Him for testing you and refining you. Thank Him for laying burdens on you that in the end made you stronger.

God, stretch me, move me, push me, test me. Amen.

What Are You Saying?

"And you—what are you saying about me? Who am I?"
LUKE 9:20 MSG

Jesus had just fed a crowd of more than five thousand when He asked His disciples, "What are the crowds saying about me, about who I am?" (Luke 9:18 MSG). It seems the crowds were pretty befuddled. Some confused Jesus with John the Baptist. Some said He was Elijah, the prophet who was mysteriously whisked away on a whirlwind up to heaven. Still others went with the vaguer concept that Jesus was some other prophet from long ago who had come to walk the earth again.

But then He asked the question of His disciples—His circle of friends. What would their answer be? He had questioned their faith before; perhaps He was doing so again.

Peter, often the one to speak up, answered, "The Messiah of God" (v. 20 MSG).

He gave the right answer. But later Peter would deny knowing anything about who this Jesus was, just as He was being prepared to be crucified.

There's *knowing* the truth, and then there's *living* the truth. Often, it's hard to do both at once. But the difficult thing is that how you live speaks to others about what you know to be true. And many times, how you live speaks much louder.

So take some time to reflect. What is *your* life saying about Jesus?

Lord, let my life speak the truth about You. Amen.

Shine

May God be gracious to us and bless us and make his face shine on us—so that your ways may be known on earth, your salvation among all nations.
PSALM 67:1–2 NIV

The golden warmth spreads across your closed eyelids. You turn up your face. The glow filters through so that even with your eyes shut tight there is no darkness. For these few moments, everything is in the light.

Humans can't comprehend the brilliance of God. Thousands and thousands of years ago, people considered the sun a god. This glowing orb hanging in the sky, lighting the entire world from the moment it broke into the morning until the last ray receded into dusk must be divine, they mused. It must have a will and a purpose. Why else would it exist at all, if it were not somehow in power? They could not imagine anything greater—a force more powerful than this ball of fire that gave life to the world. They could not imagine a power so boundless that it could simply speak the light into being.

But God does not so much want to light the world as He wants to light you. He wants your face to reflect His light, so that His ways may be known among all nations. The sun only reaches so far. The night still comes. But you, His daughter, can praise His name all the time.

Creator God, thank You for shining on me. Amen.

To Be Fair

You must have accurate and honest weights and measures, so that you may live long in the land the LORD your God is giving you.
DEUTERONOMY 25:15 NIV

It seems like there's a rule in the Bible for just about any situation. Leviticus is filled with guidance for how people ought and ought not to carry on with business, relationships, spiritual activities, and much more. The beauty in all of it is the God who cares. He cares enough to speak about the details of your life, and He knows well enough that those details are what can bring you down.

Many of these bits of advice and warnings could be summed up just by saying, "Be good, and be good to each other"—a counsel that crosses cultural lines and lives beyond time constraints. In Deuteronomy 25:15, Moses declares that the businessman should not try to weight the scales in his favor. He should be honest in his dealings. And though not many people deal with actual scales in their workplace, they can be guilty of unfairness in the way they treat each other. How many times have you manipulated circumstances to put yourself in a more favorable position? And how many times has that meant deliberately taking from someone else?

God would have you use equal measures, judging with fairness, lest you be judged with that same distorted perspective.

God, please help me treat others fairly. Amen.

The Big IF

"Wherever you go and whatever you do, you will be blessed."
DEUTERONOMY 28:6 NLT

You have met them. Maybe you are one. They're the golden people. Whatever they do seems to succeed. It's the woman who aces her exam and wins the meet in the same day. It's the mom who nails down the deal, then cooks a gourmet dinner for her family. But most of the time, when you see a person who seems to do well in everything she does, there is a reason she's doing so well. And most of the time (not always), that reason involves a lot of hard work.

Likewise, when you see a statement that promises blessing from God, there is often a framework in which that blessing comes: "If you fully obey the LORD your God and carefully keep all his commands that I am giving you today" (Deuteronomy 28:1 NLT).

There's the big *IF*. It's a lot of hard work. Obeying God and keeping all His commands is no easy task.

Now some might look at this and say, "See, your God does not love unconditionally—He will only love you 'if.'" But your God does love unconditionally. He just doesn't bless you that way. Instead, He gives you more than you need and deserve—even more than any *IF*.

Thank You, Lord, for all the generous blessings You have given me even just today. Help me maintain Your commands and abide in obedience. Amen.

Enjoying the Joke

Jesus was filled with the joy of the Holy Spirit.
LUKE 10:21 NLT

Jesus enjoyed the pleasure of a secret joke. Here in Luke 10:21, you can imagine Him smiling as He takes a moment with His Father and thanks the Lord of heaven and earth for "hiding these things from those who think themselves wise and clever, and for revealing them to the childlike" (Luke 10:21 NLT).

And it is a funny picture. Many a woman thinks that if she works hard enough, if she studies enough, if she obeys enough, if she plans enough, and if she's serious enough—then at the end of all of that, that is when Jesus will reward her with the power she wants in her life. That's when He will give her the reins. That's when she'll become important.

But Jesus turns all of that on its head. He loves you before you ever start the work, and He loves you when you have become exhausted. And though for certain there's a reward for those who remain steadfast and obey Him—the reward looks nothing like the prizes that come with gold statues and silver medals and piles of cash. Instead, it may be the weight of more responsibility, the sweat of more service, the sweet pain and blessing that comes with more love.

That Jesus—He has quite the sense of humor.

Lord, I'm glad You let me in on the joke. Amen.

Change for the Better

*"The Lord your God will change your heart and the
hearts of all your descendants, so that you will love him
with all your heart and soul and so you may live!"*
Deuteronomy 30:6 NLT

When painting a room, especially if the new color will be quite different from the old, you cannot just come in and start whacking paint splashes on the walls. (Unless you intend for the room to be a piece of performance art, but that's another story.) No, to do it properly, you have to prepare the room and prime the walls. Preparing the room means moving things out and cleaning things up. It means laying down some kind of protection. Then you prime the walls with a coat of paint that will help to cover up imperfections and allow the new paint to adhere to the surface.

Likewise, for you to become new in Christ and take up the path of obedience, you cannot do it on your own with a sinful, selfish heart. God has to change you—and so He changes your heart to want Him more. You will still sin. You will still fall into the old habit of thinking of yourself too much. But you will want to be better, do better. And the longer you travel with Him and let Him work in your life, the more your heart can conform to the shape of His love.

God, change my heart so I can love You more. Amen.

True Light

"See to it, then, that the light within you is not darkness."
LUKE 11:35 NIV

Kids love to play in a room lit with black light. It makes light and bright colors—even your teeth—seem to glow. Black light works by emitting light that's mostly invisible to the human eye—what you see from such a bulb is a soft purplish light. The light shines on items that have phosphor—a substance that converts the energy in the ultraviolet light into light you can see. But you would never want to use black light to study or read by—it's not so good for the eyes.

In Luke 11, Jesus is talking to His disciples about the kind of light they have. He says, "When your eyes are healthy, your whole body also is full of light" (v. 34). And He warns them to make sure the light they think they're carrying is not really darkness in disguise.

How many times have you felt a surge of happiness or a thrill of purpose, only to later realize that what you thought was a solid change in your heart was really created by a fleeting emotion or an artificial cause? The light of Jesus won't leave you wanting. It won't come in a moment and leave you in the next. It'll stay and grow and give warmth and banish every bit of darkness.

Lord, help me be able to discern true light from darkness. Amen.

The Confession

You, God, know my folly;
my guilt is not hidden from you.
PSALM 69:5 NIV

David, the writer of Psalm 69 was in a bad place. He was surrounded by water, and yet his thirst could not be quenched. He called out for help, and no one seemed to hear. He was sinking, sinking, and his feet could find no solid ground. His voice had worn out, and his eyes were failing. He claimed that the ones who hated him were too many to count.

And he could have settled there—he could have just blamed all his enemies for his circumstances. He could have pointed the finger at his haters. But instead he admitted his own guilt. He confessed to God his own foolish choices. And he asked God not to let those who hoped in Him be shamed due to his disgrace.

This is the beauty of knowing and living with God. When your eyes are on Him, you can see your own faults more clearly. But also you have hope that He will not leave you sinking down under the weight of those faults. He will reach down into your sorrow and your sorry-ness and lift you up into His grace.

Dear Lord who sees me, help my eyes stay trained on You. Amen.

Courage

*"Strength! Courage! Don't be timid; don't get discouraged.
God, your God, is with you every step you take."*
Joshua 1:9 msg

Maybe you have a presentation to make, a cake to bake, or an exam to take. Maybe you are facing spiders or snakes or laundry stains. Maybe you are biting your tongue—afraid to speak up, speak out, and tell your story. Maybe you think you have to wait until your knees stop shaking to take that step.

But you don't have to wait. Having courage doesn't mean you won't be afraid. It means pushing through the fear to act on what you know is right. And when you take that step into your fear, you can be 100 percent certain that God will meet you there. He will be there even when you feel like throwing up. He will stay there with you until the end.

Why do you think God kept repeating those words? "Strength! Courage!" It's a pretty good bet He knew Joshua had some fears—after all, he had just been appointed by God to lead this people of Israel (who, as you might recall, were not the most cooperative bunch) to take over the land God was giving them. Joshua needed to hear those words over and over again, to be reminded that the same God who was with Moses was still standing with him now.

*Lord, help me obey Your Word with all
the strength and courage You can give. Amen.*

Bird Business

"How much more valuable you are than birds!"
LUKE 12:24 NIV

Busy birds! Watch them for long in spring and you can see the products of their industry take shape over a few hours. They flit back and forth—building houses for their offspring-to-be. A twig there, a piece of string here. They never seem to stop and fret. They don't pull out their pocketbooks and count their savings. They just keep going about the business God has created them to do.

We can learn a lot from watching birds. Over time, humans have accelerated their lives to a breakneck pace and have set goals for which God never meant them to live—making money, retiring well, getting the "most" (meaning the most popular or most desired) out of life.

It's not that it's a bad thing to make plans—it's just a stifling thing to *live* for those plans. God wants you instead to keep going about the business He has created you to do—to love one another, to tell others about Jesus, and to love God with all your heart, soul, mind, and strength. To seek His kingdom first, and then all the rest will fall into place. That is His promise! And if this God of yours, who created such beautiful little feathered creatures, sees fit to take care of their needs, do you really believe He will neglect yours?

Father God, teach me to avoid fretting about tomorrow. Amen.

Battle Plans

"See, I have delivered Jericho into your hands."
Joshua 6:2 niv

It would be interesting to test out God's battle strategy on some military commanders today: "Want to take over that city full of hostile terrorists? Just march around it once a day for six days. Then on the seventh day, march around the city seven times and blow your trumpets. What? You don't have trumpets? Well, go get some!"

It's safe to say that plan wouldn't go over so well. But you know it did, in fact, work very well for Joshua and the Israelites. They followed God's instructions and took the whole city of Jericho without really any kind of serious opposition.

But isn't that the way with God's plans? They never look like the ones you'd come up with—not in a million years. Love your enemies. Give more than what's required. Sell all you have. Turn the other cheek. Give up your life to gain the world. Follow the star to a see the poor baby who will be the king of creation. Watch an innocent man suffering and dying to save the world.

No, His plans don't look like yours. Isn't that a very good thing?

Lord God, help me listen to Your plans for me—
even when they don't make sense. Amen.

Every Word

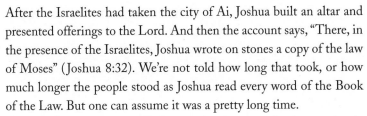

There was not a word of all that Moses had commanded that Joshua did not read to the whole assembly of Israel, including the women and children, and the foreigners who lived among them.

Joshua 8:35 niv

After the Israelites had taken the city of Ai, Joshua built an altar and presented offerings to the Lord. And then the account says, "There, in the presence of the Israelites, Joshua wrote on stones a copy of the law of Moses" (Joshua 8:32). We're not told how long that took, or how much longer the people stood as Joshua read every word of the Book of the Law. But one can assume it was a pretty long time.

So why take that time? Why not be preparing for the next battle instead?

Yet that's exactly what Joshua was doing. He wanted to remind the people who they were and why they were fighting to take this land in the first place. He wanted the new people among their group to know the promises of God. And He wanted everyone to know that they were the nation of Israel, God's chosen people, and it was their responsibility to show the world how to act like the people of God. He was preparing them for the next battle.

Spend some time in God's Word every day—especially if you know you are facing battles. Remember where you have come from.

God, remind me that I am Yours. Amen.

From Birth on Up

*From birth I have relied on you; you brought me forth
from my mother's womb. I will ever praise you.*

PSALM 71:6 NIV

There's something wonderfully strange about holding a newborn baby. To know that inside that floppy, wriggly little body is all the makings of a grown human. To look into those eyes and wonder about what questions are being asked, what observations are being made, what words are being learned. There's so much strength and yet so much weakness wrapped up in this tiny bundle.

And from the moment the baby comes out of the womb—gasping for breath and rooting for food—that child is dependent on adult hands to care for her or him.

From the moment you were born (and even before that), whether you know it or not, you began relying on God every minute of your life. He gave you the parents you have. He knitted your body into the particular shape it would be, along with molding your particular set of abilities and challenges.

So praise Him today for being there for you from day one. Praise Him for providing capable hands to care for you. Praise Him for making you who you are today!

God, I praise You for making me, me. Amen.

Jesus' Plea

"Jerusalem, Jerusalem, you who kill the prophets and stone those sent to you, how often I have longed to gather your children together, as a hen gathers her chicks under her wings, and you were not willing."

LUKE 13:34 NIV

You can feel the anguish in His words. It's the kind of pain in a mother's cries for her child who has run away—again. It's the loving anger you see in a father's pressed-together lips when his child has been led astray by some predatory friends. It's the weary grief of the guardian who feels like she's talking to a brick wall instead of an adolescent.

Anyone who has been a parent or caregiver will recognize this plea. "I just want you to be safe," Jesus seems to say. "I want to take care of you if you will only let Me."

So many times you turn Jesus away without even realizing it. You choose to ignore your own sin issues, weave webs of deceit that even fool yourself, and turn to other comforts that only seek to destroy you. Jesus calls out to you then: "Daughter, you who run away from the only One who can save you, I just want to love you. Please turn and let Me give you forgiveness and peace."

Open your ears to this heart cry of Jesus. If you have been running, turn around. Let Him love you. If you haven't, just rest in Him today.

Lord, let me stay under Your wing. Amen.

Invitations

*"When you give a banquet, invite the poor, the crippled,
the lame, the blind, and you will be blessed."*

LUKE 14:13–14 NIV

The tables are set. Beautiful floral centerpieces decorate each one. The silverware is shining, and wonderful aromas are coming from the kitchen. You have been planning this for ages and wanted to make every detail perfect.

Now, there's just one question: Who's coming to dinner?

Perhaps you haven't arranged any banquets lately. But the same question could be asked of any gathering you have organized. Do you keep your circle of family and friends fairly closed up? Or are you open to reaching out?

Even though it's nice to think humans have made great strides in this area, there are still people who get left out in today's society. And in a world where so much happens at top speed, standing in the dust is a lonely place to be.

Perhaps you are not ready to invite someone to your house for dinner. But perhaps you might try striking up a conversation with someone who is alone on the street. Or smile at the bus driver. Or help the woman in the wheelchair at the grocery store reach that can on the shelf.

It's all too easy to let the barriers stay up between you and others. Vow today to try to break them down.

*Lord God, remind me to look around and
see who I can be a friend to today. Amen.*

Consider the Cost

*"In the same way, those of you who do not give
up everything you have cannot be my disciples."*
Luke 14:33 niv

Sometimes it seems people rush to get others (perhaps children, in particular) "saved" without taking time to allow them to consider the cost of following Christ. And these verses in Luke 14 are often not mentioned when baptism is being discussed. The focus is instead on Jesus' love, forgiveness, and blessings.

But Jesus lays it out here quite clearly: You want to follow Him? Yes. Amen. Follow Jesus. But know that could mean leaving some things and some people—maybe even everything—behind. It's not that Jesus wants your couch. He doesn't need your stuff. He just needs you to be able to leave it behind. He wants you to be willing to give up anything that is getting between you and the life of abundance He wants to give you. He wants you to have a life full of healthy relationships with people who want to encourage and love one another. And that means you may have to leave some people or some stuff behind if people or stuff is standing in your way. Abiding in Jesus could be the most expensive thing you ever choose to do—but it's worth it all.

Lord, help me know what I need to give up. Amen.

Wise Justice

May [the king] judge your people in righteousness,
your afflicted ones with justice.
PSALM 72:2 NIV

Every day we read news stories about people who have been caught in some crime, sent to court, and are now facing their sentence. Our justice system is like many other systems—when it works, it's great. When it doesn't, well, people tend to get hurt in all kinds of ways.

Having people's lives placed in your hands is an awesome responsibility. As you watch the news today, consider the minds of the city leaders, judges, police officers, emergency dispatchers, and so many others who must make heavy decisions, sometimes in a flash.

Not everyone has a king these days as described in Psalm 72, but people do have leaders in government who are tasked with delivering justice and taking care of the least members of society. Every year they are faced with scores of decisions about what is ultimately the most effective way to love one another. And how do we pay for that?

Perhaps you are in one of these positions where you have to make weighty decisions. Or perhaps the heaviest decision you have to make today is what to eat for breakfast. No matter what position you hold, ask God to grant your leaders wisdom and hearts of compassion.

Dear Lord, please give wisdom, discernment,
and compassion to those who deliver justice. Amen.

Promises Fulfilled

Not one of all the LORD's good promises to
Israel failed; every one was fulfilled.
JOSHUA 21:45 NIV

When was the last time you broke a promise? If you are like most people, it does happen from time to time, and undoubtedly more often than you would like.

Sometimes, it's very hard to keep promises. Circumstances interfere. People, places, times, and availability change. You can't control all the factors, and so that promise you made suddenly slips out of your hands.

But God's promises are not like yours. He does not make promises that He cannot keep. And He keeps every promise that comes from His lips.

Do you know what promises God has made to you? Read His Word. Search for the promises of love and compassion, forgiveness and grace, reward and suffering. For He does not just promise good things will come. He also tells you that you will have trouble. You will be tempted. You will suffer for His name. But like the Israelites who had struggled for so long and spent so much time fighting their way into the Promised Land, you will also find rest on every side. If you stay with Him, He will rescue you and bring you to a land of peace. It's a promise.

God, I want to remember Your promises.
Help me keep my word, too. Amen.

Be Free

"You cannot serve God and be enslaved to money."
LUKE 16:13 NLT

You can't buy happiness or love, some people say, but you can buy comfort.

Have you examined your relationship with money lately? What kind of hold does it have on you? Are you able to give generously to others without it being painful? Do you count every penny, or are you able to budget and plan so money does not become a recurring worry?

It's easy to be enslaved to money, or rather, to debt, when you never have quite enough to make ends meet. Your mind is always consumed with how you are going to pay for the next bill, and when. When emergencies arise, your household sinks even deeper into a pit that you may never be able to get out of.

It's also easy to be enslaved to money when you are wealthy and feel the need to keep up appearances. There's so much pressure, once you have risen to the top level of society, to do all that's needed to stay there.

But followers of Jesus can be free from these concerns. Jesus has told you not to worry—God will provide your needs. And He has told you that everyone is equal in His eyes—there's no need to hang on to a certain placement in society. God won't love you more for wearing the latest shoe style.

Lord, help me let go of the hold money has on me. Amen.

Exercise of Forgiveness

"Even if they sin against you seven times in a day and seven times come back to you saying 'I repent,' you must forgive them."
Luke 17:4 NIV

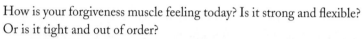

How is your forgiveness muscle feeling today? Is it strong and flexible? Or is it tight and out of order?

Forgiveness is a discipline, much like love and prayer and worship are all disciplines. To forgive well, you must practice forgiveness often. In the small moments of overlooking accidental offenses, you can practice offering grace and not being bothered. Instead of being irritated and reliving those moments, giving dramatic accounts of tiny details, why not just let them go? Put those incidents out of your mind and don't talk about them.

For greater offenses, where real hurt was meant and suffered, forgiveness may involve an ongoing program of deciding to take steps toward releasing your anger, asking God to heal your wounds, and when appropriate, restoring the relationship with the person.

Sometimes forgiveness will be as easy as saying, "No worries," and moving on with a smile. Sometimes it will be as hard as getting up every day and making yourself think the words, *I will forgive.*

But one thing you cannot do is ignore the exercise. There's a good reason Jesus commanded you to forgive and forgive and forgive again. The person who cannot forgive will never be free.

Dear God who has forgiven me so much,
help me forgive every day. Amen.

Our Portion

My flesh and my heart fail; but God is the
strength of my heart and my portion forever.
PSALM 73:26 NKJV

It's one of the mysteries of your relationship with your Creator that He loves you so much He is willing to share Himself with you. Though you, with your finite human body, may suffer in your flesh, and though your heart may refuse to beat, God is your strength. He shares His eternal life with you. He gives you a share in His kingdom—no strings attached.

And when you have loved ones who are suffering in the flesh due to illness, if they have accepted Christ, you can be confident in the fact that God is their portion as well.

What kind of portion is that? Just a piece of Him fills a person up to overflowing. A portion of God is like the eternity set in the human heart that is mentioned in Ecclesiastes 3:11—no one can find out what that means or how God works, yet each person has this longing for something more and bigger and more beautiful and far beyond what she can know or see.

Who do you have in heaven but God? No one. He is all you have. Who on earth is like Him? No one. There is no one who comes remotely close. But with God as your portion, what in the world could you possibly need?

God, thank You for sharing You with me. Amen.

God's Arbor Day

"On the mountain heights of Israel I will plant [a tender sprig]; it will produce branches and bear fruit and become a splendid cedar. Birds of every kind will nest in it; they will find shelter in the shade of its branches."
EZEKIEL 17:23 NIV

Every April thousands of people plant trees. On Arbor Day in 1907, Theodore Roosevelt said, "A people without children would face a hopeless future; a country without trees is almost as hopeless; forests which are so used that they cannot renew themselves will soon vanish, and with them all their benefits."

In Ezekiel's day, the Israelites had forsaken God and His commandments. They committed themselves to idolatry instead, and the exile was God's punishment. With Jews in exile in Babylon, their homeland had been stripped of its people like a burnt forest.

God never intended the exile to be permanent. Just as He had uprooted them, He brought them back. On God's Arbor Day, God planted a small group, a tender sprig, in Israel. It grew into a cedar that dominated the landscape.

You are a branch on the tree, the vine Jesus. Whatever your mistakes in the past, He wants you to bear fruit, grow, and offer the same to others.

Lord, make me into a branch where others can build nests.
I want to eat Your fruit and drink Your water,
both for myself and to offer the same courtesy to others.

One Thing

"What is impossible with man is possible with God."
LUKE 18:27 NIV

Who knows what motivated the man to ask the question? Perhaps he was just curious. Maybe he wanted to make a point to someone there with him in the crowd. Or maybe he had recently been made aware of his own mortality and was looking for some assurance in a life beyond the grave.

Surely Jesus knew what the man was after. But His answer wasn't so satisfactory. To get eternal life, Jesus told him, "You still lack one thing. Sell everything you have and give to the poor, and you will have treasure in heaven. Then come, follow me" (Luke 18:22).

Jesus has a knack for finding your "one thing," doesn't He? It's that one thing you are holding on to—that one thing you find so hard to give up. That one thing that keeps you from following Him completely.

His disciples marveled that if this rich man, with all his privileges, couldn't manage to make it into the kingdom, then who could? Certainly, the more you are used to having your way, the harder it is to let go. Maybe even impossible. But God can make it happen. He knows how to loosen your grip. And He has so much more for you to hold on to.

*Lord, help me let go of any one thing
that is keeping me from You. Amen.*

The Guest List

"He has gone to be the guest of a sinner."
LUKE 19:7 NIV

Imagine Jesus has come to visit your neighborhood. Someone offers to host Him and anyone else He'd like to invite. Who'd be on the list? Would you be glad to be on the guest list of sinners?

It's easy to point out sinners. And even though you may admit that you are a sinner sometimes, too, you don't really feel you belong to that crowd, right? Sinners are people who do bad things—a lot.

You make mistakes. You forget. You sometimes just don't do the right things.

But, yes, that makes you a sinner, too. And that means you need Jesus, just like everyone else.

Zacchaeus needed Jesus. He needed Him so much, he was willing to make a spectacle of himself just to get a glimpse of the Man. He climbed up into that sycamore fig tree, high above the crowd who wanted to put him down. And it worked—Jesus saw him.

What are you willing to do to see Jesus? What would you risk? How silly would you allow yourself to look?

No matter what you could give up, Jesus gave up more—and He did it for you. So, if you get a chance to sit at His table—even if your invitation is addressed to the Biggest Sinner of All—make sure you don't miss it. Be His guest.

Lord, have mercy on me, a sinner. Amen.

Hosanna!

"Blessed is the king who comes in the name of the Lord!"
Luke 19:38 niv

At the start of this month, we were celebrating Jesus' resurrection. It seems fitting then to end the month by echoing the praise of the people who first welcomed Him into the holy city. A whole crowd had lifted joyful, loud voices in praise to God for all the miracles they had seen. They spread cloaks on the road as a sign of respect and honor. Some versions of the story say they waved palm branches. They made quite a show.

As Jesus approached Jerusalem and saw these crowds, He actually wept over the city. But it seems He was not weeping because their acts of worship were so moving. He wept because it was all coming a bit too late. And the day was coming, He foretold, when their enemies would surround the city and crush them from every side. They had discovered too late what would bring peace to their city. They did not even now recognize God in their midst.

But you can. You know who Jesus is. And you can welcome Him into your heart, mind, family, household, and city today. You can sing songs of praise to Him and worship Him as your living, resurrected King, the Son of God, and the one Messiah. And you can go to Him to find peace.

Lord Jesus, show me the way to peace today. Amen.

Render unto God

He said to them, "Then give back to Caesar
what is Caesar's, and to God what is God's."
LUKE 20:25 NIV

The Pharisees were trying to trick Jesus. They wanted to ensnare Him, use His own words against Him, but the Pharisees' plan backfired. His answer was not one with which they could find fault. And so they fell silent.

They had asked Jesus this question: "Is it right for us to pay taxes to Caesar or not?" (Luke 20:22).

He asked them for a coin, and seeing Caesar's image and inscription upon it, Jesus gave His answer. "Render. . .unto Caesar the things which be Caesar's and unto God the things which be God's" (v. 25 KJV).

As a follower of Christ, consider these words He spoke so many years ago that still apply today. Be a responsible citizen. Cast your vote. Pay your taxes. Live dutifully under the authority of your government. But remember that when it comes to the matters of the heart and that which is sacred to God, He is the King to whom you bow, your highest authority.

Lord, as I seek to abide in You day in and day out, remind me at
all times that You are my sovereign God and my highest authority.
Find me a faithful servant, I pray. Amen.

Be Careful Who You Follow

"Beware of the teachers of the law. They like to walk around in flowing robes and love to be greeted with respect in the marketplaces and have the most important seats in the synagogues and the places of honor at banquets."
LUKE 20:46 NIV

Jesus warned the people against the teachers of the law. While these men were well known, they were not following God's ways. They were interested in outward appearances, but Jesus was interested in people who would serve God from the heart. The teachers prayed fancy prayers, but Jesus taught that humble prayers said in a secret place were best. The teachers paraded around showing off their wealth and authority, but Jesus, who had no place to lay His head, was a servant to all.

Heed Christ's warning here, for it remains as true today as it was when He walked the earth: be very careful whom you follow. Just because someone has a reputation does not mean he or she has good character. Look at each person's heart. Not everyone who holds a Bible in his or her hands holds its truths to be sacred. Not every preacher or prophet speaks truth. Test them. Do their words and their ways line up with scripture? Pray and ask God for discernment.

God, plant in me a discerning spirit. Show me the difference between good and bad teachers. I need wisdom that can come only from above. Amen.

Give from Your Heart

"Truly I tell you," he said, "this poor widow has put in more than all the others. All these people gave their gifts out of their wealth; but she out of her poverty put in all she had to live on."

LUKE 21:3–4 NIV

Have you ever given someone a gift anonymously? Doing so brings a special kind of joy. Knowing that the recipient received a blessing and that no credit was necessary is fun. The gift was just a blessing from God that you had the privilege of delivering!

Your Lord loves a cheerful giver! He sees not just the gift but the heart of the giver. When the widow in this story from Luke 21 gave her last coin, Jesus declared her gift the most precious of all. It was of very little value in the marketplace, but in God's economy, it was greater than all the other offerings presented at the temple that day. It was all she had left to live on, and she chose to give it to God sacrificially and cheerfully.

Give from a thankful heart. Give generously and often. In doing so, you will please God.

Dear God, help me be a cheerful giver. I trust You to provide for me all the days of my life. Your Word tells me to test You in my tithe [see Malachi 3:10]. I do so now, knowing I will always find You faithful. Amen.

God's Word Remains

"Heaven and earth will disappear,
but my words will never disappear."
LUKE 21:33 NLT

Jesus warned the people about the destruction of Jerusalem that was to come. He warned them not to get lazy but to stay alert. He warned them against getting caught up in the ways of the world. He told them that everything else would pass away but His Word would never disappear.

Jesus does not want you to be unprepared. Every day you are to put on the full armor of God and go into battle. To remain strong in the Lord, you must be deeply and firmly rooted in His Word. Satan longs to tempt you to join his team, just as he won Judas Iscariot to his side.

So many people around the world don't have the freedom to meet openly and discuss the things of God. They must hold Bible studies and worship services in secret.

Never take for granted your ability to worship God and study His Word, which is all that is lasting and true. Cling to it for life. In doing so, you will be prepared for any situation—any trial, persecution, or temptation. You will be ready when Jesus comes again.

Heavenly Father, help me value Your Word more today than I did
yesterday. And may I honor it more in my life tomorrow than I do today.
Help me love Your Word and hunger and thirst for righteousness.
In Jesus' name I pray, amen.

He Is Faithful

But then I recall all you have done, O LORD;
I remember your wonderful deeds of long ago.

PSALM 77:11 NLT

The psalmist cries out in this chapter, feeling abandoned by God. Has God stopped loving him? Have His promises failed? Before you judge this lack of faith, look to your own. Have you doubted God, felt like He has forgotten you?

God's Word points again and again to His faithfulness. Recall the Bible stories. Consider Noah hammering the final nail into a massive ark while there was not a cloud in the sky, and Abraham climbing the mountain with his beloved Isaac. Imagine the emotions of Christ's disciples those three long days between His death and resurrection. And yet each time God came through.

God is as faithful today as He was in the past. He provides. He sustains. He shows up.

When you question your Father's love, look back. Recall altars of remembrance in your own life, those constructed at places of His provision. Can you see them in your mind's eye? They are there, standing as strong as the stone monuments by which the Israelites remembered Him.

Thank God in your weakest hour for the way He came through the last time, and the time before. He is the God who sees you (see Genesis 16:13), who never changes (see James 1:17), the one whose faithfulness to you endures forever.

Thank You, heavenly Father, for Your faithfulness.
You are the same yesterday, today, and forever. Amen.

An Unseen Pathway

Your road led through the sea, your pathway through the mighty waters—a pathway no one knew was there!
PSALM 77:19 NLT

You have read the story. The Israelites, fleeing bondage in Egypt, arrive at the edge of the Red Sea with the Egyptians on their heels. At just the right moment, God parts the sea and every last Israelite passes through to the other side! And in the next instant, their pursuers are caught up in the raging waters, horses and chariots along with them.

Great story. Nice tale of long ago. Awesome movie clip. But wait. This is more than a fantasy. It really happened! And the miraculous part is that God still makes paths for you today.

When you find yourself between a rock and a hard place, cry out to God. When circumstances lead you to a dead end, lift your eyes toward heaven. God is the "great I AM," meaning that He is what you need in each moment. At times of anxiety or fear, you need the Prince of Peace. Other times, when filled with gratitude, you sing praises to the King of Glory.

Then there are Red Sea moments. At such crossroads, rely on Yahweh, the Lord who provides unseen pathways, who makes a way where there seems to be no way (see Isaiah 43:16–20)!

God, remind me that You are truly a God of miracles.
In my Red Sea moments, I trust You to make a way. Amen.

Remain Faithful

"Wherever you go, I will go; wherever you live, I will live.
Your people will be my people, and your God will be my God."
RUTH 1:16 NLT

To whom have you been called to remain faithful?

For Ruth, it was her mother-in-law, Naomi. The custom of the day would have both of Naomi's daughters-in-law return to their birth families for support after their husbands died. Only Orpah followed through with this, whereas Ruth insisted on staying with Naomi, who was widowed herself.

Because of her faithfulness to Naomi, Ruth was blessed by the Lord. She was given special privileges in the fields belonging to Boaz. He later became her husband and the father of their son Obed who became the grandfather of King David and ancestor of Jesus!

Perhaps you are in a marriage that is less than perfect. Or you may have a prodigal child or resident offspring who brings trouble and chaos into the home. Don't despair!

God is there to help you through the struggles. He honors loyalty. Stay true to your commitments. Outside of staying in a situation that is causing you real harm, stand firm. Just as God's people relied on Him in the desert and gathered only enough manna for one day at a time, trust in Him to provide.

Father, help me remain faithful. I ask You to provide
peace and wisdom in my situation today. Amen.

Impacting the Future

So the next generation would know them, even the children
yet to be born, and they in turn would tell their children.
Psalm 78:6 niv

God's ways are taught through His children. One generation learns them from the generation before them. And so it goes.

Think about the person who has had the greatest influence on your Christian walk. It may have been your mother or father. Perhaps it was a grandparent or aunt or uncle. Maybe a friend or a teacher, a church member or a pastor filled that role for you. You can likely point to someone as the person who led you to Christ. Perhaps you looked up to several people along the way—those who you knew took their faith seriously, who lived it out before you.

Your responsibility as a Christian woman is to pass on the ways of the Lord to those who come after you. Whether or not you have your own children, you have the opportunity to influence the next generation for Jesus. Consider today how you will begin to do this. If you are already well on your way in doing so, ask God to continue to reveal how you can ensure the next generation knows and follows hard after Him.

Lord, I want to be salt and light to the next generation of believers. Help me be a positive model of what it means to be a Christian woman. Amen.

See Hannah

*So in the course of time Hannah became pregnant and gave birth to a son.
She named him Samuel, saying, "Because I asked the LORD for him."*

1 SAMUEL 1:20 NIV

It's a beautiful story. Hannah prays and receives that for which she prays. But it's not that simple.

The Bible tells us Hannah longed for a child and in her barrenness was provoked by her husband's other, more fruitful wife "year after year" (see v. 7). Hannah was in deep anguish. Any woman who has longed for a child and has not been able to have one, for any reason, understands this painful longing, this brand of sorrow.

Finally, Hannah vowed to hand her yet-to-be-born son over to the Lord for His purposes. Thus, in addition to the fact that this prayer took a long time to be answered, Samuel was given to his mother at a great price. While other young boys grew up in their parents' homes, he was raised in the temple by the priest Eli.

Hannah's prayer was answered. She was granted a child who was a great blessing to her. Yet do not see only Samuel. See Hannah provoked, weeping, and praying in anguish. See her as she hands her beloved toddler over to the priest.

Never presume to know another's story or her heart.

*Father, may I see other women around me today with Your
eyes of compassion. May I never be quick to assume. Amen.*

Light in the Darkness

The light shines in the darkness,
and the darkness has not overcome it.
JOHN 1:5 NIV

A group of young girls and their camp counselor were walking through a field from the campfire back to their cabin. The campgrounds were dark and quiet because all the other groups had gone before them. No one was in sight.

The farther the group went from the campfire, the darker their path became. Only one flashlight—that of the counselor—shone light for them to follow.

Suddenly an idea came to the counselor. This was a teachable moment. She stopped and gathered the girls around her. She told them to look out ahead at their distant cabin, upon which she shone the light. Then she turned off her flashlight. "Trust in the darkness what you could see in the light," she whispered. The girls walked on a few feet, carefully, but with full knowledge that the cabin lay out there in the distance. They had seen it!

For many years after this, one of those young girls would rely on this teaching. On her darkest nights, in her loneliest hours, she would recall those wise words. "Trust in the darkness what you could see in the light."

Jesus is the Light. He is an eternal flame that will never be put out. Follow and trust in Him.

God, thank You for the Light that guides my way. Amen.

Your Ebenezer

Then Samuel took a stone and set it up between Mizpah and Shen.
He named it Ebenezer, saying, "Thus far the LORD has helped us."
1 SAMUEL 7:12 NIV

The Israelites were experiencing a great revival and a turning back to God. But they had suffered horribly at the hands of the Philistines in the past. They begged Samuel now to cry out to God on their behalf as the Philistines were set to attack. In a miraculous manner, even as Samuel presented sacrifices, God thundered from heaven and confused these enemies of the Israelites. Seeing the Philistines' hesitation, the Israelites rushed them—and were saved!

Samuel erected a stone memorial at the place where this occurred. He called the stone Ebenezer, meaning "the Lord has helped us thus far." It stood as a reminder to the people of God's faithfulness and provision.

What is your Ebenezer, and where will you erect it? Perhaps you will build it by writing down a blessing you want to remember on the pages of your Bible. Maybe you need to thank God aloud. You may choose to wear a cross necklace or carry an ichthus (the Christian fish symbol) keychain.

Whatever your memorial may look like, may it serve as a reminder to you that your God is faithful. That He has helped and will continue to help you.

Father, thank You for Your provision. Make me ever mindful
that it is by Your help that I have come this far. Amen.

Miracle Worker

This miraculous sign at Cana in Galilee was the first time
Jesus revealed his glory. And his disciples believed in him.
JOHN 2:11 NLT

What had been water, Jesus, in an instant, turned to wine. This was a sign that He was no ordinary man. Certainly Mary's son was different.

She had known this for many years. Before the tiniest bulge appeared, Mary knew she was pregnant. An angel had told her the Holy Spirit would come upon her and cause her to be with child. She would bring into the world the Son of God, the Messiah.

And it had happened just as the angel had foretold. She had laid Him in a manger for His bed. She had watched Him grow, a servant leader from the start.

And so, this wedding-day wonder was no surprise to Mary. She instructed the servants to do whatever He said. She knew He was not just a worker of miracles but a miracle Himself.

On the day Jesus turned water into wine, Mary must have smiled to herself. Now others knew what she had known all along. This was no ordinary wedding guest. This was the Messiah whose ministry had now begun.

Do you recognize Him? When Jesus shows up in your everyday life, do you watch in expectation as Mary watched that day at the wedding feast? Expect the unbelievable. You serve a miracle-working Savior.

Jesus, I want to believe in miracles. Strengthen my faith, I ask. Amen.

Born Again

*"The wind blows wherever it wants. Just as you can hear
the wind but can't tell where it comes from or where it is going,
so you can't explain how people are born of the Spirit."*
JOHN 3:8 NLT

Nicodemus was questioning Jesus about how a man could be "born again." Surely a grown man could not again enter his mother's womb! Jesus acknowledged that this rebirth is indeed mysterious. He went on to explain that humans can only give birth to a child physically and that it is through the Holy Spirit that a person is born again.

Have you experienced rebirth through Jesus Christ? If you have heard about Jesus but never accepted Him as your personal Savior and surrendered your life to His lordship, take time to do so. There is no greater celebration than that of salvation. While a natural birthday is a lot of fun with gifts and cake, spiritual rebirth provides abundant life on this earth and the promise of eternal life in heaven.

Don't be confused like Nicodemus was on this topic. Ask God to give you wisdom about what it truly means to be born again. Talk to a trusted Christian leader, a pastor, or a friend who can guide you.

If you already have assurance that you have been born again in Christ, take some time today to consider the amazing gift of your rebirth day!

God, thank You so much that through Your Son I can have new life! Amen.

Have No Other Gods before Him

They angered God by building shrines to other gods;
they made him jealous with their idols.
Psalm 78:58 nlt

God wasn't joking when He issued the Ten Commandments. The Almighty was serious when He decreed that His people have no other gods before Him. He alone is to be loved with all one's heart, mind, and soul.

The Israelites struggled with this. Remember the scene? While Moses was at the top of the mountain, they rebelled at its base, melting down gold jewelry to construct a golden calf that they planned to worship!

Before you shake your head in disapproval, look to your own life. Where do you have other gods? A god is anything you put before your heavenly Father. Has money become your focus? Do you value a relationship or even a child above God? How about your career? Your house, your car, your status, your position at your church?

Take inventory of your idols on a regular basis, rooting them out of your life just as you would dig up weeds from a garden. Other gods will choke the life out of you, steal your joy, and destroy your fellowship with your Creator.

Have no other gods before Him.

Heavenly Father, You are my God. You are the
one true God, my Creator and King. Amen.

Everlasting Water

The woman left her water jar beside the well and ran back to
the village, telling everyone, "Come and see a man who told
me everything I ever did! Could he possibly be the Messiah?"

JOHN 4:28–29 NLT

There was not a convenience store on every corner. There was no happy hour at the drive-in where she could grab a 99-cent Cherry Coke. This woman's existence relied on her water jar. That jar held life, or so she'd thought.

She was not well-liked or respected. She'd had five husbands, and everyone knew it. Other women likely gathered around the well, gossiping about her. They knew those five men by name. And she wasn't even with the fifth anymore; she was living with a boyfriend.

When the woman at the well met Jesus, truly met Him, she tossed her water jar aside. She did not walk but ran into the town to tell everyone about the Messiah.

Imagine her: skirt flying, arms flailing, a smile spread full across her sun-scorched face. The head that had once hung in shame now turned upward to heaven, a changed countenance mirroring a new heart.

What are you clinging to today? What stands between you and reckless abandon for Christ? What could you toss aside today and never miss as you, instead, soak up the goodness of everlasting water and never, ever thirst again?

Jesus, may I be like this woman who left the well,
demonstrating reckless abandon for You!

Obedience vs. Rebellion

*"Rebellion is as sinful as witchcraft, and stubbornness as bad
as worshiping idols. So because you have rejected the
command of the LORD, he has rejected you as king."*
1 SAMUEL 15:23 NLT

King Saul carried out God's instructions—well, mostly. But God wasn't interested in a "mostly" kind of leader. The Lord has a name for half obedience; it's called disobedience.

Through the prophet Samuel, the Lord had clearly told Saul to destroy the entire Amalekite nation—men, women, children, babies, cattle, sheep, goats, camels, and donkeys. But Saul allowed the king of the land to live. He also saved the best of the livestock and "everything . . .that appealed to them" (1 Samuel 15:9 NLT).

It is not up to humans to question God's commands. When God tells you to do something, do it. Just as an earthly parent teaches his children to obey, your heavenly Father disciplines those who turn away from Him in rebellion.

Saul suffered dire consequences for his rejection of the Lord's command. You, too, may pay the price for your disobedience to God. Consider what God is calling you to do. It may not be an easy task; you may not even understand the "why" of it. That's when you must simply walk in faith.

There's great reward to be found in obedience to your sovereign God.

*Help me surrender to You fully, Lord. I want to be a
daughter who is quick to obey Your commands. Amen.*

Good Shepherd

Then we your people, the sheep of your pasture, will praise you forever;
from generation to generation we will proclaim your praise.
PSALM 79:13 NIV

Although not the smartest animals, sheep can easily distinguish their own shepherd's voice from all others. That may not cause sheep to rank higher than other creatures on the IQ scale, but it shows they have their priorities straight!

Oftentimes, you may stumble through life a lot like a ewe. You go astray. You wander from the fold. You encounter dangers and snares. But your Good Shepherd remains faithful. He knows the sheep of His pasture. He watches over you. He guides you back toward home.

What a blessing it is that you can know you belong to God! Listen for the still, small voice of your Good Shepherd. He may be calling you to pursue a dream you think is unattainable, a reminder that nothing is impossible with God. He may be asking you to reach out to another woman or a child who desperately needs a word of encouragement or a bit of help. This, too, is a reminder that He will not call you to that which you cannot accomplish in His name.

Praise your heavenly Father today. Thank Him for being such a loving Shepherd. He will never lose sight of His own. May your ears always be fine-tuned to His voice.

Good Shepherd, lead me today in Your everlasting ways. Amen.

Less Is More

Another of his disciples, Andrew, Simon Peter's brother, spoke up,
"Here is a boy with five small barley loaves and two small fish,
but how far will they go among so many?"
John 6:8–9 NIV

Have you heard the expression "less is more"? Decorators have learned just a pop of color may be all that's needed. Bakers know a dash of salt goes a long way. A writer acknowledges that decluttering her text makes it more powerful. The fewer words, the stronger the message.

Yet on a day long ago, on a hillside where Jesus fed the five thousand, these words—less is more—took on a whole new meaning.

The crowds had grown larger. The more miracles Jesus performed, the more curious people became. And so they followed Him. At times the crowds were so overpowering that Christ would gather His closest twelve and withdraw. But on this day, He taught the people and decided to feed them. All of them. He did so by multiplying one child's small lunch! And ended up with leftovers!

Never wonder if your Savior has forgotten your need. He sees your longing just as He saw the hunger of more than five thousand gathered on that hillside. Never wonder if He's going to come through for you. He may not do it the way you imagine, but He will provide, and it will always be His best for you.

Miracle-working Jesus, help me remember
that nothing is impossible with You. Amen.

Bread of Life

Then Jesus declared, "I am the bread of life. Whoever comes to me will never go hungry, and whoever believes in me will never be thirsty."

JOHN 6:35 NIV

Have you ever had to feed teenage boys? They seem to be constantly growing and constantly eating! You just get done feeding them breakfast and they're back in no time for a snack before lunch!

Jesus understood the motive of the people who dogged His heels after He had miraculously fed them on the hillside. He didn't want them to be following after Him because they were hungry again but because He was the Bread of Life "that comes down from heaven and gives life to the world" (John 6:33).

This they were unable to comprehend. They knew Jesus' roots. They called the name of His earthly father, Joseph. "Isn't this man from Nazareth, the son of the carpenter?" they asked. They shook their heads in bewilderment. "How could He say He came down from heaven?" (see v. 42).

Jesus is the Son of God. He is the Way, the Truth, and the Life. Those who find the Bread of Life never go hungry again. Certainly, they will still need their fill three times a day at mealtimes. But the deepest hunger, the hunger of their souls, will be fulfilled. Forever.

*Bread of Life, fill me with contentment
that can be found only in You. Amen.*

Set Free

"I removed the burden from their shoulders;
their hands were set free from the basket."
PSALM 81:6 NIV

God reached down and saved the Israelite people from slavery in Egypt. He led them out of the land when the time was right. The exodus began with Him, through Moses, instructing the people in some strange ways. Following His directions, they smeared the blood of a Passover lamb around their door frames. They prepared unleavened bread. They walked right up to the edge of a raging sea and passed through on dry land. They looked back over their shoulders to see their pursuers swallowed up by that same great body of water.

Your God is a burden remover. He does not desire for you to remain enslaved to addiction or abuse. He wants to part the waters before you and provide safe passage. He may calm the storm and beckon you to walk on the water, or He may hold you close and calm you in spite of the storm that causes destruction all around you.

If you are downcast, look up today! Find God there, ready to call you His child, ready to loose the chains of that which binds you. Find Him faithful. Release your burden to the One who has the power to cast it out of your life.

Burden-removing Father, free me from that which
plagues me today. In Jesus' name I ask, amen.

God's Way

"But my people would not listen to me; Israel would not submit to me.
So I gave them over to their stubborn hearts to follow their own devices."
PSALM 81:11–12 NIV

Scripture says there comes a point when God turns you over to your own desires and chosen paths. That's a frightening thought!

Ever make a wrong turn? You are following your GPS, but something goes wrong. You find yourself bumping down a gravel road instead of a nicely paved highway. The GPS blares, "Turn around as soon as possible!" or "Make a U turn!" You shake your head in disbelief and talk back to the device, blaming it, in fact.

A wrong turn on the highway is frustrating but not nearly as hard to correct as veering off God's path for your life. He stands ready to guide and support you, much like that GPS that you yell at, then turn off, setting it aside to follow your own ways, which leads you into an even worse mess.

You will most likely err now and then. When you do, just be quick to ask God to get you back on the right track. Then listen to Him, submit to His wisdom, even if you don't see the logic in it. Because you do not want to be left to your own devices.

God, keep me on Your path for my life. Teach me patience to
follow Your ways even when the end isn't in sight. Amen.

One True God

The Jews there were amazed and asked, "How did this
man get such learning without having been taught?"
JOHN 7:15 NIV

Jesus is not just from God. He is God. It is a mystery Christians believe without fully understanding. The Trinity is three in One. The Father, the Son, and the Holy Spirit.

The danger in society today is that people are "okay with" God. Sound odd? Not really. The danger lies in the fact that they don't know who God is. Many believe that all of the deities are one in the same. They say Muslims call him Allah and Christians refer to him as God, but that they are one and the same. They also say there are many ways to God. These are lies.

The Bible clearly teaches there is one true God. It is only through Christ that you are saved.

When the Jews heard Christ teach, they instantly knew He was God. How else could He have such wisdom with no instruction?

Every time you hear the word god, test and measure carefully the speaker's heart and his or her definition of the word. Your God is the Almighty, the Alpha and Omega, the Beginning and the End. He is unteachable because He is, in fact, the Teacher.

God, give me discernment that I may know
You as the one true God. Amen.

Cast Not the First Stone

They made her stand before the group and said to Jesus,
"Teacher, this woman was caught in the act of adultery."
JOHN 8:3–4 NIV

It often happens on elementary school playgrounds. Children run to the teacher, pulling a troublemaker along by the arm. They just can't wait to see the offender chastised. Sometimes the accusers get their way. They stand back, pleased, as a teacher reprimands the one brought before her. But if the pack takes its prey to the wrong teacher—the one filled with compassion—the group goes away disappointed.

So it was with the religious leaders of Jesus' day. Only. . .they were adults. And their victim was a woman who'd stumbled, trapped because of a moment of weakness.

Can you imagine the words that were flying? Caught. Adultery. These were the more palatable words. Think of what they called her. You might cringe, envisioning her, head hung low. But her panel of proud judges, like the cat that drops a wounded bird at its owner's feet, thrust her before the Messiah for the expected verdict.

And. . .He loved her.

They, in utter disbelief, couldn't cast the first stone. So they went away unsatisfied.

Be Jesus to the woman in your life whom others reject. Be His smile, forgiveness, and heartbeat. Cast not the first stone. You, too, are a sinner.

Jesus, teach me to drop the stone and instead
reach out my hand to one in need. Amen.

Remain a Faithful Witness

*"Whoever belongs to God hears what God says.
The reason you do not hear is that you do not belong to God."*
JOHN 8:47 NIV

Have you tried to share your faith with a friend or relative only to be rejected? Although it may feel like a personal affront, in reality, the person is rejecting Jesus, not you.

Christ taught that the reason some people don't hear Him is because they don't belong to God. And they don't belong to God because they refuse to open up their ears and minds to what He has to say, to His truth. In effect, they're walking through life wearing ear plugs.

Be patient. Pray for those in your life who do not know Jesus, who scoff at your "religion" and smirk when you explain it as a relationship with the Savior. Know it is only through the work of the Holy Spirit that their ear plugs can be removed. In due time, and as a result of your prayers and witness, they may come to know Christ.

There is no celebration like that of a Christ rejecter turned Christ follower! Don't give up on the Sauls in your circle just because they have not heard God's voice. . .yet.

Jesus, give me the endurance I need to bear the rejection of nonbelievers in my life. I pray that one day they will come to know You as Lord. Amen.

Your Pilgrimage

Blessed are those whose strength is in you,
whose hearts are set on pilgrimage.
PSALM 84:5 NIV

This morning you may have pulled the covers back over your head after hitting the snooze button for the third time. Like many women, you are tired. Myriad demands on your time and energy are pulling you down. From the moment your feet hit the floor until you fall back into bed late at night, you are on the go.

You may not feel like you are a pilgrim, but you are. So set your heart on the pilgrimage. You, who run toward Jesus, run for a prize that is worth the struggle.

To avoid stumbling along the road, keep your eyes always fixed on Him. When someone cuts you off in traffic today, look to Jesus. When a situation at work frustrates you, stay the course. It is as if there are a million naysayers lining the sides of the track, but Jesus stands at the finish line cheering so loudly for you that His voice drowns out all the others.

You are a child of God, a daughter of the Most High, saved by grace and set on a path for success. Set your mind on the pilgrimage. God will honor your steadfastness of heart.

God, help me keep my eyes on You,
the author and perfecter of my faith. Amen.

Jesus, the Healer

"Since the world began it has been unheard of that anyone opened the eyes of one who was born blind. If this Man were not from God, He could do nothing."
John 9:32–33 NKJV

The man was blind, and then he could see. The Pharisees questioned him thoroughly regarding this miracle Jesus had performed. The man did not understand fully who Jesus was. But he understood this: he was blind, and then he could see!

He said to the Pharisees that no one in the history of the world had done such a thing—opened the eyes of one born blind. He then pointed out that if this man Jesus were not from God, He would not have been able to do this.

It didn't take an Ivy League education to figure that out. But the religious leaders of the day were, in fact, the blind ones in the story. They didn't want to believe Jesus was the long-awaited Messiah. They were looking for pageantry and grandeur, not a carpenter's son from Nazareth who didn't even own His own home.

Think about your own life. What blessing has come to you that clearly could have come only from the hand of God? Ask Him to heal your life. After all, He's the Son of God. All things are possible through Christ.

Jesus, You gave the blind sight and caused the lame to walk. Heal that which is broken in me as well. Amen.

Life vs. Death

"The thief does not come except to steal, and to kill, and to destroy. I have come that they may have life, and that they may have it more abundantly."
JOHN 10:10 NKJV

In the Garden of Eden, Satan came in the form of a serpent. He offered Eve, who in turn offered Adam, a bite of fruit. In doing so, Satan presented them with death. The fallen world was born from that choice.

Satan is nothing but a liar and a thief. His motive is never to help God's people but always to harm them.

The trouble is that the thief does not appear as a thief. He comes in disguises that are hard to discern. He seems to give good gifts when, in fact, his greatest joy is wreaking havoc in the life of a Christ-follower.

When you consider the difference between the father of lies and the Father of Lights, note this. Satan kills. Christ gives life. Satan destroys. Christ builds, and rebuilds. Satan steals. Christ gives good gifts.

Live the abundant life that is offered to you as a believer. Reject the temptations of the devil. Run to Jesus. In Him there is life abundant and free.

Jesus, You are the Giver of all good gifts. Bind Satan from my life that I might follow You always. Amen.

Call on God

In the day of my trouble I will call upon You,
for You will answer me.
PSALM 86:7 NKJV

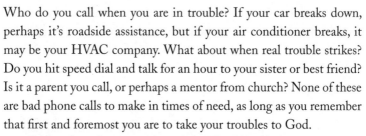

Who do you call when you are in trouble? If your car breaks down, perhaps it's roadside assistance, but if your air conditioner breaks, it may be your HVAC company. What about when real trouble strikes? Do you hit speed dial and talk for an hour to your sister or best friend? Is it a parent you call, or perhaps a mentor from church? None of these are bad phone calls to make in times of need, as long as you remember that first and foremost you are to take your troubles to God.

God is there for you night and day. His Word tells you He never sleeps. When you are depressed or lonely, He's there. When you don't know what to do, He's there. There's no trouble you could encounter that would cause God to turn His back on you. He's ready and waiting for you, His daughter, to call out to Him.

Think about the best earthly father you know. Would that daddy desert his children in a time of need? Would he ever be too busy to come running? How much more does your heavenly Father long to attend to the needs of His own?

God, I know that You are always ready to help.
May You be the first one I turn to with my troubles. Amen.

Apply the Brakes

So David sent and inquired about the woman. And someone said, "Is this not Bathsheba, the daughter of Eliam, the wife of Uriah the Hittite?"
2 SAMUEL 11:3 NKJV

King David woke in the night and went out on his balcony. Nothing wrong with that. He saw a woman bathing. He found her beautiful. Hmm. Next he inquired about her. He found out she was married. This is where the brakes should have been applied. But, like a soap opera, the story continued to unfold. David slept with Bathsheba. The next thing we know, she was pregnant with David's child and the web became even more tangled.

What can you learn from David's mistakes? When you step outside of God's will, things tend to get messy fast.

David suffered dire consequences for his sin. This doesn't mean God stopped loving him. It means David and those around him had to suffer because he chose wrong over right.

The story would not be nearly as juicy if David had simply drawn the blinds and gone back to bed that night. But it would have saved many people, including himself, a great deal of grief.

Where do you need to apply the brakes before things get out of control? God stands ready to give you the strength you need. His will and ways are always best for you.

Father, I don't want to wander from Your ways.
Help me rely on You for strength. Amen.

Jesus Is Always Right on Time

When Mary came where Jesus was, and saw Him,
she fell down at His feet, saying to Him, "Lord,
if You had been here, my brother would not have died."
JOHN 11:32 NKJV

When Jesus arrived, Mary thought He was too late. She knew Jesus, the Son of God, could have saved her brother. But now her beloved Lazarus was dead.

Yet, the fact is that Jesus is always right on time. This may be hard for you to understand because you are human. And humans operate on an earthly timetable. But Jesus, the Son of God, is beyond time and space. He can always be trusted to do what is right. He didn't "mess up" and have to fix any mistake in the story of Lazarus's death.

Lazarus had been dead four days. And yet Jesus asked that the stone blocking the entrance to the tomb be moved. An unusual request. But that's because something unusual was about to happen.

Jesus called for Lazarus to "come forth" (John 11:43 NKJV), and Lazarus did! The Savior had shown up and given life back to a dead man.

"Trust in the LORD with all your heart, and lean not on your own understanding" (Proverbs 3:5 NIV). Looking for a miracle in your life? Hold on. Jesus is never late.

Jesus, thank You for this reminder that Your
power and timing are always perfect. Amen.

Cry Out to God

GOD, you're my last chance of the day.
I spend the night on my knees before you.
PSALM 88:1 MSG

The psalmist was in misery and cried out to God. He felt as though he were near death. Been there?

In one form or another, every woman experiences extreme despair in her life. It may be due to the loss of a loved one. You may find yourself abandoned by a family member, dealing with a chronic illness, or desperate over a prodigal child who makes one bad choice after another.

Whatever the cause of your heartache, if you have not yet been in the depths of despair, at some point in your life you will be. Human existence brings with it times that are simply unbearable on your own.

During such times, you must rely on God. You may not feel Him or sense His presence, but His Word declares that He will never leave you nor forsake you.

Talk to God first thing in the morning and just before your head hits the pillow at night. He is your refuge and your strong tower in times of trouble. A brighter day will come. Joy comes in the morning. Hold on tight to God. Find strength in knowing you are never, ever alone.

God, I find comfort in knowing You are always with me and
will always see me through to the other side of sorrow. Amen.

The Cost

"Anyone who loves their life will lose it, while anyone who hates their life in this world will keep it for eternal life. Whoever serves me must follow me; and where I am, my servant also will be."
JOHN 12:25–26 NIV

A student planted the one-hundred-dollar bill on a desk in a physics class—getting all the juniors' and seniors' attention—and then they discovered it was actually a tract containing the Ten Commandments and Jesus' teachings from the Sermon on the Mount.

As it was passed around, a classmate balked at what he read. "Does this mean that if you even look at a woman with lust in your heart, you have already committed adultery? How is it possible not to do that?" While he was right—and thus humanity's great need for Jesus' saving grace—this student, like so many people who hear God's weighty, life-changing commands, counted the cost and said "no thanks" without ever meeting the One whose love makes all the difference.

Jesus Himself said that abiding in Him wasn't going to be easy. You already know how faithfully living for Christ tests your endurance and commitments. Yet you hold on to this hope and promise: The fruit you will bear and the depth you will reach in your relationship with Him are greater than anything you may leave behind. Look up (see Hebrews 12:2)! He has already cleared the path ahead.

Father, as I follow You, help me keep Your Son in my sights.

Drawing Near

For who in the skies above can compare with the LORD?
Who is like the LORD among the heavenly beings?
PSALM 89:6 NIV

In John 13 Jesus caused no small amount of consternation as He, the esteemed teacher, took on a Jewish household's lowliest job to wash His disciples' feet. Though a shock (to Peter especially), this was just one of many humbling acts that Jesus did in His earthly life. There is no one like Him—"he is more awesome than all who surround him" (Psalm 89:7 NIV)—yet Jesus came to dwell with His creation, to display His perfect love by walking with humanity side by side. The complete picture of His humility is that Jesus "loved [His followers] to the end" (John 13:1 NIV) by laying down His perfect life to redeem all humankind's imperfections.

Have you pondered how Jesus "washes" your feet? He cleansed you by His saving work, yet does confessing your sin make you shrink back from prayer?

Do not hang back as Peter did at first. Your big Brother Jesus invites you to prop up your feet and let Him see your dirty, well-worn soles—no sin of yours is too dark, no hurt too scarred, for Him to heal. Confess and repent before your Savior, and feel His gentle, loving, and protective hands washing you clean.

Jesus, thank You for humbling Yourself so
I can draw near and be renewed by You.

To Love Like Him

"A new command I give you: Love one another. As I have
loved you, so you must love one another. By this everyone
will know that you are my disciples, if you love one another."
JOHN 13:34–35 NIV

"Let go of that which does not serve you" is a popular mantra used in yoga and meditation. It can help you identify anxious behaviors, but many times it's used as permission to write off difficult people in your life. That mantra doesn't fit with Jesus' command to His followers— aside from toxic or abusive relationships, which must be considered prayerfully and with godly counsel.

Jesus does not say, "Love the Christians who make you feel your best"; you are to love all your brothers and sisters in the way He already loves you. Present and strong before you ever loved Him back (see Romans 5:8), His love is steadfast, unchanging, persevering, nurturing, encouraging, and forgiving, even in your worst moments.

Jesus knows the difficult people in your life, your church. And because He loves them and you, He will help you live out His love toward them. Dwell on His Word and His abundant mercy; as you witness His steadfast love and seek to obey His commands, He will grow your heart's capacity beyond what you thought possible, His love through you encircling those who before felt beyond your reach.

Holy Savior, I trust Your love's perfect power to change and strengthen me!

Armed with Wisdom

She spoke, saying, "They used to talk in former times, saying, 'They shall surely seek guidance at Abel,' and so they would end disputes. I am among the peaceable and faithful in Israel. You seek to destroy a city and a mother in Israel. Why would you swallow up the inheritance of the LORD?"

2 SAMUEL 20:18–19 NKJV

Joab showed up to destroy the city of Abel to get to Sheba, a troublemaker who had led the men of Israel (minus the tribe of Judah) to follow him and not David (see 1 Samuel 20:1–2). However, as Joab and his men battered the city wall to gain access, a wise woman of Abel spoke up. She knew that God's law allowed a city to attempt to make peace with its attackers (see Deuteronomy 20:10), and she convinced Joab not to destroy the city to kill only one man. Her wise, timely words, borne out of her faithfulness to God's Word, saved all those around her!

You, too, like this unnamed mother in Israel, can be wise by arming yourself with God's Word to speak up with godly counsel when the occasion arises. Walk humbly in the light of the Lord's countenance each day (see Psalm 89:15), deepening your knowledge of His character and commandments so you can lead and protect others with His truth.

*Father, thank You that You grant Your wisdom
to the woman who asks for it in faith.*

Tried and True

As for God, his way is perfect; the word of the LORD is tried:
he is a buckler to all them that trust in him.

2 SAMUEL 22:31 KJV

Amid his many troubles, David, the man after God's own heart, fully believed in God's promises to him. One important promise stands out—that David would be king and there would always be a king from his line on Israel's throne ever after—a promise that would culminate in the eternal rule of Jesus, the King of kings (see Psalm 89:28–29; Matthew 1).

If you feel like you are forever waiting and praying for God's promises to be fulfilled in your life, David would understand completely. The psalms show how David wrestled through many bleak days to keep his hope fixed on the Lord. But finally, after being on the run from Saul and fighting numerous enemies, David assumed the throne and sang today's song of praise! David would be quick to tell you that though your hope feels small, his God is trustworthy—He is your strong shield, His promises tried and true.

Today, no matter what you are up against, spend some time with David's song of praise, recounting the victories and grace the Lord has given you. Reminding yourself of His goodness and His help in the past will give you hope for the waiting—just as it did for one famous shepherd-king.

Lord, I praise You for being tried and true!

Sacrifice of Praise

The king said unto Araunah, Nay; but I will surely buy it
of thee at a price: neither will I offer burnt offerings unto
the LORD my God of that which doth cost me nothing.
2 SAMUEL 24:24 KJV

Though Araunah the Jebusite was willing to give David his oxen, yokes, and threshing equipment for the king to sacrifice to the Lord, David insisted on paying Araunah, refusing to offer a sacrifice to God that cost him nothing. David's statement is convicting. Most every woman would rather give out of her abundance than give till it hurts, but the One who saved you with His best—His very life—is worthy of your best.

Since Christ fulfilled the need for burnt offerings, how can you bring a "sacrifice"—something that costs you—to honor Him today? Hebrews 13 gives some guidance: Aside from your tithe, are you giving God a "sacrifice of praise. . .the fruit of [your] lips giving thanks to his name" (v. 15 KJV)? Does your worship involve doing good and sharing with others? "For with such sacrifices God is well pleased" (v. 16 KJV).

Let David's example give you courage to examine yourself. Ask God how He would have you deepen your worship—whether that's in giving Him praise, serving others, or giving sacrificially of what He has given you—and not just settle for what's easy to give.

Father, thank You for Your boundless generosity to me.
What would You have me give?

Eternity Now!

This is life eternal, that they might know thee the only
true God, and Jesus Christ, whom thou hast sent.
JOHN 17:3 KJV

Rapture fervor never gets wilder on Christian college campuses than during finals week. Fueled by caffeine and fear, students take help in whatever way they can get it—"Come, Lord Jesus! Before 10:00 a.m. on Friday!" Though you might laugh, you and the harried junior pleading for the Second Coming from beneath her pile of organic chemistry flash cards aren't that different. How often have you looked at the mess you are in and wished for heaven?

And that's not bad! The hope of heaven's restoration is a weighty truth, especially when the decay of the broken world presses in. But eternal life's hope isn't just future; it's now. According to Jesus, eternal life isn't dependent on a time, but a relationship with Him—knowing Him by trusting, depending, leaning on Him. If you belong to Jesus, you already participate in the eternal conversation that will sustain you until you can continue it with your Savior face-to-face.

Your King has "overcome the world" (John 16:33) and gives you peace; His sustaining presence and care are near, His restoration power strong (see Psalm 119:151; Isaiah 43:19). Whatever lies ahead, o-chem final or worse, He will always be with you, to the very end and beyond . . .starting now (see Matthew 28:20).

Jesus, thank You for eternal life! Show me how to trust You more today.

He Is for You

*"I do not pray for these alone, but also for those who will believe
in Me through their word; that they all may be one, as You, Father,
are in Me, and I in You; that they also may be one in Us,
that the world may believe that You sent Me."*

JOHN 17:20–21 NKJV

In the Psalms reading for today, the psalmist asks God to "teach us to number our days, that we may gain a heart of wisdom" (Psalm 90:12 NKJV). Perhaps you have tallied your days and felt frustrated that you aren't closer to God or that you are not done with that sin already. Look at Jesus' prayer for you in John 17—you who believed by the disciples' witness passed down through the centuries. He did not ask that your behavior be perfect, your devotional time impressive, but that you would be unified with Him as He is with the Father. And because Jesus prayed according to God's will, God will answer that prayer (1 John 5:14)!

Number your days, and don't forget to number His mercies. May your Savior's prayers encourage you when you feel like you are failing at following Him. Jesus is for you; He will continue to intercede for you before the Father until the joyful day He presents you "faultless" before the throne (see Romans 8:34; Jude 1:24).

*Jesus, thank You for Your prayers for me!
Help me be with You as You are with Father God!*

His Beauty Your Foundation

*Let Your work appear to Your servants, and Your glory to
their children. And let the beauty of the LORD our God
be upon us, and establish the work of our hands for us.*
PSALM 90:16–17 NKJV

When God told Solomon He would give him anything he asked for,
the new king requested God's wisdom in leadership and justice instead
of riches. God granted his desire, making Solomon the wisest man who
ever lived (see 1 Kings 3:9–12). The fame of Solomon's beautiful, just
decisions spread; his subjects regarded him with awe when he discerned
which of the two prostitutes was the true mother of the living child (see
3:19–28), and rulers of the nations surrounding Israel came to hear his
wisdom—his three thousand proverbs, many songs, and encyclopedic
knowledge of plant and animal life (see 4:32–34).

But Solomon would have just been some other king if God hadn't
given him the tools to be a great one. Perhaps you know believers whose
flourishing work is built on their love for God, and you wonder how
you could ever measure up to their "holiness." Leave the comparison
game behind and turn to Your Maker; examine His glorious work in
scripture, in your life. Ask Him to show you His beauty and establish
the works of your hands wherever you labor—in your community,
workplace, church, or home. He will answer.

Lord, may Your beauty establish the works of my hands!

Living in His Shadow

*He who dwells in the secret place of the Most High shall abide under
the shadow of the Almighty. I will say of the LORD, "He is my
refuge and my fortress; My God, in Him I will trust."*

PSALM 91:1–2 NKJV

Ever heard the phrase "living in someone's shadow"? Maybe you grew
up in a family with high expectations or with a sibling who seemed to
outshine you no matter what you did, leaving you feeling a bit invisible.
If you are thinking about this phrase in modern English, Psalm 91:1
sounds like a dubious blessing.

But consider Israel, the land of the psalm's original hearers—hot,
arid, desertlike in places. On a blistering day, a traveler would see the
shadow of a tall rock as a welcome place of rest and safety from the
scorching sun. In the rest of this psalm's imagery, God presents Himself
as a place of safety: Like a protective mother bird, He covers you with
His feathers; as the Deliverer He rescues you from traps and dangerous
diseases; and His truth is a shield, knocking away the lies that your
enemy Satan hurls at you.

So perhaps there's a Person whose shadow you wouldn't mind living
in, One who is ready and able to come to your aid, ready to welcome
you to hide yourself in Him.

*Father, I rest joyfully in the security of Your shadow,
the blessing of Your refreshing presence.*

Made to Be Makers

King Solomon sent to Tyre and brought Huram. . . .
Huram was filled with wisdom, with understanding
and with knowledge to do all kinds of bronze work.

1 KINGS 7:13–14 NIV

Imagine gazing up at the temple's two towering bronze pillars, their capitals adorned with pomegranates, entwined chains, and lilies. Inside, the burnished bronze of the sea catches your eye; holding twelve thousand gallons of water, its delicate lily-shaped rim is ringed with cast gourds, its base twelve bulls. Huram's wisdom in his handiwork and designs is evident, even down to the coal shovels!

Perhaps Huram's gifts are daunting, but did you know you have been given creativity, too? Whether it's fabric arts, visual arts, music, baking, gardening, dancing, running, writing, or something else, God loves it when you are creative—since you are made in His image, the Creator made you to be a maker! No matter the amount of your talent, He delights in your creativity.

Maybe creativity feels like a splurge to you or someone told you it's not as important as other pursuits. But God intends for you to use and develop all His good gifts. Ask Him to give you courage to explore your creativity, to give you the wisdom and freedom to make as He does. Who knows what beautiful, truthful, excellent things He has in store for you to create?

Father, thank You for making me creative like You!
Help me use my gifts well.

A Temple Not Made with Hands

"Will God really dwell on earth? The heavens, even the highest heaven, cannot contain you. How much less this temple I have built!"

1 KINGS 8:27 NIV

In his prayer of dedication for the temple, Solomon was right—neither heaven nor the temple could contain God. But Solomon would have been knocked off his kingly feet had he known that, to dwell with His creation, God's Son would be born into a regular Jewish family!

In John 19, Jesus' role as Emmanuel ("God with us") reaches its fullness as He gives up His life on the cross to heal the rift between humanity and God—forever changing how humans would relate to Him. Hundreds of years before, Solomon had exhorted God to turn His ear to those who would pray to Him in the temple (see 1 Kings 8:30), but now God's followers no longer have to pray to Him in a specific place. As Jesus told the Samaritan woman, God's children will worship Him in spirit and in truth (see John 4:24). If you have faith in Jesus, your heart becomes His home (see Ephesians 3:17).

How amazing to think that Jesus considers your heart, with all its fears and joys, to be a more glorious dwelling place than Solomon's temple! And no matter how worthy or unworthy you may feel, because of Christ's faithful love, He will never leave you (see Hebrews 13:5).

Jesus, thank You for dwelling in me. Let me feel Your nearness each day.

Right on Time

He asked her, "Woman, why are you crying? Who is it you are looking for?"
Thinking he was the gardener, she said, "Sir, if you have carried him away,
tell me where you have put him, and I will get him." Jesus said to her,
"Mary." She turned toward him and cried out in Aramaic,
"Rabboni!" (which means "Teacher").
JOHN 20:15–16 NIV

Surely you have wondered why Mary assumed Jesus was the gardener.
Was it because He spoke from behind her (see John 20:14), or was it
because she didn't recognize Him? But the fact remains: there she was,
mourning Jesus, and suddenly there He was. Instead of chiding her for
not believing His words, Mary's loving Savior comforted her, dispelling
the grief from her heart and replacing it with joy—and purpose. Jesus
told her to bear witness to His resurrection by telling the disciples she
had seen Him.

On your heavy-heart days, you might not really expect Jesus to
show up. But turn around, dear friend! Your Savior calls you by name,
and His grace is always right on time. Think back on how Jesus has
renewed your joy in the past: sending just the right scripture, a call from
a friend, or a surprise refund when your paycheck was beyond stretched.
With Mary, bear witness to His love and presence today!

Thank You, Jesus, that You are always on time.
Your grace is enough; You are enough.

The Flag of the Free

The LORD reigns, he is robed in majesty; the LORD is robed in majesty
and armed with strength; indeed, the world is established, firm and secure.
Your throne was established long ago; you are from all eternity.
PSALM 93:1–2 NIV

Today Americans celebrate the day in 1777 when the Second Continental Congress adopted the flag that would go on to be waved in victory after the colonies won their independence from Great Britain. Though our nation is 242 years young, the pride for our country's flag runs deep, especially when Americans consider the freedoms it represents—freedom to worship, assemble, express ourselves in the press, and peacefully change who is in power.

Yet flags may fade and countries may disappear into obscurity. In the midst of this world's turmoil, there is one ruler whose power will never change—your heavenly Father. Robed in majesty and armed with strength, He sits on His throne, which is established for all time. His truth "stand[s] firm" and holiness adorns His house "for endless days" (Psalm 93:5 NIV), and true freedom is with Him (see John 8:36).

Really, you are just a pilgrim here in the United States, only temporarily affiliated with the Stars and Stripes. As you seek to be a good citizen in the land you love, draw close to the true ruler. He has everything under control.

Father, thank You that I can trust You and depend on You no matter what.

Plan to Trust

The LORD knows all human plans;
he knows that they are futile.
PSALM 94:11 NIV

Ever have your plans blow up in your face? In 1 Kings 12, King Jeroboam of Israel had a pretty good plan to keep his kingship out of trouble, but it backfired in a big way. God had promised a throne for Jeroboam and his descendants if he was obedient to His commands, but Jeroboam was worried about one little detail—the temple in Jerusalem. He feared that if his people traveled to Judah to worship, they would defect to King Rehoboam, his rival. So Jeroboam made golden calves in Israel as a stand-in for the temple. As did Aaron, Jeroboam severely disobeyed God's commands by doing this, and while it didn't happen immediately, his kingly line disintegrated.

Certainly you have made plans for a secure life: working toward a full savings account or keeping your family healthy or other good goals. But what's driving your plans—fear of the future or faith that God's grace will be there for you in the future? Every Christian struggles with this. But relying on anything for security apart from God never ends well. . .and it puts distance between you and Him. Where is fear steering your way? Pour out your worries to Him, and He will restore your heart with His abiding peace (see John 16:33).

Jesus, help me plan to trust You; teach my
heart to expect Your grace in what's ahead.

Restoring the Kingdom

"You shall receive power when the Holy Spirit has come upon you;
and you shall be witnesses to Me in Jerusalem, and in all
Judea and Samaria, and to the end of the earth."

ACTS 1:8 NKJV

The forgotten glory of Israel was on the disciples' minds when Jesus preached about the kingdom of God. They were expecting Him to restore Israel's political power and to drive out the Romans from the land, so after His resurrection, they asked if the time was now. But Jesus' answer surprised them all. Instead of a timeline, Jesus gave them a charge that opened up the doors for the Gentiles to become a part of God's people: Equipped by the power by the Holy Spirit, the disciples would spread the word about Him to the ends of the earth.

The disciples' charge and promise is also yours. You may feel powerless when you see the brokenness in your community, but you are not; God has given you His Spirit to empower your work in His plan to restore the world, and He has prepared the work for you to do (see Ephesians 2:10). As you lean on His power to serve your community, ask Him to give you wisdom and courage to bear witness to His hope to everyone around you—with your words, your hands, your life.

Father, I want to give Your hope to my community!
Show me my part in Your plan to bring restoration.

Good Examples

Asa did what was right in the eyes of the Lord,
as did his father David.
1 Kings 15:11 nkjv

If you have spent any time around kids (related or not), you have heard their little voices echo your words back to you. . .and maybe you started wondering if duct tape could help you be more like Jesus. Today's 1 Kings reading demonstrates how important it is to be a godly example to the young: Unfortunately, King Abijam learned from his father Rehoboam's example and "walked in all the sins of his father, which he had done before him" (1 Kings 15:3).

Verses like that can give rise to terrifying thoughts: I'm going to ruin these kids! But thankfully, God's grace extends beyond your best (and worst) efforts. Though Abijam didn't follow God, his son Asa's heart "was loyal to the Lord all his days" (v. 14).

So push back the panic. Your perfect heavenly Father entrusted those little ones to you, and He knows you are imperfect! He never meant for you to teach them without His help. So, through your stinging foibles, remember, God will take care of those kids. . .and you.

Continue to let God teach you: watch how He, the Good Shepherd, tenderly cares for you, "the sheep of His hand" (Psalm 95:7 nkjv). As you grow closer to Him, He will give you grace to be a good example.

Father, thanks for Your amazing grace!
I trust You with the children in my life.

Help in Doubt

For the LORD is great and greatly to be praised;
He is to be feared above all gods.
PSALM 96:4 NKJV

When the widow's son was brought back to life, she declared to Elijah, "Now by this I know that you are a man of God, and that the word of the LORD in your mouth is the truth" (1 Kings 17:24 NKJV).

It's interesting that she didn't say this after Elijah showed her the miracle of the flour and oil. Perhaps she'd wondered, Was that really the God of Israel who rescued us from starving? Maybe it was one of the local gods. But she put her full trust in Jehovah when her son was restored to her; no other god could reverse death's curse.

Maybe pain is running rampant in your life or you are looking at what's happening in the world and wondering where God even is. But He's here, and He's powerful—the God who brought the widow's boy back from the dead also raised your Savior. . .and resurrected your heart to new life.

When doubt strikes and death seems triumphant, immerse yourself in His truth. Don't fear your doubt, for God doesn't; abiding in Christ sometimes looks more like clawing to catch hold of Him. Seek Him; He will show you the truth the widow knew—that He is present and mighty—and fill your heart with what it needs.

Father, thank You that You will help me when doubt strikes.

Wilderness Days

*So he said, "I have been very zealous for the LORD God of
hosts; for the children of Israel have forsaken Your covenant,
torn down Your altars, and killed Your prophets with the
sword. I alone am left; and they seek to take my life."*
1 KINGS 19:10 NKJV

After the Lord's triumph at Mount Carmel, Elijah spent forty days in
the wilderness, despondent beyond belief, thinking he would soon die
at the wicked hands of Ahab and Jezebel. Despite all of his work for
God, all Elijah saw was the death of God's prophets, and God's people
going way wayward. He cried out, "It is enough! Now, LORD, take
my life, for I am no better than my fathers!" (1 Kings 19:4).

Instead of God giving Elijah a pep talk—"Remember all My
miracles? My ravens feeding you by the brook? Get back in the game,
Elijah!"—He sent an angel to sustain him in his grief. At the end of
the forty days, God showed his servant His nearness in the still, small
voice after the earthquakes and the wind and fire.

Maybe you have beaten yourself up for not doing more or being more
for God. Or maybe you feel like your efforts go unseen or your resources
are exhausted. But during your wilderness days, your compassionate
God is by your side, too, and He always has more grace than you expect.

Lord, thank You that You are near on my wilderness days.

Open Homes and Hearts

*So continuing daily with one accord in the temple, and breaking bread
from house to house, they ate their food with gladness and simplicity
of heart, praising God and having favor with all the people.*
ACTS 2:46–47 NKJV

The early church in Acts is famous for its generosity—they sold property
to meet their members' needs (Acts 2:45)—but they were also known for
their hospitality. These believers were in one another's lives on a daily
basis—going from house to house to share meals and their joy in God.

These believers ate meals together with "simplicity of heart." Perhaps
the word hospitality generates "complexity of heart" in you, whether you
fear judgment ("My home's not that big, and it's a mess!") or comparison
("I can't cook as well as she can"). But those things aren't the heart of
hospitality. Instead, hospitality is the intentional practice of making space
for sharing life with others anywhere—in your home, a coffee shop, or a
park. For believers, hospitality provides opportunities outside of church
to be "Jesus with skin on" for one another: to listen, to eat together, to
lend strength and encouragement on heart-weary days. And you get to
model God, who keeps a place open for you at His table to nourish your
spirit. Whom could you invite to spend time at your table?

*Father, Your love is amazing! Help me
share it with everyone who enters my home.*

Shining Brightly

Light is sown for the righteous, and gladness for the upright in heart.
Psalm 97:11 kjv

If you live in the northern hemisphere, the days of the year dance from short to long, then back again. This journey of lengthening daylight culminates in today, the first day of summer, the most light-filled day of the year.

Though you are used to the changeability of everything on this earth, the light of the Lord does not fade, and what a promise that is! The Amplified Bible says light is "strewn along" the "pathway" of the righteous—that through the suffering and pain of a broken world, the way for God's people is lit with truth and joy, "the irrepressible joy which comes from consciousness of His favor and protection" (Psalm 97:11 ampc).

Until heaven comes and God's light fills the Holy City, making the sun and moon obsolete (see Revelation 22:3, 5), be confident that Jesus, the Light of the World, is lighting your way; as you spend time in the Word and prayer, He will help you cultivate joy in the midst of uncertain bends in the path. As the season of summer blooms—months of bustle and fruitfulness, of gardens and relationships growing in the sunshine—may you reap a harvest of irrepressible joy as you grow closer with your faithful God who lights your pathway through any darkness, through any valley (see Psalm 23:4).

Father, fill me with Jesus' joy so I may shine just as brightly!

Celebrate Justice. . .and Grace

*So the king died and was brought to Samaria, and they buried
him there. They washed the chariot at a pool in Samaria. . .and
the dogs licked up his blood, as the word of the LORD had declared.*
1 KINGS 22:37–38 NIV

The prophecy made Ahab quake in his sandals—his kingly line would
fall, and the dogs would lap up his blood (see 1 Kings 21:19–22). Well
aware of the trouble he was in, Ahab tried to escape his fate by dressing
up like a common soldier when he went to battle, but an arrow drawn
"at random" caught him "between the sections of his armor" (22:34 NIV),
showing that God's justice cannot be fooled.

Maybe you did a little victory dance when you read that Ahab got
what he deserved. But. . .have you considered your sins' consequences
recently? Surely you haven't stolen and committed murder as Ahab did,
but sin in any form creates distance between you and God and hurts
your fellow man. And its consequences reverberate. So celebrate His
justice, but be sure to fall on His grace.

As you come into God's presence through Jesus, confess your sins
with reverence and awe for His unfathomable holiness and grace, and be
restored. Humbly thank Him for the forgiveness He gave in Christ—
because you have only escaped the true weight of justice through grace.

*Father, let me never forget that my relationship
with You was bought by Jesus' sacrifice.*

On Your Side

[The Sadducees] arrested the apostles and put them in the
public jail. But during the night an angel of the Lord
opened the doors of the jail and brought them out.

Acts 5:18–20 niv

Arrested and imprisoned out of jealousy (see v. 17), the disciples were no doubt praying about how to handle this new setback when an angel of the Lord flung open the jail doors. The heavenly being told the astonished believers God's command: " 'Go to the Temple and take your stand. Tell the people everything there is to say about this Life' " (Acts 5:20 msg). And so they did, leaving behind the still-locked prison and a befuddled captain of the guard (vv. 21–24).

If God has something for you to do, what's going to stop you? Perhaps you have seen His prison-breaking handiwork in your community: funds coming in for adoption fees; closed countries approving visas for undercover missionaries; parents taking their baby girl home after months in the neonatal intensive care unit when they'd been told she'd had little chance of survival; a text from your sister, who has shown no interest in Jesus, wanting to talk about spiritual things.

No one and nothing can stop what the Lord has planned for you to do to glorify Him. Though you will have your jail-cell nights, wait for His power to fling open those doors and then tell everyone about what He's done!

Jesus, thank You that You are on my side!

Practicing His Compassion

Know that the LORD is God. It is he who made us,
and we are his; we are his people, the sheep of his pasture.
PSALM 100:3 NIV

In Old Testament days, few people were more defenseless than widows and orphans. Yet God's love for the vulnerable is demonstrated across the Bible and in today's reading: Through God's power, Elisha provides for the widow's debt. With the miraculous continual supply of oil from her little jar, she was able to save her sons from being sold into slavery (see 2 Kings 4).

James says that truly living out your faith—"pure religion and undefiled"—involves loving widows and orphans, "to visit [them] in their affliction" (James 1:27 KJV). As were the apostles and early church in their provision for the widows in today's Acts reading (6:1–6), God's people should be marked by their love for the marginalized or forgotten.

Practicing being like God in His compassion helps you grow closer to His heart. You will learn to love as He loves, helping people who feel overlooked to know, through your care, that He is the God who sees, who provides. As you draw strength from your Good Shepherd's compassionate care toward you, how will you share His love with the vulnerable people around you?

Father, Your love is so beautiful. Lead me to the hurting people who need Your love today so I can share the hope You have given me.

Seal of Approval

*I will be careful to lead a blameless life—when will you come
to me? I will conduct the affairs of my house with a blameless
heart. I will not look with approval on anything that is vile.*
Psalm 101:2–3 niv

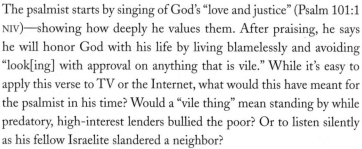

The psalmist starts by singing of God's "love and justice" (Psalm 101:1
niv)—showing how deeply he values them. After praising, he says
he will honor God with his life by living blamelessly and avoiding
"look[ing] with approval on anything that is vile." While it's easy to
apply this verse to TV or the Internet, what would this have meant for
the psalmist in his time? Would a "vile thing" mean standing by while
predatory, high-interest lenders bullied the poor? Or to listen silently
as his fellow Israelite slandered a neighbor?

Entertainment isn't the only area where "vile" things are condoned.
Sometimes it happens when people turn away from those crying out
under the weight of a wicked government or when their rights are
being trampled by profit-hungry companies. It's not easy to seek justice.
But when you spend time in the Word, your idea of justice will start
to align more with God's. Ask Him humbly, and He will deepen your
understanding of what it is to walk blamelessly before Him, of when
to speak against vile things. Amplify your song of His eternal love and
justice with action!

*Father, You love justice. I want to love Your ways
and help bring comfort in an unjust world.*

"His Eye Is on the Sparrow," Part 1

*I am like a pelican of the wilderness; I am like an owl of the desert.
I lie awake, and am like a sparrow alone on the housetop.*

PSALM 102:6–7 NKJV

The circumstances of the psalmist's prayer could have been anything—chronic pain, an enemy's affliction—but the psalmist lays it all out before the Lord, describing how his "bones burn like glowing embers" and he is "reduced to skin and bones" (Psalm 102:3, 5 NIV). In his suffering, he felt alone, like a solitary bird on the roof.

Though the psalmist felt alone—as maybe you sometimes do—it doesn't mean he was overlooked. For God sees every sparrow, and His children are worth much more than the birds of the air (see Matthew 10:29–31). You are seen; your pain does not go unnoticed.

As tempting as it is to put on a brave front and swallow your pain, don't withhold your lament from the Lord. Lamenting is different from complaining—it's not blaming God but crying out for His mercy. Follow the psalmists' example: There are more psalms of lament than any other type. Lamenting is part of abiding—for it is waiting patiently through your tears, waiting in expectant hope for the help of the One who hears, the One who will answer.

*I sing of Your truth, Father, trusting You: Your eye is
on the sparrow, and I know You are watching me.*

"His Eye Is on the Sparrow," Part 2

He shall regard the prayer of the destitute,
and shall not despise their prayer.
PSALM 102:17 NKJV

After lamenting, the psalmist continues his prayer and expresses his expectation that he will see the Lord's goodness—that God will "arise and have compassion" (Psalm 102:13 NIV). He cries out in full confidence of God's answer—not because he has anything to offer (feeling "destitute"), but because of God's immense love for him. The psalmist's key to enduring suffering is to turn his focus to God's eternal nature, to His promised plan to show mercy to His people.

Endurance in trials comes not from an immediate alleviation of your circumstances but the expectation that you will see the character of the One who holds you fast; that you will see His mercy and favor (see v. 13), His glory—beheld by all the nations of the earth (see vv. 15–16); that you will witness those things in your own life as you entrust your life to His care.

Whether you feel destitute—of inspiration, willpower, love, physical strength, holiness—He hears you. He doesn't despise you in your weakness but draws near to you, for nothing can separate you from His love (see Romans 8:38–39). Keep holding on—He will give you strength in the prayer-filled wait for restoration.

Father, when I feel I have little to offer,
thank You that You always hear my prayer!

Nothing Is Wasted

At that time a great persecution arose against the church which
was at Jerusalem; and they were all scattered throughout
the regions of Judea and Samaria, except the apostles.

ACTS 8:1 NKJV

Dismayed that their neighbors had turned away from centuries of religious tradition, many in Jerusalem rose up to persecute Jesus' followers to the point that the Christians fled the city. While it was terrible at the time, in the end the Christians could echo Joseph's words, "You meant evil against me; but God meant it for good" (Genesis 50:20 NKJV). Because the Christians took the Gospel wherever they went, their persecutors' attacks backfired spectacularly!

Jesus warned that Christians will experience suffering, especially persecution (see Matthew 5:10, John 16:33). But God's Word also promises that whatever happens, your story fits perfectly into the big picture of His plan (see John 9:1–3; Romans 8:28). Nothing is wasted, not your victories and hard work, your sins or pain or attacks from others. He fashions every part of your life for your good and His glory. Whatever you endure now, God will not waste it.

Will you open your pain to Your heavenly Father, trusting that He will use it beautifully as a conduit for His glory? Rest in and be empowered by His promise of working all things together "for good" (Romans 8:28), knowing that "He who promised is faithful" (Hebrews 10:23 NKJV).

Father, thank You for being the Author of my
story and that You are in charge of it all!

Divine Appointments

Then Philip ran up to the chariot and heard the man reading
Isaiah the prophet. "Do you understand what you are reading?"
Philip asked. "How can I," he said, "unless someone explains it
to me?" So he invited Philip to come up and sit with him.
ACTS 8:30–31 NIV

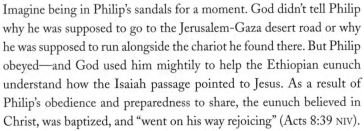

Imagine being in Philip's sandals for a moment. God didn't tell Philip why he was supposed to go to the Jerusalem-Gaza desert road or why he was supposed to run alongside the chariot he found there. But Philip obeyed—and God used him mightily to help the Ethiopian eunuch understand how the Isaiah passage pointed to Jesus. As a result of Philip's obedience and preparedness to share, the eunuch believed in Christ, was baptized, and "went on his way rejoicing" (Acts 8:39 NIV).

In results-oriented terms, you might wonder if it would be worth the miles and time to preach to just one person, but apparently God thinks so—every lost sheep is worth His time and attention (see Luke 15:4–7). Spending time with Him in the Word and prayer will help you prepare for witnessing, whenever and to whomever He sends you; when you are abiding in the Truth, you will start getting nudges from God to show up in places or relationships you may not have expected. Keep your calendar open for these divine appointments!

Lord, ready my heart and words to minister
to the people You bring to me on my way.

Powerful Mercy

"But Lord. . . I've heard many people talk about the terrible things this man has done. . .! And he is authorized by the leading priests to arrest everyone who calls upon your name." But the Lord said, "Go, for Saul is my chosen instrument to take my message to the Gentiles."

ACTS 9:13–15 NLT

Ananias had good reason to ask God to clarify why he would be helping Saul—a man who was beyond zealous for the Jewish faith, who approved Stephen's death and dragged believers to jail. Yet God chose Saul as a "vessel" to preach to the Gentiles, proving no one is beyond God's salvation.

Henry Gerecke trusted God's amazing power to redeem, too. A Lutheran minister, he served as a "spiritual helper" to Nazi officers before and during the trial of Nuremberg. By his own account, he saw some of those beyond-notorious men repent and turn to Christ. God's promise of forgiveness is staggering; for anyone who repents, He will remove his sins "as far from [him] as the east is from the west" (Psalm 103:12 NLT).

In His mercy, God redeemed Saul, giving him a new name (Paul) and task, for which he praised Him ever after (see 1 Timothy 1:15–17). When you think of people who seem too far from God, don't rule them out but boldly pray for transformation—that they will witness firsthand the beautiful reach of God's mercy.

Loving Father, teach my heart to be as merciful as Yours.

Something Like Scales

Immediately, something like scales fell from Saul's eyes,
and he could see again. He got up and was baptized.
Acts 9:18 niv

Saul was the least likely candidate to become a Christ-follower. He was a Jew among Jews and a persecutor of Christians. All this changed when he met Jesus in a bright light on the road to Damascus! At that time, Saul was temporarily blinded. And then a disciple named Ananias was sent by God to lay hands on Saul and restore his vision.

Scripture says "something like scales fell from Saul's eyes." He was a new man. He was soon to receive a new name—Paul. Paul would become a faithful apostle of Christ, a great evangelist, and the writer of many books of the Bible! From Christian-murderer to Christian-maker, he was truly a new creation!

This story is a powerful one.

Ponder for a moment the "Saul" in your life. Who is the least likely candidate to become a Christian? Think about that coworker or friend who scoffs at you for being so "religious." The world has its claws dug deeply into this individual. He or she is wearing spiritual blinders.

Pray for this person today. Ask God to remove the scales covering his or her eyes. He's done it before and He can do it again. You serve a miracle-working God!

God, please open the eyes of _____. Draw _____ to yourself
by the power of the Holy Spirit. In Jesus' name, amen.

Boundary Lines

You have set a boundary that they may not pass over,
that they may not return to cover the earth.
Psalm 104:9 NKJV

God is the Creator and ruler of the earth. At the sound of His voice, mountains tremble. At His command, storms begin and end. He is so powerful that the human mind cannot begin to comprehend His strength.

God, at one time, flooded the entire earth because it was evil. He saved only one man and his family and two of each animal. It has become a popular children's toy and story—the cute wooden ark filled with animals. But in reality, it was horrendous. Everyone died—except the chosen few related to a man God found righteous.

After the flood, God put a rainbow in the sky as a promise. He made a covenant with humans that He would never again flood the earth. He told the waves they would never come forth with such a vengeance again.

God sets forth boundaries in your life as well. Those "boundary lines" fall for you in "pleasant places" (Psalm 16:6 NIV).

Even if you are facing your own "flood" in life—unemployment, loss, disappointment, or depression—God is your portion. Your joy is found in Him, not your circumstances. He will never give you more than you can bear and will draw the lines for you. He is always with you and always has your best interest at heart.

God, thank You for being all I need. Amen.

Work and Rest

Man goes out to his work and to his labor until the evening.
PSALM 104:23 NKJV

Way back in Genesis 2:3, God set a pattern for humans to follow: He worked six days and rested on the seventh. In Exodus, God commanded His people to "remember the Sabbath Day [the seventh day] by keeping it holy" (20:8 NIV) and to rest and worship on that day. In Ecclesiastes 3:1 (NIV) Solomon wrote, "There is a time for everything" (NIV, emphasis added).

God knows you need both work and rest (preferably, the daytime for work and the nighttime for rest, for doing so follows the natural rhythms of your body). For if you never work, your muscles will weaken; your mind, atrophy; your spirit, sadden. You will feel purposeless and empty. And yet if you work all the time and never rest (ideally sleeping seven or eight hours each night and taking off at least one day per week), your body will fail you.

So go about your day and accomplish the tasks at hand. Whether you work in the home or outside of it, paid or unpaid, do all that lies before you today for the glory of God. But when it's time to rest, never feel guilty for doing so. God created man and woman. He made the day and the night. He created the first workweek, and the Sabbath was His idea!

God, help me find the right balance between work and rest. Amen.

Pray for America

O Lord, how many and varied are Your works! In wisdom have
You made them all; the earth is full of Your riches and Your
creatures. . . . These all wait and are dependent upon You.
PSALM 104:24, 27 AMPC

On this, your nation's birthday, pray.

Pray for your nation. Lift up your leaders by name. Offer thanksgiving to the Lord for the freedoms you enjoy—including the freedom to worship God, read the Bible, study His precepts. Remember those who've given their lives for all those freedoms.

But most of all, remember that even on this Independence Day, you remain dependent on God the Father, Jesus the Son, and the Holy Spirit. And as you remain dependent on them, they remain dependent on you to spread the light, the glory, the wonder, and spirit of the Good News—news that is not limited to one nation but goes beyond borders.

If you are not sure where to begin spreading the light, start with yourself. Realize your dependence on God. Drink, eat, and abide in His Word, knowing that it is life itself. With God's wisdom and in His power, the Holy Spirit will instruct you from there.

God, I lift my nation and its leaders up to You. Thank You for all the
freedoms I enjoy, especially the freedom to abide in and worship You.
Use me, Lord, to spread Your light beyond my border.

Attitude Makes the Difference

I will sing to the LORD all my life;
I will sing praise to my God as long as I live.
PSALM 104:33 NIV

Have you ever noticed a difference among elderly individuals? Some seem depressed. They go through their days focusing on their ailments and woes. Others are bright and happy with cheerful spirits and never a word of complaint. Are the chipper seniors healthier? Have they been spared arthritis, diabetes, heart issues, and digestion troubles? Not at all! The difference lies in a little thing that makes a big difference—the attitude they choose to take!

If you determine to sing to the Lord all the days of your life, as the psalmist did, you will have a hard time listing off all your troubles to everyone who will listen. It's pretty tough to sing praises to Jesus while whining about what aches.

Happiness is a choice. If you have the joy of the Lord planted deep within your soul, you will be able to shine for Him, regardless of your circumstances. Commit today to praise Him all the days of your life. It will make all the difference in the world!

Heavenly Father, You are so good. You are my provider and my
companion. Whether I have plenty or am in need, whether I am among
others or on my own, You are my God and I will praise You. Amen.

Praise the Lord

Give praise to the LORD, proclaim his name;
make known among the nations what he has done.
PSALM 105:1 NIV

It's good to praise the Lord, to let others know you honor God in your life and proclaim Him as the Lord of lords and King of kings.

When others notice something about you or praise you in any way, point them to the Lord with a statement such as, "God has blessed me with this ability, and I'm thankful for the opportunity to use it for His glory." This takes the focus off of you and puts it where it belongs—on God.

Praising the Lord takes many forms. You can do it by singing and tithing. Being a part of a local body called the church is another. Praise Him with words but also through your actions, because faith without works is dead (see James 2:20).

When you receive a blessing, rather than just being happy, discipline yourself to immediately thank God. Praising the Father for who He is and thanking Him for all that He does go hand in hand. And gratitude, as it turns out, increases your sense of well-being! It's a win-win!

You are called to make God's name known throughout the nations. This starts by praising Him in your own home, workplace, and community. Wherever you are, whatever you do, remember the importance of praising God!

Father, I praise Your holy name. May I
always remember to worship You. Amen.

Sharing the Gospel

Through [Jesus] everyone who believes is set free from every sin,
a justification you were not able to obtain under the law of Moses.
ACTS 13:39 NIV

Paul spoke these words to Jews in a synagogue. He was on a missionary journey with Barnabas. When he had seen the light on the road to Damascus, his life had been turned upside down. A Jew among Jews, Saul (as Paul had formerly been known) had followed the letter of the law. He knew the scriptures backward and forward. But suddenly his eyes had been opened. He knew Jesus was the Messiah, the fulfillment of the prophecies. And he could not keep the good news to himself!

The greatest news Paul had ever heard was that through Christ people could be forgiven of their sins. He shared fervently with all who would listen that this forgiveness couldn't be obtained under the law of Moses. Paul's chains had been loosed. His freedom was in Christ, and he longed to see others set free as well!

Do you share Christ with those around you? Do you dare to speak of Him as boldly as Paul did? Are you afraid of what others' reactions might be? Challenge yourself this week to share your faith with at least one person. God will bless your efforts even if your message is rejected.

God, help me have the boldness of the apostle Paul.
I want those around me who are lost to be saved. Amen.

God of Miracles

He listened to Paul as he was speaking. Paul looked directly at him,
saw that he had faith to be healed and called out, "Stand up on
your feet!" At that, the man jumped up and began to walk.
Acts 14:9–10 niv

Paul and Barnabas were traveling around, sharing the Gospel message. They preached it boldly. Many accepted, while others rejected their message. When they were in Lystra, Paul was given power by the Lord to heal a lame man, a man who had never walked—until now! Through the power of the Holy Spirit, Paul healed him, and scripture reveals to us why this man was selected: when Paul looked at the man, he could see "that he had faith to be healed."

Do you believe as this man did? Do you wake up each day expecting the Lord to do great things? Or have you given up and laid to rest a big dream in your life?

You serve a God who is powerful enough to make a lame man stand up and walk! Believe in Jesus. He's above and beyond all you can imagine. He can bring beauty from ashes in your life. He can make dry bones live again.

God, give me hope again where I am hopeless. You are a God
who still works miracles in Your children's lives. Help me
believe. Help me stand up on my feet again! Amen.

Leaders in the Church

Paul and Barnabas appointed elders for them in each
church and, with prayer and fasting, committed them
to the Lord, in whom they had put their trust.
Acts 14:23 niv

Paul and Barnabas had front-row seats to rejection. As the two men moved about on their missionary journey, many people accepted the good news of Jesus. But at the same time, many—especially Jews—rejected the Gospel. These two bold preachers were often threatened. In fact, Paul was stoned and left outside one city, believed to be dead.

At times the two would leave a town and move on, shaking the dust off their sandals as a warning to the citizens there. They were not just rejecting Paul and Barnabas; they were rejecting Jesus Christ, the only way to the Father!

Paul and Barnabas saw the trials and temptations that were going to befall new believers. They knew the local churches needed leaders. So they put into place elders, then painstakingly prayed, fasted, and committed these leaders to the Lord.

Who are the leaders in your church? Do you have elders or deacons? There may be community group leaders or other shepherds who are leading your local congregation. Respect them. Remember to pray for God to protect and use them.

Lord, remind me of the great respect I should
have for the leaders in my church. Amen.

Out of Nowhere

He opened the rock, and water gushed out;
it flowed like a river in the desert.

PSALM 105:41 NIV

Has a blessing ever appeared in your life that seemingly came out of nowhere?

The Israelites experienced this phenomenon time and time again as God led them out of Egypt. He opened the Red Sea, and they walked right through it on dry ground. He fed them bread from heaven called manna. He even opened a rock, and water gushed forth to sustain them.

You may be walking through a desert right now in your own life. Perhaps the job that seemed so secure is suddenly gone. Or a relationship has crumbled around you. Or a loved one has passed away. Regardless of the barren land in which you find yourself, know God hasn't forgotten you.

Abide in Christ. Read His Word. Stand on His promises. He has called you more than a conqueror (see Romans 8:37), has promised you hope and a future (see Jeremiah 29:11), and will never leave nor forsake you (see Hebrews 13:5).

You may never see water flood out of a rock, but get ready. There are blessings ahead of you that will seem to come out of nowhere! God has a bright future in store for you and is able to do above and beyond what you can imagine in your wildest dreams.

Father, help me believe in miracles. I know
You have a good future for me. Amen.

Working Together

Paul and Barnabas stayed on in Antioch, teaching and preaching the Word of God. But they weren't alone. There were a number of teachers and preachers at that time in Antioch.
ACTS 15:35 MSG

Have you ever been part of a group that simply had "too many chiefs"? It's hard enough when there are not enough leaders. It's even harder when there are too many!

Paul and Barnabas had been spreading the Gospel. New leaders had grown out of this movement, many of whom were chosen by Paul and Barnabas to help handle the burgeoning workload of shepherding new believers.

If you are a leader in your church or in a ministry, learn from Paul and Barnabas. Delegate to others. You do not need to be the only leader! If you are working under a leader, consider ways in which you can grow and take on more responsibility to lessen your leader's load.

Sharing the work of the Lord is a good practice. God established the church for this very reason. He also made the body of Christ one but made up of various parts. Each part been given different gifts and abilities. Determine your talents and how you can use them and your time for the Lord. And be sure to encourage all of those within your sphere of influence in all their endeavors.

Dear God, help me be a faithful follower, an effective encourager, and a loyal leader. In Jesus' name, amen.

Remember God

They soon forgot His works; they did not wait for His counsel.
PSALM 106:13 NKJV

Humans are quick to forget. Just as the Israelites forgot God's magnificent works in their lives, you, too, may turn your back on the Father. You forget the good and dwell on the bad. You get hurried and harried. You go out before Him instead of waiting on His hand to lead you in the right way at the right time. You accuse Him of withholding good gifts. Admit it. You are just as bad as an Israelite at the foot of Mount Sinai. Your face shines in the golden glow of the calf—or whatever idol you have fashioned to replace the King.

Stop today. Erect for yourself an altar of remembrance. Name the places and times God has blessed you beyond measure. He longs to do so again. In the moments when the grass appears greener, yesterday or tomorrow, rest in the unsettledness of today. It's okay if you cannot see the way. You know the Way Maker.

God is for you. Just as His heart was for the Israelite people, His heart beats for all who call Jesus Lord and Savior. Remember Him. Count your blessings. Trust God, who is the same yesterday, today, and tomorrow.

Father, help me be faithful. To remember the wheres and
whens of your hand of blessing on me and my life.
Find me loyal and thankful this day. Amen.

Strengthened by the Lord

*Because God helped the Levites, strengthening them as they
carried the Chest of the Covenant of GOD, they paused
to worship by sacrificing seven bulls and seven rams.*
1 CHRONICLES 15:26 MSG

The ark of the covenant was not too heavy for the men carrying it. So why does the Bible tell us that God helped them carry it? In what ways did they need strengthening?

These same men had witnessed Uzzah fall dead for merely touching the ark to steady it (see 1 Chronicles 13:9–10)! The remaining Levites probably trembled at the thought of transporting it. But God calmed their fears. He strengthened them emotionally and mentally for the task. Not only this, but He helped them.

Often, when you are going about the business of the church, you may forget God. Although you are capable of carrying out a lot of well-laid plans in your own human strength, let this verse serve as a reminder for you to seek and rely on God's help.

You may not feel you need God to assist you. But without God, you wouldn't take your next breath, much less carry out the missions you may have created in your own limited thinking. So before you stumble, reach out to the Lord. Ask Him to lead, guide, and strengthen you on the way.

*Heavenly Father, help me in all I do today. You are my strength,
my steady rock, my ultimate helper. In Jesus' name I pray, amen.*

God's Plans Are Best

When your days are over and you go to be with your ancestors,
I will raise up your offspring to succeed you, one of your own sons,
and I will establish his kingdom. He is the one who will build
a house for me, and I will establish his throne forever.
1 CHRONICLES 17:11–12 NIV

David wanted to build a temple to house the ark of the covenant. He felt guilty that he was living in a fine home built of cedar and that the ark had no home. His heart was in the right place. But God had other plans.

The prophet Nathan delivered God's word to King David that his son Solomon was the one God would allow to build the temple. God wanted a man of peace to construct it. Although the message wasn't exactly what David expected, it pleased him nonetheless. The warrior David accepted Nathan's news and was beyond thankful to the Lord for establishing his family to be used in God's service.

Even if you feel your plans are God-centered and for His glory, He may have His reasons for thwarting them. So if something isn't going the way you had envisioned, resist the urge to blame God. Trust Him. He will use you as He sees fit. His choices and His timing are always perfect.

God, help me rely on Your wisdom rather than my own,
for You see the big picture. Amen.

Judgment Day

"For he has set a day when he will judge the world with justice by the man he has appointed. He has given proof of this to everyone by raising him from the dead."
Acts 17:31 niv

One day every knee will bow and everyone will declare Jesus Christ as Lord. Paul preached this truth in his day, and it is still being preached today. Yet many people wander aimlessly, never accepting Christ, never seeing the Light of life.

If you have accepted the free gift of salvation, you don't have to fear the day of judgment. When you are asked why you should enter heaven, your answer will be simply, as the old hymn "Jesus Paid It All" puts it; "All to Him I owe. Sin had left a crimson stain. He washed it white as snow."

Can you imagine living life either oblivious to salvation or in rejection of it? Pray for those you know who are rebuffing Christ. Ask that God use the Holy Spirit to remove spiritual blinders. Be open to God using you to share the Gospel message, even if it is rejected.

Father, I pray for all of those who don't know You or refuse to know You. May they come to seek and love You as I do so that at Your judgment seat they, too, may proclaim freedom and acceptance through my Savior. Amen.

Share Your Story

Let the redeemed of the LORD tell their story—those
he redeemed from the hand of the foe, those he gathered
from the lands, from east and west, from north and south.
PSALM 107:2–3 NIV

You have a story. Whether you came to know Christ as a natural consequence of growing up in a Christian home or found Him later in life, you have a story.

Scripture commands God's people to tell their stories. Never feel that your story is boring or that you haven't much to say. Jesus Christ saved you from eternal separation from a loving God. That's a great story—one worth sharing!

Statistics show that most people come to know Jesus as their personal Savior through a family member or friend. Someone shares the Gospel, and another soul is won for the kingdom of God.

Spend some time before God today. Ask Him to show you that person in your sphere of influence who needs to hear your story. Perhaps you have long believed that others will see Jesus through your actions. This is true, but others may not know why you live as you do. Although they may see a difference in you, they will still be wondering what it is. Rather than waiting to be asked, step out in faith and share your story.

Father, give me the boldness I need to share how You saved me.
I want others to know Your goodness and grace. Amen.

Free from Depression

He brought them out of darkness, the utter darkness,
and broke away their chains.
PSALM 107:14 NIV

Do you struggle with depression? It's a state of being, a state of despondency that may be caused by chemical changes in your brain. It's a condition that can shackle your heart and take captive your mind. It's a place in which you feel like a prisoner.

The word depression comes from the Latin verb *deprimere*, meaning "to press down," to subjugate, or to bring down in spirits. This pressing down can take you to some very dark places. But God never leaves His children in the dark. He is a God of light—and He wants you with Him, standing tall in the Sonshine.

When you are in the abyss, when all you can see is the darkness, God will provide you with a helper, for you were never meant to live life in your own power. God has created physicians, psychologists, counselors, and even friends and family members to help you. So reach out to someone standing outside of the pit, someone in the light, who can lift you up and out.

If you are not in such a dark place, take inventory of those around you. Reach out to one who may need help in loosing his or her own chains.

Heavenly Father, thank You for Your promise to rescue those
who are in darkness. You are glorious, everlasting Light. Amen.

Share the Load

He sent two of his helpers, Timothy and Erastus, to Macedonia,
while he stayed in the province of Asia a little longer.
ACTS 19:22 NIV

The apostle Paul was an amazing leader. Yet he knew he couldn't be all things to all people. He was limited by time and space, just as you are. So he sometimes sent helpers instead of always making a trip himself.

Are you, like many women today, so busy trying to do everything yourself that you cannot do any one thing well? If so, ask God for wisdom in learning how to manage your time and energy. When you are with your family, be fully present. Give your fam face-to-face time by turning off all electronic communication devices. When you are working, focus on each task and complete it for the glory of God, whether you are sending emails or folding laundry.

Consider assigning chores to your children rather than doing them yourself. This not only helps lighten your load but prepares them for life as adults. Don't deprive them of this training just because they may whine a bit or may not do a task exactly as you would have done it.

Rest when needed. When you return to the tasks at hand, you will be refreshed and ready, at ease and focused, leading to a job for the Lord well done.

Father, I know I cannot be all things to all people at all times.
Help me be wise with my time and energy. Amen.

Getting Out of the Desert

He turned the desert into pools of water
and the parched ground into flowing springs.
PSALM 107:35 NIV

Do you find yourself in the desert? Is life dry and boring? Are you parched from the sameness of it all? Look up! God is more than able to bring you out of that place. He can turn your desert into pools of water and bring new life to the lifeless.

Have you considered your gifts? What abilities or talents has God given you? Are you using them? Often when one becomes too self-focused or is not using her gifts, life becomes stagnant.

Maybe you are good with your hands. Could you volunteer with a local group that constructs homes for the poor? Or help with crafts in a kids' Sunday school class? Do you have musical ability? Nursing homes are always looking for someone to come and play an instrument or lead music for the residents. Or maybe your church's worship team needs help. These are just a couple of ideas. Get creative! Find a way to use a gift God has given you today.

When you are busy about God's work, you won't have as much time to feel bored with life. You will find that He can bring joy to replace sorrow, and a feeling of value that trumps that desert place every time!

God, lead me today as I consider ways to use the gifts
and abilities You have bestowed on me. Amen.

God-Centered Request

Solomon son of David established himself firmly over his kingdom,
for the LORD his God was with him and made him exceedingly great.
2 Chronicles 1:1 NIV

David's son Solomon got a firm grip on the kingdom of Israel not because he was self-centered but because He was God-centered. And because Solomon stuck so close to God, God stuck close to Solomon—"and made him exceedingly great."

Later in 2 Chronicles, Solomon seeks out and worships the Lord's presence at the Tent of Meeting. That night God appears to Solomon in a dream, saying, "Ask for whatever you want me to give you" (1 Kings 3:5 NIV). Solomon doesn't ask for his enemies to be killed, wealth, fame, or a long life. Instead, he asks for wisdom with which to lead God's people.

Because what Solomon asks for is coming from the bottom of his heart and is a selfless request, a very-pleased God grants his request for wisdom—and grants him great wealth as well!

Solomon was a person totally devoted to God, who stuck close to and sought God while He was near (see Isaiah 55:6–7), a great example for any human to follow!

What would you like to ask God for? If your request is heart-centered, God-serving, and selfless, God will surely grant it—and more besides!

God, help me search my heart, find the request I want to
make of You that would further Your kingdom. May it please You.

You Are Loved

For great is your love, higher than the heavens;
your faithfulness reaches to the skies.
PSALM 108:4 NIV

God's love for you is higher than the heavens. His faithfulness reaches to the skies—and beyond. Rest in that love today.

Regardless of where love has led you in the past, you can trust God. He will never withdraw His love from you—no matter what.

Perhaps a man pledged his love to you at an altar and you believed in him, later to be left with a big, expensive photo album full of memories—no husband in sight. Perhaps earthly parents let you down in some way. Siblings turned their backs on you. Friends who pledged their love and loyalty forever have dropped out of sight.

Let those hurts and memories go. And know this: God loves you. He is your true husband, father, brother, and friend. He has your name written on the palms of His hands (see Isaiah 49:16). And He will love you from here to eternity. For "He is good; his love endures forever" (2 Chronicles 5:13 NIV).

With God, there is no time or space. He is not limited by feelings or circumstances. He has no earthly constraints. He promises in His Word that He will never leave you. Bank on it. Today, start living like a daughter of the King. Hold your head high. You are dearly and infinitely loved.

Thank You, Father, for Your great love for me. Amen.

Promise-Keeper

"You have kept your promise to your servant David my father;
with your mouth you have promised and with your
hand you have fulfilled it—as it is today."
2 Chronicles 6:15 NIV

God keeps His promises. All of them.

God promised to allow David's son Solomon to build the temple. And He did.

God promised never again to flood the earth as in Noah's day. He put a rainbow in the sky to reflect that oath.

God has given you His Word that He will never leave you nor forsake you. And He won't.

Are you a person of your word? Do you, as a child of the living God, follow His example?

Maybe you are true to big promises but find others less significant. The writer of Ecclesiastes advises you, "It is better not to make a vow than to make one and not fulfill it" (5:5). Although it's important to keep all your promises, this is especially so when it comes to kids. Not only are they more fragile than adults, but they will mimic your promise-breaking or promise-keeping behavior.

Thank God that He's a promise-keeper. Then ask for the wisdom to make promises only if you know you will be able to keep them.

Father, help me be true to my promises. Show me that sometimes it's wiser to say, "I'll try," or "I hope we can make that happen," than "I promise," so that I can stay as true to my word as You are to Yours. Amen.

Pointing Others to God

"Praise be to the LORD your God, who has delighted in you and placed you on his throne as king to rule for the LORD your God."
2 CHRONICLES 9:8 NIV

The queen of Sheba had heard about King Solomon's great wisdom and fame. She came to see for herself, and was she ever impressed! The interesting point to notice from her visit is that she acknowledged God's hand in what she witnessed.

The queen knew that Solomon could not have, in his own power, risen to such high levels of intellect, wealth, and wisdom. She gave credit where credit was due. She acknowledged the power of Solomon's God, who did not bless Solomon with wisdom for Solomon's own use and glory but for God's greater purposes.

When Jesus came, He told His followers, "Let your light shine before others, that they may see your good deeds and glorify your Father in heaven" (Matthew 5:16). He wanted them to be as transparent as Solomon was to the queen of Sheba when it came to recognizing and giving glory to the true Gift Giver.

When others notice your good works, attributes, or talents, do you let them see past you to the true source of your power and worth?

*Heavenly Father, I want to shine for You today—
and every day! May others see good in me so that
they will praise You and give glory to You. Amen.*

What Shall I Do, Lord?

" 'What shall I do, Lord?' I asked. 'Get up,' the Lord said, 'and go into Damascus. There you will be told all that you have been assigned to do.'"
ACTS 22:10 NIV

Paul, bound in chains, shared his dramatic personal testimony before the commander and all those who would listen outside a Roman barracks in Jerusalem.

He told them that he, Paul, then known as Saul, a persecutor of Christians, had been struck by a bright light on the road to Damascus. Then he heard the voice of Jesus, who asked why he was persecuting Him. Paul had been on that road to gather some Christ-followers and bring them to their punishment. Suddenly blinded, he was instead now asking Jesus, "What shall I do, Lord?"

At this, one of the greatest persecutors of believers was instantly converted. In a moment, Paul's life and mission changed. What had it taken? A personal encounter with Christ.

Do you have a personal encounter with Christ each day? Do you go before Him asking, "What shall I do today, Jesus?" If not, start today. See where the Lord takes you. But be as pliable as Paul. Be ready to carry out whatever mission Christ may set before you.

Savior, what would You have me do today? If You need to stop me in my tracks as You did Saul on the road to Damascus, please take that liberty in my life. Amen.

Jesus Stands Near

The following night the Lord stood near Paul and said,
"Take courage! As you have testified about me in
Jerusalem, so you must also testify in Rome."
Acts 23:11 niv

Paul had been beaten, arrested, and put in chains. Some people had been ready to kill him. He had earlier escaped with his life only due to his Roman citizenship. And now he was already on the chopping block again! What would he do?

This is when the Lord stood near him, telling him to be brave and to share his testimony again. Did you catch that? The Lord stood near him. What strength is the believer's when he or she has Jesus literally standing near!

Christ stands with you every single day of your life. Listen. Do you hear Him now? He whispers words of affirmation, which He spoke over your ancestors, words He will speak to your descendants. Be still now. Hear Him:

You are Mine. You are a beloved sheep of My pasture, and I am your Good Shepherd. Be bold in My name, for I have declared you more than a conqueror. I've breathed new life into you. You are cherished. Be strong and courageous because I go with you into battle. I'll help you share your story. Your testimony will draw others to My side so that I may stand near to them as well!

Father, help me remember that You are always standing near me. Amen.

The Maze of Life

The fear of the LORD is the beginning of wisdom;
all who follow his precepts have good understanding.
PSALM 111:10 NIV

Have you ever tackled the challenge of a corn maze? It can be frustrating. Just when you think you have discovered the way out, you run into another wall of stalks! With twists and turns galore, you find yourself backing up, plotting your path again and again. Eventually you find the way out, usually with the help of a friend calling to you from the exit!

Life isn't that different from a good old-fashioned corn maze. But the good news is that Psalm 111 tells you how to find wisdom. The starting point in the crazy maze of life is fear of the Lord. This isn't a shaking-in-your-boots kind of fear, for you know God is love. But it's a very healthy respect, an awesome respect, for a Sovereign Lord who is above all things. And the second step is that because of that respect, you will follow His ways, which will lead to good understanding.

Like a faithful friend at the end of the corn maze, God is constantly speaking to, encouraging, and calling out directions to you. It's your job to listen. Fear the Lord. And follow His instructions. These steps will give you a great jump start as you navigate through an uncertain life.

Heavenly Father, develop in me a healthy fear of You.
Guide me as I follow Your ways. Amen.

No Fear of Bad News

They will have no fear of bad news;
their hearts are steadfast, trusting in the LORD.
PSALM 112:7 NIV

Have you ever waited in a doctor's office to discuss results of a blood test or biopsy? Waiting is hard, particularly when there's a good chance you may receive bad news.

The Bible tells us that those who walk with God need not fear bad news. Nothing can touch a believer's life that has not been filtered through the fingers of a loving God.

God is good—all the time. Not just on the days when the college acceptance letter shows up in your mailbox or the love of your life proposes marriage. He's just as good on the day that the doctor says the C word or you stand at the graveside of one you cherished.

Scripture does not say you will not face trouble. It does not claim that bad—really bad—things cannot touch your life. What it does promise is that you, Christian sister, will never go it alone. God is at—and on—your side.

Stay true to Him. Put your faith in the One who will hold you tight and walk with you when bad news does come. Trust He knows what's best for you. He's got this.

Thank You, God, that I need have no fear of bad news. Amen.

Stand Firm When Persecuted

*"I found he had done nothing deserving of death, but because he
made his appeal to the Emperor I decided to send him to Rome."*
ACTS 25:25 NIV

Paul had done nothing wrong. Much like his Savior before him, he was
an innocent man whom many feared and hated because he spoke truth.

You may be wrongly accused at different times in your life. You
may be misunderstood or may even experience persecution. If these
things come to you because of your faith, rest assured that your Judge
and King will take care of it for you.

From the beginning of time, innocent men and women of faith
have been mistreated for standing up for what is right. The Bible assures
God-followers this will only get worse. In the last days, God's people
will be persecuted.

Even though you are living in difficult times, you need not sink
down in despair. For Jesus is your Redeemer, your Savior. He provides
the way for you to stand completely guiltless and stain-free before God.
And until that day, He is about the business of watching over His own.

Stand up. Never shrink in the face of persecution for being a follower
of the Master. It will all be worth it in the end.

*Father, give me strength to stand for You even
if I am misunderstood or falsely accused. Amen.*

Pray for Unbelievers

Paul replied, "Short time or long—I pray to God that
not only you but all who are listening to me today
may become what I am, except for these chains."
Acts 26:29 niv

Paul, appearing before King Agrippa, was allowed to give his defense. He explained that he had not broken any laws but was merely following what Jesus had commanded him to do. Agrippa scoffed at Paul and asked if he truly believed that in such a short time he could convince the king to become a Christian.

Paul's answer should be the same as every Christian's: "Short time or long—I pray to God that not only you but all who are listening to me today may become what I am."

No matter how long it takes, Christ followers should remain prayerful that all would come to know Jesus. They ought never give up preaching the Gospel through action and words. It's a matter of life and death!

The Holy Spirit is the only one who can open the eyes of the spiritually blind and draw them to salvation. But you, as a believer, play a major role via prayer.

Keep lifting up those you long to see become Christians. If God can turn Saul the persecutor into Paul the apostle, surely He can save anyone!

God, I pray that today You would begin drawing _____
and _____ close as I continue to lift them up to You! Amen.

God vs. Gods

Our God is in heaven; he does whatever pleases him.
But their idols are silver and gold, made by human hands.
PSALM 115:3–4 NIV

Would you bow down, worship, or pray to something formed by human hands?

While people throughout the history of the earth have worshipped golden calves and stone figures, there are other types of idols that are just as dangerous. Perhaps more so!

Anything placed above God is an idol and has the potential of becoming, in fact, a god. A good question to ask yourself to test if you have allowed idols to creep into your life is, "What do I spend the most time doing or thinking about?"

Could social media be an idol? You bet! Compare the amount of time you spend scrolling through posts or sending messages with the amount of time you spend in God's Word. Which one wins? Which one leads you closer to the one true God? Which one might be a "lowercase g" god in your life?

These questions are the litmus test. The challenge is to root out other gods from your life. Your God is a jealous God. You shall have no other gods before Him. (See Exodus 20:3–5.)

God, help me take the first step and identify any idols
in my life. Once I've named my idols, give me the
strength to stamp them out of my life. Amen.

"Pride Goeth before a Fall"

But after Uzziah became powerful, his pride led to his downfall.
He was unfaithful to the LORD his God, and entered the temple
of the LORD to burn incense on the altar of incense.
2 CHRONICLES 26:16 NIV

King Uzziah started out on the right track. He was blessed because he honored God. In fact, he was "greatly helped until he became powerful" (2 Chronicles 26:15 NIV). But the proverb "Pride goeth before. . .a fall" (Proverbs 16:18 KJV) had Uzziah's name written all over it. When he took his eyes off God and placed them on himself, things began to go very wrong!

Uzziah took the liberty of entering the temple to perform a duty reserved for priests. This was not his place. He was reminded of this by a group of about eighty priests who followed him into the temple to reprimand him.

Instead of listening to them, Uzziah grew very angry, which led to his demise. The Lord had had enough. He struck Uzziah, who had once been a God-fearing king, with leprosy.

This story serves as a reminder that God will not tolerate pride. For He alone is the true source of all you have and are. So to keep things clear and avoid tripping up, keep your focus on Jesus!

God, thank You for reminders in Your Word that teach me to avoid pride.
May I always remember that You are the Giver of all good gifts. Amen.

Bending an Ear

*Because He has inclined His ear to me,
therefore I will call upon Him as long as I live.*
PSALM 116:2 NKJV

The best friends are those who listen. They sit with you and let you vent about your latest source of stress. They don't interrupt or interject their solutions. They don't judge or jump to conclusions. They just attend to your words and nod their heads. They lean in close and look you in the eyes so you know they're really paying attention.

How wonderful is the picture painted by the psalmist's words: "He has inclined His ear to me"! Picture the Creator leaning over to hear your prayers—not because His hearing is lacking, but because He wants to show that He is listening to every word. Father God bending to attend to the requests of His daughter. The psalmist states that because of this care and attention from the almighty God, he has been led to pledge his lifelong loyalty to the Lord.

One wonders how many might come to know God if those who are His representatives spent more time bending an ear than they do wagging fingers, placing blame, or cultivating divisions. If you make a pledge every day to have ears willing to listen, what difference could that make to those who are weary and struggling, stressed and despairing? Perhaps it could make all the difference in the world.

Lord, let me be like You and bend to listen to others. Amen.

Proud

*For I am not ashamed of the gospel, because it is the power
of God that brings salvation to everyone who believes.*

ROMANS 1:16 NIV

Think of the last time you had a really good story to tell. Maybe it was a story of your own or another's achievement. Maybe it was the account of an animal rescue. Maybe it was an anecdote about a celebrity you'd met, the tale of a well-negotiated deal, or the news of record sales for your business.

A woman loves to tell stories like these. She wants others to hear them because it's exciting to share good news. Besides, positive reports can lift people's spirits and spark ideas.

That's especially true when it comes to sharing the good news of salvation. When you share this story, you share the power and excitement of Jesus' resurrection. You spread hope of eternal life. You offer an opportunity to receive God's gift of grace.

Why then does it feel so difficult sometimes to tell this particular story? Perhaps it's because you have told it before and gotten a negative or dismissive reaction.

The key to the success of any story is to know your audience. Jesus spoke in parables so the everyday people could understand. Matthew explained the Gospel to Jews, Mark to the Romans, Luke to the Greeks, and John to everyone.

So consider who your audience is and try telling the story again.

Lord, help me find success in telling others about You. Amen.

Fighting for Us

*"With him is only the arm of flesh, but with us is
the Lord our God to help us and to fight our battles."*
2 Chronicles 32:8 niv

Hezekiah had been working hard for God, undertaking the service of God's temple. But after all this hard work, King Sennacherib of Assyria came to make war against Jerusalem.

Hezekiah gathered his people and made plans. He delivered a rousing speech that could have come straight out of a Hollywood movie—telling his people not to be afraid of the king of Assyria, "for there is a greater power with us than with him" (2 Chronicles 32:7 niv). And it worked! The people "gained confidence" (v. 8 niv) and stood up to the Assyrian army.

Then Hezekiah and Isaiah prayed and the Lord sent an angel "who annihilated all the fighting men" (v. 21 niv) of Assyria. So the Lord saved Hezekiah and Jerusalem, just as He had saved His people before, and just as He would do again and again.

This same God is continuing to fight for you today—answering your prayers and giving you confidence to do battle against any kind of power that seeks to control your heart. You may not ever have to fight off kings and armies, but you can count on your Lord to give you strength to defend your peace.

Lord, thank You for helping me fight my battles. Amen.

Obedience Is Necessary

For it is not those who hear the law who are righteous in God's sight,
but it is those who obey the law who will be declared righteous.
ROMANS 2:13 NIV

The child reaches toward the dancing, flickering, yellow thing. It's so pretty. Her fingers grow warm as she inches closer.

"No playing with the candle. Don't go near it," her mother had warned her.

She'd heard the words. She especially heard "no" and "candle." She understood those words very well. But when she saw the beautiful light, she couldn't resist getting closer to it.

Obedience can be a very, very difficult thing. Obedience in the face of temptation can be dangerous—especially when you are a child close to a flame.

But many times you are in that exact same spot. You have heard the words. You understand the words. But the attractive thing is so beautiful. Perhaps the look of it makes you forget. Perhaps you think you know better.

Hearing the words doesn't even get you halfway to where you ought to be. You have to listen, heed, and follow God's words. Those who are attentively abiding in God day and night are those who are so totally yielded to Him that they cannot help but obey. They have, by the power of God's Spirit, worked hard to remember the words, follow the words, and deny self. That's why they are declared righteous.

Lord, help me develop the strength to obey You. Amen.

All Fall, All Free

All have sinned and fall short of the glory of God, and all are justified freely by his grace through the redemption that came by Christ Jesus.
ROMANS 3:23–24 NIV

Several verses in Romans are often used as a kind of shorthand for sharing the Gospel of Jesus Christ. The verses above are the starting point—they describe the state of human beings. All have sinned. All fall short. There are no divisions between those who have sinned a lot and those who have sinned a little. Murderers, liars, adulterers, and gossipers are all thrown into the same group. If you have ever known a right thing to do and chosen instead to do wrong, you have sinned. If you are human, you have sinned. And if you have sinned, you are not worthy of the glory of God.

But thankfully the story doesn't stop there. Everyone has fallen, but everyone is made worthy by the gift of the grace of God. It's a mysterious gift—one that doesn't just add to who you are or what you have, like other possessions that bestow some added honor or wealth. It's a gift that changes where you stand. Without this grace, you sink to the bottom of the sea. With it, you can walk on water to meet your Savior.

God, thank You for my gift of grace! Amen.

Be Glad

The LORD has done it this very day;
let us rejoice today and be glad.
PSALM 118:24 NIV

The feeling of gladness often carries with it a sense of relief and gratitude. A student may be glad to find out she passed the driving test. A husband and wife may be glad to hear the news that they are pregnant (or not!). An employee is glad to receive a raise.

This psalmist was very glad. He had been surrounded by his enemies. He had been pushed back and was about to fall down and be conquered, but the Lord helped him. God came to the rescue, and instead of dying that day, the writer had lived. He says, "The LORD is my strength and my defense; he has become my salvation. Shouts of joy and victory resound" (Psalm 118:14–15).

What has God done for you already this day? Open your eyes and see the works He has performed. Maybe He kept you safe on your commute to work. Maybe He sent rain to water dry fields. Maybe He cleared the clouds and gave you a bit of sunshine to start your morning. God shows His love and care for you every day all day long in both big and small ways. Don't forget to look around and see what God is doing for you and for others today. Then rejoice and be glad!

God, I'm so glad You love me! Thank You! Amen.

Access Door

*Therefore, since we have been justified through faith, we have peace
with God through our Lord Jesus Christ, through whom we have
gained access by faith into this grace in which we now stand.*
ROMANS 5:1–2 NIV

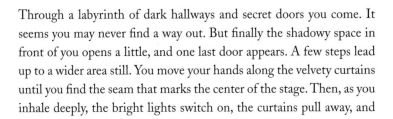

Through a labyrinth of dark hallways and secret doors you come. It
seems you may never find a way out. But finally the shadowy space in
front of you opens a little, and one last door appears. A few steps lead
up to a wider area still. You move your hands along the velvety curtains
until you find the seam that marks the center of the stage. Then, as you
inhale deeply, the bright lights switch on, the curtains pull away, and
there you are—standing in the spotlight.

Accepting Jesus as your Lord and Savior gives you special access
to the center stage of God's theater. You don't have to stay in the shadows watching a more joy-filled life go by. God invites you to step into
His light and live boldly in the scenes He has written just for you. He
is your director and guide, your manager and your adoring audience.
And He is the author of your life, the gifter of grace.

Though you may sometimes get butterflies in your stomach, you
don't have to be afraid to use your voice. You can find peace in the
certainty that God will be with you, every minute.

God, thank You for the grace in which I stand. Amen.

Dead or Alive?

Count yourselves dead to sin but alive to God in Christ Jesus.
ROMANS 6:11 NIV

Have you ever met people who seemed to be living with one foot in the grave? Their faces show signs of wearying schedules, bitter rejections, and stressful worries. They do not move with quick, purposeful steps, but shuffle along in indecision and under the weight of past mistakes. They cannot help anyone because they cannot see past their own self-absorption.

That's what it's like to live as a slave to sin.

Sin keeps you so wrapped up in yourself, you can't see any other way to live or any other person to live life with. The only way to escape that kind of existence is to kill it—to die to sin. To be baptized into the death of Christ and raised in new life with Him.

Does dying to sin mean you will never sin again? Never make a mistake? Never choose to do wrong? No. Accepting Christ does not make you perfect—at least not all at once. It does, however, give you purpose. And that purpose becomes the driving force behind your choices and actions. What is that purpose? To love the Lord our God with all your heart, mind, soul, and strength, and to love others as you love yourself. That's really living!

God, thank You for making me alive in You. Amen.

Under Construction

"Do not interfere with the work on this temple of God."
EZRA 6:7 NIV

King Darius wasn't messing around. He had uncovered a decree, originally issued by King Cyrus, to allow the temple of God to be rebuilt in Jerusalem. So Darius sent a message to the regional officials, ordering them to leave the Jews alone as they built the house of God. And in the last paragraph, he added a warning: "I decree if anyone defies this edict, a beam is to be pulled from their house and they are to be impaled on it" (Ezra 6:11).

Yes, indeed—King Darius was serious.

Don't you wish sometimes that someone could send out a decree on your behalf? "I hereby decree that everyone leave [insert your name here] alone while she gets her life together. And if they don't, they are to be impaled on their satellite dish." Well, maybe that's a little harsh.

These days you don't go to one temple to talk with God, but God does live inside you, and you are under construction—a work in progress, so to speak. He's busy every day building you up into the person He created you to be, making you into a temple of the Holy Spirit.

Make sure you don't let anyone or anything—even you!—interfere with this work.

God, thank You for working on me. Help me not get in the way! Amen.

Worthless Things

Turn my eyes from worthless things,
and give me life through your word.
PSALM 119:37 NLT

Cute cat videos. The latest celebrity selfies. Political commentary. Pictures of people's dinners posted the night before. This week's sales ads.

Thanks to the marvels of modern-day technology, you can now see these and many more worthless things before you even get out of bed in the morning. But what kind of way is that to start the day?

The thousands of amusing, alarming, and even admirable articles you find on the Internet can be harmless diversions, but they are still diversions. They divert your attention from events that are more important, from ideas that are worth spending time thinking through, and from building relationships that matter. They divert you from your connection to God through prayer and reading His Word. They divert you into accepting a virtual life instead of really living.

How much better might your days be if you started the morning off by listening to what God has to say to you, dwelling in His Word, and memorizing some Scripture that might help you get through your days?

Anyway, there will always be another cute cat video. Don't miss your chance to hear what God has to say to you today.

Lord, help me remember to look in Your
Word before I go out in the world today. Amen.

In All Things

*We know that in all things God works for the good of those
who love him, who have been called according to his purpose.*
ROMANS 8:28 NIV

Through the traffic-snarled highway home and on the quiet path through peaceful parkland; in the tense, executive office conference and it the chatty cafeteria atmosphere; on the phone with distant relatives or sitting together around a family campfire—God can work in all kinds of places and circumstances for the good of those who love Him.

You may think about God working only when you are sitting in a worship service or reading the Bible or on a prayer retreat. Or maybe you think about Him working only when something good happens—when a prayer is answered, a relationship mended, or a crisis averted.

But God is always at work. He doesn't take vacation days. He doesn't ever stop knitting you together and unfolding His grand story. Even at the times when you feel your weakest, when you don't even know what to pray for and can't find the words to say, the Spirit helps you and speaks for you. No matter how you feel, where you are, what you are doing, or who you are with—God is working for your good.

*God, I want to join You in Your work.
Teach me to be a good servant for You. Amen.*

A Start

"Let us start rebuilding."
NEHEMIAH 2:18 NIV

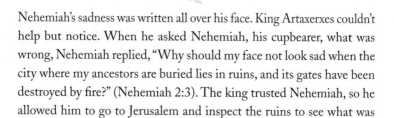

Nehemiah's sadness was written all over his face. King Artaxerxes couldn't help but notice. When he asked Nehemiah, his cupbearer, what was wrong, Nehemiah replied, "Why should my face not look sad when the city where my ancestors are buried lies in ruins, and its gates have been destroyed by fire?" (Nehemiah 2:3). The king trusted Nehemiah, so he allowed him to go to Jerusalem and inspect the ruins to see what was needed to rebuild the walls.

The state of a city says something about the state of its people. The Jews of this time were broken and scattered, much like the rubble of Jerusalem. But God had spoken hope and purpose into Nehemiah's heart, so even when he saw the destruction with his own eyes, he didn't become discouraged. And his confidence, founded in the strength of his God, passed through his words and into the hearts of the other Jews. "Let us start rebuilding," they said. They were ready to begin.

When you feel God nudging you to do something, don't ignore it. When you see a problem or hear of trouble and you don't know how to fix it, ask God to help you find a way. He will lead you in the right direction and give you the courage to take up the work. And that courage will lead others to join you.

God, help me be bold in inviting others to serve You. Amen.

Artist and Author

Your hands made me and formed me;
give me understanding to learn your commands.
PSALM 119:73 NIV

Ten tiny, round toes. Ten chubby, curled fingers. Little lips forming a wee, yet perfectly shaped O. Soft, kissable cheeks and sweet-smelling wisps of hair. When a newborn is in your arms, it's almost impossible not to acknowledge the handiwork of God.

The same Artist who shapes a newborn's elbows and carved out mountains is the Author who is writing the story of your life and laid out plans to guide you along the way.

Yet, although you may be grateful for the body He has given you, you are often not as grateful for His commands. You want to do things your own way—find your own path. You think you can figure out the answers. Sometimes you just want to be satisfied in the fastest way possible—you don't even consider other options.

You may spend several hours wondering at the hand of the Artist but then skip right over the words of the Author.

You need to pray the prayer of the psalmist: "Give me understanding to learn your commands." This understanding doesn't come along with those tiny toes and sweet cheeks—you have to seek it out, to ask for it. Sometimes you might even have to start by asking God to grant you the spirit to want to understand.

God who made every part of me,
help me learn every part of Your Word. Amen.

Work of Salvation

You're not "doing" anything; you're simply calling
out to God, trusting him to do it for you.
ROMANS 10:10 MSG

Strong arms lift you up into the seat. You hold on tight to the chains. Seconds later, two hands press firmly on your back, propelling you forward. One, two, three, away! Your seated body flies back through the air, and then up, up, up into the sky. Your toes reach out to touch the clouds. Then just as soon as you are launched, you come whooshing back, hair flying, knees bent, ground in a blur passing under your heels, and fingers clenched tighter yet around those chains.

You are swinging. And yet you are not swinging. You are being swung. You are pushed into the air like the pendulum on a clock. You, especially tiny, not-quite-two you, have very little control over your actions or your locations.

All you did was ask, "Swing me, Mama, please?" All you did was trust that she would put you in the seat and push you in the air and not let you fall.

That's what you do with God. You call out to Him and ask Him to save you. But you do not do the saving. He lifts you up, puts you on the path you are supposed to go on, and gives you a push. You just have to stay in the seat and trust Him.

God, help me trust You more. Amen.

Every Generation

Your faithfulness extends to every generation,
as enduring as the earth you created.
PSALM 119:90 NLT

She beat the eggs carefully and poured them into the bowl of flour. She smiled as she turned the wooden spoon over in her hand. The spoon had belonged to her mother and to her mother's mother before her. Perhaps it had even once rested on the stove of her great-great-great-grandmother.

There were nicks on the handle from some particularly hard taps on the edge of a pot. And on one side there was a small burn mark from when someone had left it sitting too close to the flame. As she stirred together her ingredients, she wondered how many stories it could tell of kitchen successes and messes. How many times had it been swirled around the old stoneware mixing bowl?

She considered how much this spoon was like the stories of faith that had been passed down through her family from generation to generation—stories of preachers who had spoken out against slavery and of soldiers who had been noble in battle. From early childhood she had enjoyed listening to the tales of her faithful forebears—strong men and women who loved God and worked hard to serve Him.

As she licked the batter off the spoon, she thanked God for His faithfulness—from generation to generation.

Thank You, Lord, for always being with me. Amen.

The Sacred Mundane

"Take your everyday, ordinary life—your sleeping, eating, going-to-work, and walking-around life—and place it before God as an offering."
ROMANS 12:1 MSG

Wake up. Turn off your alarm. Get up and get dressed and get moving. Pour the cereal and brew the coffee. Brush your teeth. Grab your keys and go.

Doesn't seem like much, does it? Just a regular person going to a regular job on a regular day. But God wants all of it. He wants your mundane minutes and your sacred seconds and everything in between. Why? Because that is one of the best ways you can worship Him—by giving over body, mind, and soul as an act of living, breathing sacrifice.

But there's another reason, too. If you are giving every moment to Him, then it will be easier for you to stay set apart from this world—and "be transformed by the renewing of your mind" (Romans 12:2 NIV). Instead of just following the same old routine that everyone else does, if you actually actively gave over your schedule to God, praying through your day and committing to honor Him in your actions, how do you think that might change you? What might happen to your day if you offered every piece of it to God?

Lord, take my body and my time—I offer them to You.
Please show me Your will, and I will serve You all my days. Amen.

Empathy

Rejoice with those who rejoice; mourn with those who mourn.
ROMANS 12:15 NIV

Toward the end of his long letter to the Romans, Paul urges his readers to love one another. He gives them several ideas about what that means. He tells them to put others first, to share with people in need, and to open their homes to one another. He tells them not to be proud or conceited but to "live in harmony with one another" (12:16).

Perhaps the best way to live in harmony with others is to practice empathy. Empathy is not pity—it's not feeling bad for someone. It's the act of understanding someone's experience and feeling it with them.

Empathy is practiced not just by sending flowers but by going to the funeral home, sitting beside the casket, holding the mourner's hand, and crying with her. Your tears are real. You feel sad because you can imagine her sadness. You mourn with her because you can understand her loss, and you grieve that anyone has to experience that loss.

Empathy is practiced not just by congratulating someone, but by embracing that person in her joy and feeling happy because she is happy. It's being genuinely glad for her celebration—even if her victory has nothing at all to do with you.

When you get close enough to practice empathy, it's very hard to be divided. And that's the whole point.

Lord, help me feel what others are feeling. Amen.

Acceptance

Accept the one whose faith is weak,
without quarreling over disputable matters.
ROMANS 14:1 NIV

Christians can be vastly different from one other. Some worship in churches with stained glass windows and pipe organs. Others worship in cinemas and pipe in rock music. Some follow strict orders of service. Others change what they do from week to week. Some maintain particular diets and styles of dress. Others eat and wear whatever they like.

Who is stronger or weaker in faith isn't the point. What is clear from Romans 14 is that part of loving one another means caring for others' needs first and not judging others. Caring for one another means that if someone you know is a believer and he has a conviction about not eating meat, then when you invite him to eat at your house, you provide him with a vegetarian option. Don't give him a hard time. Don't try to get him to eat as you do. It's just not that important. Paul put it well in verse 20: "Do not destroy the work of God for the sake of food." And you could add to that: "for the sake of clothing, music styles, carpet choice, political persuasion, and so forth."

Make every effort to speak, act, and be friends to others in such a way as to lead to peace instead of discord. And build others up instead of tearing them down.

God, help me accept others as You accept me. Amen.

Hovering

Every day he walked back and forth near the courtyard of the harem to find out how Esther was and what was happening to her.

ESTHER 2:11 NIV

Are you guilty? Have you been the kind of parent, guardian, grandparent, or friend who hovers? You always have a piece of your mind and heart engaged in wondering how and what your children are doing. You can't help it!

Letting go is hard. Mordecai knew this. He had raised his cousin Esther as his own daughter after her parents died. Then this daughter was taken to the king's palace as a new queen candidate. But this wasn't just any beauty pageant. If the king did not like Esther, she could be thrown out, or worse. And her Jewish background made her status all the more uncertain. It's no wonder Mordecai paced outside the courtyard, hoping to glean some bit of information. He had told Esther to keep her background quiet, but would she?

So many times, those who raise children have moments of letting go, from those first baby steps to sending them off into the world. It's in those moments you have to trust that the God who loves you knows how to love your children, too—even better than you do. He had a plan for Esther—and He will have a plan for your kids, too.

God, thank You for loving my children better than I ever could. Amen.

For Such a Time

*"Who knows but that you have come to
your royal position for such a time as this?"*
ESTHER 4:14 NIV

Esther didn't have just one moment of truth—she had several! When she went before the king the first time, when she went without being asked, when she invited him to her house—there were many points when she could have caved in to fear and hidden away from the amazing responsibility in her hands.

Why didn't she?

Because that's how she was raised. When Mordecai took her as his daughter, he loved her, raised her as his own, teaching her the traditions of the Jews. He told her the stories of God's protection and faithfulness and of courageous men and women of faith who were her ancestors, men and women who stood strong in times of trouble.

Little girl Esther knew love and safety. She knew her earthly father Mordecai would be there for her. And she knew her heavenly Father God had a plan for her people that was bigger than anything she could see.

So when the chance to make a difference fell into her hands, she knew her father was right. She'd been made queen for a reason. Then she did what she had been doing since she was a girl. She knelt before her heavenly Father and prepared to stand in His story.

*God, help me see the part You want
me to play in Your grand story. Amen.*

Come and Find Me

I have wandered away like a lost sheep; come and find me.
PSALM 119:176 NLT

Sheep are funny creatures. Left to their own devices, they meander through fields, searching for the next choice mouthful. Their stomachs guide them. That's why they sometimes get themselves into precarious situations. That's why they don't always see their enemies until it's too late.

Have you ever acted like a ewe? Wandering through life, seeking to feed your desires? Looking for the next thing you think might satisfy you?

Everyone wanders away sometimes. And every time it's stupid. It's as stupid as the sheep who willingly steps out of sight of her one and only protector.

Face it. There's no good argument for leaving the Shepherd. He knows you. He's the only one who knows every thought you have ever had, every word you have ever said or left unsaid. And He still loves you and wants you to be with Him. Can you really think of a good reason to leave Him?

But undoubtedly you will. Everyone will stray. Everyone will turn their backs. Again and again.

"Come and find me," you will pray. And He will. Your Shepherd will come with grace and mercy. He will come and pick you up and take you back to the flock again. Maybe this time you will stay.

Lord, help me to understand that my best safe place is with You. Amen.

Awake

He who watches over you will not slumber.
PSALM 121:3 NIV

You push the little button on your phone for the hundredth time. What does that say? 3:35? In the morning?

But still you sit, in the same chair you have been sitting in for the last five hours. Because you dare not move. If you move, she might wake up. And if she wakes up. . . Oh, no.

She woke up.

You go over to quiet her once again. You pat her back, feel her forehead. The fever seems better, but her breathing is so congested. She's still crying, so you pick her up in your leaden arms. And you plop back down in the rocking chair, throw a blanket over both of you, and close your eyes as you listen to her sobs begin to slow.

If you have ever taken care of a small child who is sick in the night, you know what it's like not to slumber. Even when you get so tired that your eyelids won't stay open, you can't really get into a deep sleep. A small sound—a sniffle, a cough, raspy breathing—wakes you.

God watches over you like a parent watching over a sick child in the night. Except God's eyes never shut, and He never tires. He is always there to comfort you, guide you, and hold you in His strong arms.

*God, thank You for watching over me even
when I don't realize You are. Amen.*

Foolish Wisdom

Has not God made foolish the wisdom of the world?
1 CORINTHIANS 1:20 NIV

People have the wisdom of the world at their fingertips. Through the reach of the Internet, they can take classes at the world's best universities, listen to some of the most intelligent speakers, and read a large portion of all the best books ever written.

But having easy access to all of that hasn't seemed to make people all that much smarter. They still flounder in their foolishness and get caught up in their chaos. They're still, by and large, fighting against one another more than living in harmony. Somehow everyone has all the answers, but no one can work out the solutions to the problems.

Why is that?

Well, it could be that they don't ask the One who is the source of all wisdom.

Just as in the days of the first disciples, people are still looking for signs. They look out in the world for answers, reasons, and evidence. They look to each other for guidance.

"But we preach Christ crucified" (1 Corinthians 1:23).

If you go to Jesus, you will find the answers. If you study His life, you will see the order to your chaos. If you accept His grace, you will find who you were meant to be.

A seeming fool to the world. But, in reality, a wise woman of God.

God, if Your story is considered foolishness to the world,
then let me be a fool, too. Amen.

Searching

The Spirit searches all things, even the deep things of God.
1 Corinthians 2:10 niv

The beginning of the seas. The source of darkness. The reason for evil. The end to suffering. The birth of souls.

Can you even begin to fathom what it must be like to search the deep things of God?

Paul wrote to the Corinthians, "For who knows a person's thoughts except their own spirit within them? In the same way no one knows the thoughts of God except the Spirit of God" (1 Corinthians 2:11).

What an awesome gift God has given you! He has given you His Spirit, sent to live with you, so that you can have access to God—to understand what He has told you through His Word and what He speaks to you in your prayer times and all through your life.

But this kind of gift does not come all at once, like a cake in a box. It's more like a seed that gets planted and, if taken care of, grows into a strong tree, with branches reaching ever upward to the sun and outward across the sky.

You dare not think that just because you have His Spirit, you suddenly can understand all there is to know about God. But you can study Him, and as you walk with Him, you can get to know Him better day by day.

Holy Spirit, help me understand what God has freely given me. Amen.

What Grows from Grief

Those who plant in tears will harvest with shouts of joy.
PSALM 126:5 NLT

You are crushed. All your hopes for your future, that beautiful dream of a life you had painted in your mind, have blurred—like a chalk drawing washed away by a storm. Maybe it was a lost job, a lost friend, or a lost romance—but something significant has changed in your life, and the disappointment threatens to tear you apart.

The people of Israel knew sorrow and disappointment. So many times, either through their own wrong actions or the actions of others, their lives were thrown into turmoil. And suddenly the Promised Land seemed too far to reach, or the temple crumbled, or the enemies appeared on every side—and there was no way out.

But God always came back for them, and as the psalmist records here, He brought them home to Jerusalem.

God will remember you, too. So start again. Take up the faith of the farmer and plant your seeds, watering them with tears. Trust in the One who can make anything grow—even in the wilderness of grief.

Just remember, when your harvest comes and your happiness returns, to give God the glory. Sing praises to Him. Remember your brokenness, and rejoice in the work of the One who restores.

Lord, sometimes life seems so hard. Help me remember that You are always with me and that Your promises never fail. Amen.

A Hope to Be Heard

"Though he slay me, yet will I hope in him."
JOB 13:15 NIV

Job had suffered the loss of almost everything he valued. And he couldn't understand why.

His friends tried to give him advice. They told him what his attitude toward God should be. They suggested there must be a reason he was suffering—that perhaps it was even Job's fault. That he shouldn't question God. That he should just move on.

But Job was a man of God. Job 1:1 says that he was "blameless and upright; he feared God and shunned evil" (NIV). Job knew God. In Job 12 he launches into a beautiful description of the power and might and justice and righteousness of God.

Knowing all of this—knowing who God is and what He has done— Job proclaims that he wants to argue his case before God. He wants his day in God's court. He wants to hear God's testimony against him and understand why everything had been taken from him.

And even though he knows God could crush him, Job still wants to come before God because he trusts Him. His hope is in God. His understanding is that God is good. His experience is that God is truth.

May you yourself aspire to have the faith of Job—the faith that will keep you turning to God even in the darkest times.

God, let my hope always rest in You. Amen.

Deleted

If you, LORD, kept a record of sins, Lord, who could stand?
PSALM 130:3 NIV

The answer to the psalmist's question is an easy one.

No one. No one in the world would be able to stand. No one's record is pure. Every human on the earth has sinned or will sin.

Imagine for a moment what your record of sins might look like. Would it be a short volume with just a few pages in it? Or would it be a giant, heavy tome, with small, cramped printing filling every space on every single one of its thousands of pages?

No matter what your record might entail, if you accept Jesus as your Savior, all those entries will be deleted.

Erased.

Cleaned.

Wiped out.

You still have to deal with the consequences of those sins. You still bear scars. But you can stand because, with God, there is forgiveness.

And God asks you to forgive others in the same way. The consequences—broken relationships, hurt feelings, damaged people—won't be erased. But God does not want you to hold things over people all their lives. If you try to do that, you will only end up with tired hands from clenching on to darkness. God wants you instead to delete those records of wrongs, open your fists, and bring your empty hands to serve Him.

*Lord, my Savior and Redeemer, help me forgive
others in the same way You forgive me. Amen.*

Not Your Own

You are not your own; you were bought at a price.
1 CORINTHIANS 6:19–20 NIV

"I wanna do it by my own self," the child shouts, stomping his little foot. From the time humans can speak, they try to get their own way. Even toddlers with no words will run the other way as soon as they sense others trying to corral them. Everyone likes to be able to do their own thing.

But the trouble is, people are not their own thing. They are God's things.

Only God knows what's good for people. As Paul put it, "'I have the right to do anything,' you say—but not everything is beneficial" (1 Corinthians 6:12). Because people aren't perfect creatures, and definitely not perfectly good, they often get it wrong when they are making decisions about what's good for them or calculating how their decisions will affect others. People need God's help.

That's why it's so important to spend time in God's Word every day. We have to be reminded about what's good and what's not. We have to be reminded to go toward the Father and not run off in the opposite direction.

You were bought at a price—at the immeasurably high price of Jesus' life on the cross. Once you have accepted His sacrifice, you cannot behave as though you are on your own anymore. And really, who would want to?

Lord Jesus, thank You for giving Your life for me.
Help me live like I know it! Amen.

Different Gifts

God gives the gift of the single life to some,
the gift of the married life to others.
1 CORINTHIANS 7:7 MSG

Maybe you are a happily married woman. You have built a life with your spouse and you love each other as best you can. You enjoy being able to serve God together and share your days.

Maybe you are a single woman. You enjoy your independence and being able to do things on your own schedule. You serve God with your friends and your church family.

No one is better than the other. The married woman has to balance her responsibilities to job, home, spouse, and perhaps children with her service to God. The single woman has to balance her job life, home life, family life, and social life with her life in Christ.

Everyone has different circumstances. Everyone has different gifts.

Do you consider your life a gift? Or do you find yourself wondering if there's a better life out there somewhere?

Take a good look at your blessings. Those who are married, think of all the ways you are grateful to have a partner with whom to go through life. Those who are single, think of the scope for service that's available to you.

Be thankful for the gift of where you are now, and show your gratitude in how you live and love and work for God.

Lord of all, thank You for showing me
all the ways I am blessed, right now. Amen.

Potluck Heaven

How good and pleasant it is when God's people live together in unity!
Psalm 133:1 niv

The aroma is amazing. It's a mix of baked ham, garlic chicken, rosemary potatoes, apple pie, and fifty other delicious dishes. And the sight of the casseroles! It's like a patchwork food quilt: individual rectangles of golden corn, green beans, emerald broccoli and sharp yellow cheese, golden-brown chicken, chili-red pepperoni roll, sunshine mac and cheese, and bright orange sweet potatoes. There's food from diverse cultures—tamales, cannolis, kebabs, egg rolls, and papadum—representing people from diverse cultures all eating under one roof. And the dessert table is heavy with sweet, rich, luscious calories—chocolate cake, five kinds of pie, brownies, cookies, muffins, several things that involve whipping cream (do you even have to know more than that?), two kinds of cheesecake, and cupcakes with sprinkles!

Potluck dinners represent all that's good and pleasant about God's people living together in unity. When Christian community is working as it should, people come together to share resources, talents, caring, friendship, families, and, yes, food.

They come to talk and laugh together. They come to spend time getting to know one another. They come to hear one another's stories.

And in these moments of laughing and talking and telling and hearing—each one gets just a little glimpse of heaven.

Anyone want another piece of pie?

God, help me reach out to others who are different from me. Amen.

Build

Knowledge puffs up while love builds up.
1 CORINTHIANS 8:1 NIV

Knowledge is a beautiful thing. To know a person, to understand a little of what makes her tick and what she likes and doesn't like, is part of constructing a relationship. You ask questions and listen to answers because you want to know: Who are you—you, sitting there—living, breathing, talking, walking, doing, going, human being?

But knowing is not the same as loving. And knowledge you hold on to too tightly or depend on too much can sometimes raise a wall between you and another instead of building a bridge. In that moment when you claim, "Oh yes, I see how you are," instead of confessing, "Oh yes, I see how we are alike," a wall begins to go up.

Paul cautioned the Corinthians not to dedicate so much time to attaining knowledge. Knowledge can puff you up full of pride and suppositions, full of your own views about the world. You learn to the point you think you know it all, and then you shut out anyone else's opinions.

But love builds up, imparts humility. Love cultivates in you a desire to understand more—to always ask another question, see another side, walk another mile in someone else's shoes.

If you think you know something, you should think again. And maybe, try loving instead.

God, keep me humble. Knock me down if I get too full of myself. Amen.

Live in the Light

"This is the way God works. Over and over again He pulls our souls back from certain destruction so we'll see the light—and live in the light!"
JOB 33:29–30 MSG

Upon experiencing the unexpected death of a loved one, you may go through a sort of numbness. But eventually you will begin to feel again—possibly hurt, anger, bitterness, and deep grief. The cold emptiness of your life may reflect what you feel in your heart. Your loved one's absence sucks all the warmth and light out of you.

Although your phone rings, you ignore it. You don't want to talk to anyone. You haven't really even talked to God but know you need to. You sense it's time to open up and invite God into your grief. So even though you may not feel like it, you begin to pray: "God, I need you. I feel like I died, too. I need to feel alive again."

Suddenly a warm, bright light fills the room. You feel God's presence and His peace surround you. You feel a surge of strength and know that God is with you. He will help you begin again. He will pull your soul back from the darkness and bring you back into the light.

God, I have hurts and have experienced loss. It's easy to isolate myself and pull away from You. But I need You. I invite You to shed Your light on my hurts and heal my brokenness.

Holding the Pieces Together

*But God is faithful [to His Word and to His compassionate nature],
and He [can be trusted] not to let you be tempted and tried and assayed
beyond your ability and strength of resistance and power to endure,
but with the temptation He will [always] also provide the way out
(the means of escape to a landing place), that you may be capable
and strong and powerful to bear up under it patiently.*
1 CORINTHIANS 10:13 AMPC

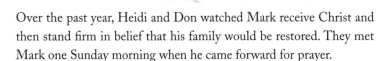

Over the past year, Heidi and Don watched Mark receive Christ and then stand firm in belief that his family would be restored. They met Mark one Sunday morning when he came forward for prayer.

Soon they got to know Mark and developed a friendship. They watched as he overcame drug and alcohol addiction, and continued to ask God to save his marriage and family. After nine long months, his wife, Janna, saw the change in him and allowed his children to attend church with him. A few months later she joined them.

Finally, that day came when they had the privilege to see Mark, along with his entire family, be baptized. God held the pieces when things fell apart, but over time, He put the pieces back together.

*God, when there seems to be no hope in sight, I refuse to give up.
You make a way for me, always. Help me hold on and patiently
see Your perfect plan come together for my life.*

Your Job Matters

"God's voice thunders in marvelous ways; he does great things beyond our understanding. He says to the snow, 'Fall on the earth,' and to the rain shower, 'Be a mighty downpour.' So that everyone he has made may know his work, he stops all people from their labor."

JOB 37:5–7 NIV

Ah, Labor Day. The last day of what, hopefully for you, was a three-day weekend. A time to rest from your labors.

Labor Day is important to many people who come from a long line of hard workers. It's a time to be thankful not only for the work ethic instilled by parents but to recognize the importance of doing what God has given you to do with everything within you. Whatever you do. Whether your job is to tend children, attend school, do volunteer work, or work for pay outside the home every day.

It's also important to take time today to rest and thank God for the purpose He has placed in you and the ability you have been given to do it. So give God thanks today.

Lord, thank You for revealing my purpose to me and giving me everything I need to fulfill it. It is only through Your power within me that I'm able to fulfill my destiny. Thank You for this day of rest from all the labor You have given my hands to do. And for reminding me that what I do matters to You.

Let Your Life Be a Song for Him

I will praise You with my whole heart; before the gods I will sing
praises to You. I will worship toward Your holy temple, and praise
Your name for Your lovingkindness and Your truth; for You
have magnified Your word above all Your name.

PSALM 138:1–2 NKJV

A music store is filled with potential—beautiful instruments just waiting for the musician to play them. From the majestic grand pianos and sea of colorful and sleek guitars, to elegant violins and harmonious flutes—every single instrument holds within it the potential for beautiful and creative music. But without someone to play them, they can never achieve their purpose.

You were born to worship—to live, to move in God. You were created to be an instrument of praise. Worship from your lips ushers you into His presence and brings Him pleasure.

One of the greatest gifts you can give God—aside from your heart through salvation—is worship. Take time to fully express your adoration of Him. Invite Him to show you who He has created you to be. As you become one with Him, your life becomes a song sung for Him.

Lord, I praise You. Thank You for Your lovingkindness and truth.
I want to be an instrument of praise to You. May my
life bring You pleasure in all I do.

Even When You Don't See, Believe

Yet God has made everything beautiful for its own time.
He has planted eternity in the human heart, but even so, people
cannot see the whole scope of God's work from beginning to end.
ECCLESIASTES 3:11 NLT

Seeing your loved ones suffer is difficult. Mothers especially know this, for good mothers tend to feel their own child's pain, whether it's caused by physical addiction, illness or injury, divorce or other loss, spiritual doubt or confusion, financial bankruptcy or debt, or mental issues—the list can go on and on.

The concern you, as a woman, have for others can almost consume you. You imagine a thousand things that could come from the current situation and another thousand ways you could possibly fix things. You find yourself wanting to wrap your arms around your loved one and tell him it's going to be okay. But deep down you know it's going to hurt for a while.

Chin up, woman. You know God is at work behind the scenes. He makes all things beautiful in His time. He is there to heal your loved one—and you. Yes, God will make it beautiful again. You just have to believe it till you see it.

God, You are making all things beautiful in Your time. Amid the
turmoil in my life and the lives of those I love, I will trust You.

The Greatest Is Love

And so faith, hope, love abide [faith—conviction and belief
respecting man's relation to God and divine things; hope—
joyful and confident expectation of eternal salvation; love—
true affection for God and man, growing out of God's love
for and in us], these three; but the greatest of these is love.
1 Corinthians 13:13 AMPC

One morning Kristin suddenly felt compelled to detour from the usual walking route she and her dog, Jasper, normally took. Instead, they turned the opposite direction and strolled toward the shopping center.

Kristin made a point to look people in the eye, smile, and say hello. Introductions were easy because Jasper was so cute. As Kristin and Jasper passed a man sitting on a bench outside the grocery store, she said, "Hello," and he said his name was Robert. She listened to his story. He had seen a doctor at the hospital for an infection in his foot. After asking her for money, he paused, and she said, "I don't have any money with me, but I'd like to pray for you if that's okay. Do you know Jesus?" she asked.

He nodded yes, and his eyes filled with tears. Kristin placed her hand in his and began to pray for him. When she finished, they both knew God had touched him.

God, fill me with compassion to see others in a new way.
Use me to show Your love to them.

God Is Always Thinking about You

You saw me before I was born. Every day of my life was recorded in your book. Every moment was laid out before a single day had passed. How precious are your thoughts about me, O God. They cannot be numbered!

Psalm 139:16–17 NLT

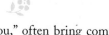

The words "I'm thinking of you," often bring comfort in the midst of a personal struggle or family crisis. It's soothing to know someone cares—and that you are in his or her thoughts.

Have you ever wondered what God thinks about you? Not a moment passes that you are not in His thoughts. From the very beginning of time, your Father's thoughts for you compelled Him to send His Son, Jesus, to the cross so you could have an eternal relationship with Him. Even amid the most trying personal crisis of Jesus' life—while hanging on the cross—you were on the heart of the Father.

What a powerful revelation to know you are on God's mind. Take time today to contemplate this news from a novel perspective. Let this truth sink into your heart as you begin to understand how God thinks about you.

God, thank You for reminding me that because every day of my life is recorded in Your book, nothing about my life catches You off guard. That even when my mind is full of things, sometimes even crowding out thoughts of You, You are still thinking about me.

Precious Time with Him

I say to the LORD, "You are my God." Hear, LORD,
my cry for mercy. Sovereign LORD, my strong deliverer,
you shield my head in the day of battle.
PSALM 140:6–7 NIV

Often we are distracted by life to the point that we are too busy to connect with the Lord.

Regardless of today's workload or your planned to-dos, resist the pressing urge to jump into your busyness first thing. Instead, determine to spend some time with the Lord.

Pour a cup of tea and sit in your favorite chair. Look out your window to whatever nature might surround you. Better yet, take a nice leisurely walk around your neighborhood or in a park. Either way, begin to pray quietly. Stop for a moment to drink in your surroundings, the beauty that reflects your Creator.

If you are outside, notice that just as the air escaping your lips is normally unseen in other seasons, fall exposes the presence of God. Notice that those things that often are invisible seem to be shouting out God's presence with each step you take.

How wonderful that in these quiet moments, God takes every means to remind you that He cherishes the precious time you spend with Him.

Lord, forgive me for being distracted. I will make time for You—
especially today. Give me a visible glimpse of You.

This Is the Way

The heart of the wise inclines to the right,
but the heart of the fool to the left.
ECCLESIASTES 10:2 NIV

Perhaps you are tired of all the confusion life presents. Somehow you may have lost your way, veered off the path. Distractions, selfishness, grief, and disappointment have pushed you in the wrong direction for too long. You lie in bed wide awake, unable to sleep, thoughts spinning around and around.

You turn off the droning television. Walk to the nearest prayer nook. Search for your Bible. Wait. It may have been a very long time since you have opened it. Perhaps the best place to start is with prayer.

You sit and have a chat with the One who has loved you since the beginning of time and longs to hear your voice. Tears flow. You begin to pray: "God, I'm lost. I'm confused. I'm sorry I stepped away from You. I need You. Please forgive me. Show me what to do."

Suddenly you feel snug and warm in the once chilly house. You feel God's familiar embrace and hear a soft whisper: "I've always been with you." Your eyes open. Then you spy your Bible and, with a smile, pull it out from underneath a stack of books and begin reading.

God, thank You for sticking with me all the way.
Help me keep my feet on Your path.

His Arms of Unconditional Love

*Set me as a seal upon thine heart, as a seal upon thine arm:
for love is strong as death; jealousy is cruel as the grave: the coals
thereof are coals of fire, which hath a most vehement flame.*
SONG OF SOLOMON 8:6 KJV

The sound of her niece's feet pitter-pattering across the wood floor brought a smile to Sheila's face. As she opened the oven to put the cookies in, she could hear Nikki's sweet voice asking the same question again, "Uncle Sam, will you read me a story 'bout Jesus."

Sheila peered over the kitchen counter just in time to catch a glimpse of her husband, Sam, setting his laptop aside and pulling the two-year-old into his lap. Sheila loved how this little girl brought out a completely different, often unseen side of her husband. She turned to set the timer on the stove as Sam's normally gruff voice melted away into a sing-song rhyme as he read to Nikki. The toddler giggled and wiggled as she helped him turn the pages of one of their favorite books.

Sheila's thoughts turned to her heavenly Father. *Lord, that's how I feel when I come to You. You are never too busy—You always have time for me.*

*Father God, I praise You for Your faithfulness. You always
answer when I call. Thank You for always lifting me up
and welcoming me into Your arms of unconditional love.*

Heart Work

Be alert and on your guard; stand firm in your faith (your conviction respecting man's relationship to God and divine things, keeping the trust and holy fervor born of faith and a part of it). Act like men and be courageous; grow in strength!
1 CORINTHIANS 16:13 AMPC

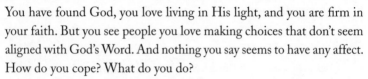

You have found God, you love living in His light, and you are firm in your faith. But you see people you love making choices that don't seem aligned with God's Word. And nothing you say seems to have any affect. How do you cope? What do you do?

You could lose a lot of sleep with worry. Or you could try another tack and go to God, praying: "Lord, it's so hard to watch someone I love choose things she knows are wrong. Why does it seem her heart is so hard toward you? Yet I know that she belongs to You, and I know You love her more than I do. So I leave it in Your hands. Help me trust You."

Deep down in your heart, you listen for the Lord's promising reply: "I'm taking care of it. No worries." Then you open your eyes, confident in His promise, and let Him do the heart work.

Lord, help me avoid overthinking things. It's not my place to make things happen in the lives of those I love. Only You can work in the heart. Thank You for peace to trust Your plan.

Through the Test

Then the LORD will create over all of Mount Zion and over those who assemble there a cloud of smoke by day and a glow of flaming fire by night; over everything the glory will be a canopy. It will be a shelter and shade from the heat of the day, and a refuge and hiding place from the storm and rain.
ISAIAH 4:5–6 NIV

Remember when you took your driving test? Although you may have taken drivers education, you didn't have much practice behind the wheel. So chances are your hands held the steering wheel with a white-knuckled grip, and butterflies ricocheted around inside your belly.

One part of you, wracked with doubts and nervousness, may have prayed for the Lord to help you, after which you tried to relax and allow Him to remind you of all the things you'd learned. But another part of you may have wished Jesus could just take the test for you.

Since that time, there have likely been many other situations during which you wished the same thing. The important thing to remember is that God is always with you, walking you through every situation, helping you come out victorious—but you have to take the test. So do so knowing you can do all things because He gives you strength.

Lord, I don't ever have to go through a test without You. You lead me, guide me, and give me the strength to face any adversity.

Drink of His Glory

I saw the Lord sitting on a throne, high and lifted up, and the train of His robe filled the temple. Above it stood seraphim; each one had six wings: with two he covered his face, with two he covered his feet, and with two he flew. And one cried to another and said: "Holy, holy, holy is the LORD of hosts; the whole earth is full of His glory!"

ISAIAH 6:1–3 NKJV

The earth truly is full of God's glory. In the busyness of life, so filled with distractions, it's easy to miss the wonder and majesty of His glory. Yet each new day, God takes the time to paint the sunrise and fill the evening sky with a light show.

Consider the works of His hands—the beauty and variety of flowers growing wildly, the powerful crashes of the ocean's waves, the majestic heights of a mountain range.

He wants you to step outside of the everyday chaos that tries to hem you in to experience His presence and His glory. He speaks to you in the little and big things found in His creation. Your heavenly Father pours out His artistic beauty simply for your joy and pleasure.

Heavenly Father, thank You for filling the earth with Your glory. I appreciate the little and big things You give me each day that demonstrate Your love for me.

The One You Can Count On

*Blessed be the LORD my Rock, Who trains my hands for war,
and my fingers for battle—my lovingkindness and my fortress,
my high tower and my deliverer, my shield and the One in
whom I take refuge, Who subdues my people under me.*

PSALM 144:1–2 NKJV

David learned at an early age that he could count on God. Although small in stature, he killed a lion and a bear, protecting his father's sheep from certain death. His courage and boldness came from within, from strength in his relationship with God.

His brothers, onlookers, and especially his enemy, the Philistine giant Goliath, laughed at him when he stood before them declaring he would take down Israel's enemy. He knew he could count on God. He had faith that God would go before him and give him victory in the battles he faced.

God has been with you and prepared you for what lies before you. You don't have to go into battle alone. When you know God as the One you can always count on, you can stand in the face of the giants in your life and come out of your battle a giant-slayer!

God, You are so faithful. Thank You for being with me in the battles I've faced. I know I can count on You to go with me now and see me through to become the champion You have destined me to be.

Dependent on Him

It is not that we think we are qualified to do anything
on our own. Our qualification comes from God.
2 CORINTHIANS 3:5 NLT

You are in a hurry, and your patience begins to evaporate with each breath you take. Your preschooler is taking forever to get ready and now sits down on the floor, pulling his left shoe toward him.

Exasperated, you say for the second time, "Please, let Mommy help you with your shoes."

But, of course, he wants to do it himself and works at it at a snail's pace. After what feels like hours, you make it into the car, drop him off at preschool, and head to work.

When you finally reach your destination, you suddenly realize, as you pull into the parking lot, that you often treat God like your child treated you that morning. You begin to imagine how God felt when you tried to do things on your own.

This is the moment to breathe deep and bow your head in prayer, inviting God to help you to depend more on Him—He who is your strength and your defense (see Isaiah 12:2), your protector, and your rescuer, He who is merely a breath away (see Psalm 145:18–20).

Father, I know You stand ready to help me with whatever
task is at hand. I don't want to do it in my own ability,
but instead surrender completely to do things Your way.

Supernatural Assurance

We are hard pressed on every side, but not crushed; perplexed, but not in despair; persecuted, but not abandoned; struck down, but not destroyed.
2 CORINTHIANS 4:8–9 NIV

After Whitney and Vince miscarried, the doctor finally gave them the okay to try to conceive again. They asked the Lord to heal their hearts of the deep grief and give them a healthy baby.

After trying to get pregnant for two weeks, Whitney prayed, "Lord, just be with me and give me a sign that it will all be okay."

That night around two a.m., Whitney woke up and looked over at Vince, who was sound asleep. Suddenly Vince sat up, grabbed her arm and said, "It's all going to be okay." The voice was different—a sweet voice, loud—but not a whisper.

A few weeks later, the couple found out they were pregnant. Today they have a beautiful, healthy two-year-old girl. Vince doesn't remember speaking that night, but Whitney is certain the Lord used him to give her supernatural assurance they would make it through.

The Lord can speak to you in many ways. No matter how dark the night, He will give you what He knows you need to make it through.

Lord, I am listening. When my heart trembles,
thank You for speaking to me clearly and filling me
with a supernatural assurance that only You can give.

Made New

*Therefore if any person is [ingrafted] in Christ (the Messiah) he is a
new creation (a new creature altogether); the old [previous moral and
spiritual condition] has passed away. Behold, the fresh and new has come!*
2 CORINTHIANS 5:17 AMPC

The day had started with a shining sun, but suddenly you find yourself
caught in a heavy downpour of rain. Short on time and patience, you
tighten your grip on your bags of just-bought groceries and walk briskly
to your car. Once behind the wheel, you realize you are completely
soaked, but you don't even care.

Some days everything seems to go wrong and you just want to sit
down and cry. Maybe you need a good cry. Just don't forget to follow
it up with prayer. Let God know you need more of Him. That your
focus has been elsewhere. You have let too many things get in the way.
Ask Him to wash away the old and tired, and bring back the new—the
dedication and love you experienced when you first came to know Him.

Then take a deep breath. Feel His embrace. He will help you make
a clean start.

*God, life fills up so fast. I don't want to get lost in the busyness.
Help me continue to experience the newness of who You have
created me to be. Help me embrace the new each day.*

God's Partner

In everything we do, we show that we are true ministers of God.
2 CORINTHIANS 6:4 NLT

When you turn on the television to glimpse the evening news, you are immediately reminded of the fallen world you live in. Danger, calamity, and terror are all around, yet you have hope in God's mercy because you know who you are.

- You are God's partner (see 2 Corinthians 6:1).
- You patiently endure troubles, hardships, and calamities of all sorts and sizes (see v. 4)
- You know that God's power is working in you (see v. 7).
- Your heart may ache, but you have eternal joy (see v. 10).
- You may be poor but give spiritual riches to others (see v. 10).
- You may own little but have everything (see v. 10).
- You have no lack of love within you, even though others withhold their love from you (see v. 12).

In other words, as God's partner, you see the world with His eyes. You know He's living in you. He's your safety zone. As you abide in Him, nothing can touch you.

So, as God's partner, don't panic. Instead, praise Him for what He is doing in your life. And continue to show others that no matter what happens in the world, you have peace because you are a true woman of the Way.

Father, thank You for allowing me to be Your partner in patience, power, joy, richness, and love as I abide in You.

The Family Table

O LORD, You are my God; I will exalt You, I will praise Your name,
for You have done wonderful things, even purposes planned
of old [and fulfilled] in faithfulness and truth.
ISAIAH 25:1 AMPC

Esther sat down at the long dining room table. At eighty-nine she still got around well, but her granddaughter, Emily, insisted she take her seat at the table while she called the rest of the family together for Esther's birthday meal.

She could hear the great-grandchildren's squeals and laughter as they took turns washing hands. She smiled as she raised the tablecloth up a little and peeked at the worn, hard wood. Her husband's father had made the table when his own family needed a big table to gather around. She closed her eyes, thinking about how her loving God met with each generation at this very table year after year.

"Grandmom," Emily said, "What are you thinking about?"

Esther smiled. "I was remembering how God met us for generations around this table. Many prayers were prayed and Bibles read around this table."

Emily smiled. "Maybe you should say grace today and remind us of what a beautiful heritage we have."

Esther replied. "I'd be honored."

God, thank You for giving me a godly heritage. You have
blessed me with the truth of Your Word. Help me live each day
according to Your truths so that I can pass that heritage on to others.

Your Vineyard Keeper

"In that day, sing about the fruitful vineyard. I, the LORD, will watch over it, watering it carefully. Day and night I will watch so no one can harm it."

ISAIAH 27:2–3 NIV

While sitting quietly in your front-row seat and watching your son say his wedding vows to his beautiful bride, don't be surprised if images of his childhood flash before your eyes. Such a beautiful baby and curious toddler, you remember. An artistic and creative child. Then the teenage and college years interrupt your sweet thoughts. Those years were so hard because your boy had turned away from God.

But God, you think, *You were always there. You knew exactly who he'd grow up to be. You kept him, watched over him.*

Your son had definitely been a vineyard that the Lord had faithfully tended all those years. In times when it seemed there would never be fruit again, you'd see a bloom of hope. Then, when you saw your son come back to the Lord, you witnessed his life flourishing.

Back to the reality of the wedding scene before you, you realize your heart is full today. Not only are you happy for your son on his wedding day, but you are even more thankful to God for keeping His promise. You raised your son in the way he should go, and he returned to the path of truth.

Lord, thank You for being my vineyard keeper.

A Quiet Confidence

For thus said the Lord God, the Holy One of Israel: In returning
[to Me] and resting [in Me] you shall be saved; in quietness
and in [trusting] confidence shall be your strength.
ISAIAH 30:15 AMPC

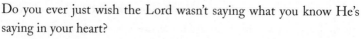

Do you ever just wish the Lord wasn't saying what you know He's saying in your heart?

That question may sound confusing, but have you ever felt aggravated to hear the Lord tell you to wait, or rest, when it's really not what you want to do? After all, you had plans.

You may go through some very difficult times. And your life may look very different from what you expected. But you also know that God has been, and will be, faithful through all the health challenges, financial obstacles, relationship difficulties, job losses, heartbreaks—everything you have faced and may still be facing in life.

So make it a point to return to God daily. Rest in Him. Stop your running around (mentally and physically) and be still and know that He is God (see Psalm 46:10). In so doing, you will be saved. And as you quietly and confidently trust in Him, you will find unlimited strength.

Lord, thank You for a quiet confidence in times of waiting.
Thank You for taking my hand and leading me through this
season. Help me be obedient to all You have asked me to
do. Help me hear You and respond with confidence.

Your Place of Peace

My people will live in peaceful dwelling places,
in secure homes, in undisturbed places of rest.
Isaiah 32:18 NIV

Marissa's hands shook a little as she set the laundry basket filled with books, electronics, and things she might need over the next week into the back of her SUV. She scanned the items already packed in her car. She was probably taking too much but didn't know exactly how long she'd be gone or what would remain when she got back.

New to Charleston, she'd never had to evacuate for a hurricane before. Thankfully her fiancé lived only four hours away, and it was far enough west to be out of harm's way. She made one more quick look through the house, checked the windows and doors, and locked it up.

Once on the interstate, traffic was the worst she'd ever seen. She'd never had to drive in traffic like that before. She looked down at her hands and realized her knuckles were white. She reached over and turned on some praise music. "Lord," she prayed, "I need your strength."

Suddenly the words of a song washed over her, reassuring her of the Lord's promise of His presence and peace. She no longer felt alone.

Know that no matter where you go, if you are abiding in God, you will find peace and security in the fiercest of gales.

Lord, in times of uncertainty, You give me security
and hope no matter what storms I face.

Whispers with God

*"Come and listen to my counsel. I'll share
my heart with you and make you wise."*
Proverbs 1:23 nlt

Prayer is an exchange, a conversation often uttered in whispers between God and His child. A man named Jonah called to God to deliver him from the belly of a large fish. Many of David's heart-wrenching prayers are recorded in the book of Psalms. And we cannot forget Jesus' prayer in the Garden of Gethsemane.

God called to Moses from a burning bush in the desert and gave him the assignment of his life. God whispered to Samuel in the middle of the night while he was just a child, to warn him of things to come in the prophet Eli's house. And Jesus questioned a Christian-persecuting Saul, who soon became the apostle Paul.

As you build your relationship with God and grow in knowing His voice, you learn to follow His lead. There are no perfect prayers or right ways of talking to God. He is ready and willing to hear your heart and answer the big and small questions in life.

God, thank You for your gentle nudges and whispers of love. Through prayer You provide everything I need for my life. Help me ask the right question, hear Your voice, and live in a way that pleases You.

God's Grace through the Detour

But he said to me, "My grace is sufficient for you, for my power
is made perfect in weakness." Therefore I will boast all the more
gladly about my weaknesses, so that Christ's power may rest on me.
2 CORINTHIANS 12:9 NIV

You may be struggling. A situation is out of your control. Someone has made a decision that affects you—and you are not very happy about it.

Take heart. Such things happen often throughout life. You thought you were on a particular path, but the plans, circumstances, or parameters changed. And right now you may feel as though God interrupted your life. But here's the thing: God always has permission to interrupt. And even though you may be having a hard time understanding what it all means, rest assured that you are just on a detour right now—and you cannot detour out of the reach of God's grace.

So there's no need to worry—a detour always puts you right back on the path you are supposed to be on!

Your job is just to take this time to relax and enjoy the scenery.

God Almighty, when You interrupt my life with a detour, help me
embrace it. I choose to trust You to take care of the details. I let
go of the expectations I have for this journey. Help me live
in the moment and experience Your grace along the way.

Show 'Em Who Lives in You

Examine yourselves as to whether you are in the faith. Test yourselves.
Do you not know yourselves, that Jesus Christ is in you?
2 CORINTHIANS 13:5 NKJV

Perhaps you have heard the phrase "Show 'em what you're made of." It is used to encourage someone to demonstrate his or her true character, often in the face of adversity or judgment from others.

When you choose to live for Christ, you have the opportunity to reveal to others who you are in Christ and who He is living in you. It gives others the chance to see your faith at work as you choose to follow Jesus' example.

Paul wrote, "I don't just do what is best for me; I do what is best for others so that many may be saved. And you should imitate me, just as I imitate Christ" (see 1 Corinthians 10:33–11:1 NLT). When you abide in Christ, His character—His nature and all of His attributes—shines out from within you. You are God's sanctuary; His Spirit lives in you. Christ in you is the hope of His glory demonstrated to those all around you (see Colossians 1:27). Each day, choose to show 'em who lives in you!

Christ Jesus, You live and dwell in me. Let my life shine for
Your glory. Let Your purpose and presence in my life point others
to a relationship with You because of the choices I make today.

I Am Your God

Fear not [there is nothing to fear], for I am with you; do not look around you in terror and be dismayed, for I am your God. I will strengthen and harden you to difficulties, yes, I will help you; yes, I will hold you up and retain you with My [victorious] right hand of rightness and justice.

ISAIAH 41:10 AMPC

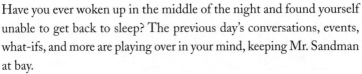

Have you ever woken up in the middle of the night and found yourself unable to get back to sleep? The previous day's conversations, events, what-ifs, and more are playing over in your mind, keeping Mr. Sandman at bay.

That's when you know the challenge is on. You get up quietly, careful not to disturb your snoring dog, cat, husband, child—whatever—and head for where you left your Bible the night before. You sit down and open God's Book to the verse above, then read Isaiah 41:13: "For I the Lord your God hold your right hand; I am the Lord, Who says to you, Fear not; I will help you!" (AMPC). Having set a firm foundation of faith, you enter into the Psalms, reading aloud King David's words of praise. As the minutes tick by, you feel God's presence. As you abide in Him, your eyes grow heavy and you find sleep in His arms.

Father, sometimes I live in my head. I let my worrisome thoughts take over. Thank You for bringing me back into Your presence, strength, and peace.

Strength in Him

What actually took place is this: I tried keeping rules and
working my head off to please God, and it didn't work.
So I quit being a "law man" so that I could be God's man.

GALATIANS 2:19 MSG

Imagine you are visiting your new church for the first time and notice that it lacks friendliness. Still, you know God directed you here. It's your new home. You also know that to have friends, you need to be friendly.

So, determined to obey the Lord and connect with your new church family, you enter the foyer the next Sunday morning intent on making a go of it, even though this is way out of your comfort zone.

Then you remember you don't have to depend on your own ability to befriend others. As you step out in faith, Christ will help you do what He has asked of you. You are God's woman, and His life has shown you just what you need to do and enabled you to do it.

Surprised by your newfound confidence, you stretch out your hand and introduce yourself to a family standing near you, thinking, "I have been crucified with Christ. My ego is no longer central. . . . Christ lives in me" (Galatians 2:20 MSG). Whew! What a relief!

Thank You, Lord, for living through me, for turning me
into Your woman, for giving me strength to do what
I cannot do on my own. My confidence is in You.

Showers of His Presence

"You heavens above, rain down my righteousness; let the clouds
shower it down. Let the earth open wide, let salvation spring up,
let righteousness flourish with it; I, the LORD, have created it."
ISAIAH 45:8 NIV

Exhaustion hung heavy on Leigh. She felt like someone was forcing her to carry heavy sandbags across her shoulders. But her mother needed her more than ever. She was her mother's only advocate in these last days before she succumbed to the sickness taking her life.

She walked through the kitchen and relaxed a little when she realized her children had cleaned the kitchen and put away the leftovers from dinner. She opened the microwave and retrieved the plate one of them had set aside for her. She moved it to the refrigerator, too tired to eat, and headed to the shower.

In the shower, she let go of her emotions and cried. God, "I need You," she whispered, "now more than ever." Suddenly it was much more than the warm water she felt. God was with her, pouring His love over her. She felt the weight on her shoulders slowly wash away as He embraced her with peace.

God, sometimes I feel the weight of so much on me. I know it's not Your
desire for me to carry the pressures of this world. I release them to You.
Wash away the heaviness and pour out Your peaceful presence on me now.

Daughters of Promise

And now that you belong to Christ, you are the true children of Abraham.
You are his heirs, and God's promise to Abraham belongs to you.
GALATIANS 3:29 NLT

The amazing thing about today's devotion is that each of the readings in your Bible reading plan (from Isaiah, Proverbs, and Galatians) contain verses that work together to give you great guidance.

Galatians 3:29 tells you that because you belong to Christ, you are a true daughter of Abraham—and, as such, an heir to the promise God made to Him. And what was God's initial promise? That if Abraham left all he knew behind and went to a new place God would show Him, there God would bless him (see Genesis 12:1–2).

In other words, God wants you to step out—and when you do step out in faith, He will direct you to where He wants you to go. And He reiterates this idea all through the Bible, including in Isaiah 48:17, where He says: "I am the LORD your God, who teaches you what is good for you and leads you along the paths you should follow."

The bonus is that He will not only teach and lead you but will take you "into his confidence" (Proverbs 3:32 NIV) along the way.

Because you are God's daughter and an heir to His promises, there's no way you can go wrong. Trust God. He knows.

Father, thank You for making the way clear for me, a daughter of promise.

Isolated but Not Alone

"Can a mother forget the baby at her breast and have no compassion on the child she has borne? Though she may forget, I will not forget you! See, I have engraved you on the palms of my hands."
ISAIAH 49:15–16 NIV

Jesus prayed in the Garden of Gethsemane. He knew He stood on the brink of the biggest battle of His earthly life. He craved companionship—support from His friends. He asked His disciples, those closest to Him, to pray, but He discovered them sleeping instead. Then in the night, Judas gave Him away with a kiss. His disciples abandoned Him, friends forgot Him, and Peter, the one who promised to have His back, denied even knowing Him.

As Jesus' captors dragged Him away, He saw no supportive, familiar faces in the crowd. Isolated, He held tight to God. Even when the Father turned away, Jesus called to Him for assurance. Jesus gave up His life and died, fully committed to the Father's plan. He faced death, burial, and resurrection—isolated but not alone. His faith remained unshaken because He knew God would never abandon Him.

No matter what circumstances you are facing today, God has not forgotten you. When you feel isolated, remember that you are never alone.

Heavenly Father, just as You were with Jesus, I know You are with me. When others forget me and fail to support me, I look to You. You are my strength. You are always with me.

Healthy Heart

Pay attention to what I say; turn your ear to my words. Do not
let them out of your sight, keep them within your heart; for they
are life to those who find them and health to one's whole body.
Proverbs 4:20–22 niv

How's your heart health? The health of your heart, the source of all your emotions, is critical to the well-being of your entire body. Unfortunately, there can be toxic waste accumulations within your heart that need to be brought to light and replaced with brilliant truth.

God commands you to put His truths into your heart by meditating on His Word. Truths transform your thoughts. Truths toss out lies you have believed about yourself. You live in a broken world; therefore, your mind requires a heavenly wipe down, a renewal that transforms you. After reading this devotion, take a few words from a verse that means something to you and turn them over all day in your mind.

God stresses the importance of guarding well your heart where His truths are stored, truths that bring you life and healing. When you hear the voice in your head, the one that says you are a failure, stupid, too much or not enough, raise your shield and grab your sword. Meditate on what God says about you. You are holy, without blame, more than a conqueror, a beloved child of God, alive in Christ.

God, help me replace my earthly thoughts
with Your heavenly truths. Amen.

No Biting

For everything we know about God's Word is summed up in a single
sentence: Love others as you love yourself. That's an act of true freedom.
If you bite and ravage each other, watch out—in no time at all you will
be annihilating each other, and where will your precious freedom be then?
GALATIANS 5:14–15 MSG

God wants His children to get along and not be in strife with one another. To accept the limitations and uniqueness of others instead of making judgments or even sarcastic remarks. For such cutting statements are like biting and devouring. And such "bites" hurt not only the receiver but the giver as well.

Judgments about others puts you in the seat reserved only for God. And sarcasm toward others is no better. Interestingly enough, the word sarcasm comes from a root word meaning "to strip off the flesh." Bite! Munch! Devour! That's a feeding frenzy during which everyone ends up being consumed.

There's another way to live, and God tells you that it fulfills His whole law as well as puts you on the path of freedom. You can love those around you like you love yourself. Doing so includes stopping the judgments and sarcasm—and embracing the absolute freedom of letting others be themselves. No biting required.

Father God, forgive me for times when I have judged the people You love.
Help me love and accept everyone just as they are. Amen.

Springs of Water

*"The LORD will guide you always; he will satisfy your needs in a
sun-scorched land and will strengthen your frame. You will be like
a well-watered garden, like a spring whose waters never fail."*
ISAIAH 58:11 NIV

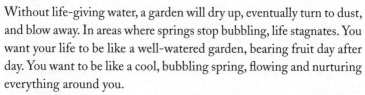

Without life-giving water, a garden will dry up, eventually turn to dust,
and blow away. In areas where springs stop bubbling, life stagnates. You
want your life to be like a well-watered garden, bearing fruit day after
day. You want to be like a cool, bubbling spring, flowing and nurturing
everything around you.

Abiding close to the heart of God is the secret to being replenished
by the Master Gardener. God knows that living apart from Him leaves
you with scorched places within. Time with Him renews you with
waters that never fail. No matter your circumstances, step into the lush
oasis created by God for those who seek Him. Linger there, gaining
refreshment of soul and clarity of mind.

God desires His children to love each other well. When you treat
others by God's standards of justice, He promotes healing and strength
in your life as described in this chapter of Isaiah.

Physical strength provides stamina and health to dry bones. Strength
of spirit allows you to be brave in uncertainty. The strength God provides
is a sure and solid power. It will not leave you faltering or failing—but
ever fruitful and flowing.

*God, thank You, my Master Gardener,
for tending me with Your loving hand.*

Delightfully You

You [Judah] shall no more be termed Forsaken, nor shall your land be called Desolate any more. But you shall be called Hephzibah [My delight is in her], and your land be called Beulah [married]; for the Lord delights in you, and your land shall be married [owned and protected by the Lord].

ISAIAH 62:4 AMPC

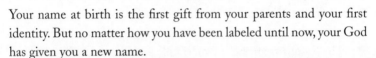

Your name at birth is the first gift from your parents and your first identity. But no matter how you have been labeled until now, your God has given you a new name.

The terms "Forsaken" and "Desolate" call forth images of a dry, deserted, barren land where nothing grows or flourishes. But "My Delight" is the new name God gives you. Captivated by you, He adores spending time with you. He awakens you with a brilliant sunrise and lulls you to sleep with a glowing moon and twinkling stars, heavenly displays that show how much pleasure He takes in you.

Let go of the other names you have accumulated: Too Heavy, Too Tall, Not Smart Enough, Not Pretty Enough, Too Much Trouble. You are enough. . .and not too much. God is not seeking perfection, beauty, or grace. He is seeking you. Bloom in the love of a Father who has renamed you His Delight.

Father God, thank You for delighting in me. Help me fully accept my new name and live as one accepted and adored by her Father. Amen.

Lessons from an Ant

Go to the ant, you sluggard; consider its ways and be wise!
It has no commander, no overseer or ruler, yet it stores its
provisions in summer and gathers its food at harvest.
PROVERBS 6:6–8 NIV

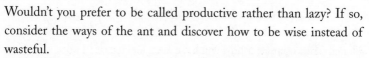

Wouldn't you prefer to be called productive rather than lazy? If so, consider the ways of the ant and discover how to be wise instead of wasteful.

The lessons from the ant are simple and threefold: First, the ant "has no commander." So find a way to motivate yourself, something that will keep you working without having someone standing over you making sure you do the task before you. Second, the ant has a strategy, one that follows the seasons. So plan your own course. Determine steps to achieve your goal—with God's input, of course. Third, the ant gathers and stores. So should you take action. Scrutinize obstacles that have held you up before, and sidestep them. Go after your dreams, making sure your heart's desires also match God's.

By studying the ant's habits, you will gain wisdom that will benefit your life. God knows productivity will produce a happier and more satisfying life for you. But be sure to schedule time for rest and relaxation to live a truly balanced, godly life. Queen ants are known to sleep nine hours a day, and worker ants enjoy power naps!

God, thank You for instilling good habits in the ant.
Help me incorporate their ways into my daily life. Amen.

Fullness

I pray that you, being rooted and established in love, may have power. . .
to know this love that surpasses knowledge—that you may
be filled to the measure of all the fullness of God.
EPHESIANS 3:17–19 NIV

God's fullness infuses you when you understand how deeply you are loved, to the brim.

What keeps you from accepting God's love? Perhaps feelings of unworthiness and guilt block your heart. Or the shame of secret sins isolates you. Yet the One who knows you best accepts you the most completely. Christ's blood was more than sufficient, and you stand before God faultless and beloved. Let go of any thought that you must earn the affection that God pours into you freely.

The fullness of God is like the deep pool at the base of a mountain waterfall, deep enough for you to plunge into, laughing with joy. Immerse yourself in the great incomprehensible mystery of who God is—an all-knowing and all-powerful being who chooses friendship with you. He is enduringly faithful but forgives all of your unfaithfulness. He is God the mighty warrior of the Old Testament and Christ the gentle lamb of the New.

Though God is unfathomable, He delights in revealing Himself to you so that you may be filled to the brim with the fullness of God.

Father God, help me absorb the deep and extravagant
love with which You fill me to the brim. Amen.

Forget Me Not

Does a young woman forget her jewelry, a bride her wedding ornaments?
Yet my people have forgotten me, days without number.
JEREMIAH 2:32 NIV

Have you forgotten something recently that you later felt lost without?

Forgetting a cell phone is highly inconvenient, as is leaving home without sunglasses, keys, or a wallet. How about forgetting a carefully planned shopping list when you are in a time crunch?

Have you ever forgotten to spend time with God in His Word? When you do so, you miss out on the joy and peace that comes from God, causing your soul to begin to feel dry and lonely.

Each morning God is smiling when you open your eyes. He wants to talk with you. Time in His Word is like sitting down to coffee with the best of friends. He meets you there and prepares you for your day.

When it's time to get dressed, remember to slow down long enough to add your most valuable accessory: a spirit warmed and refreshed by the Spirit of God. Just as a woman remembers to put on earrings or a necklace, take a mental and spiritual moment to clothe yourself with the truth of God. And just as a bride places a veil on her head, pause and adjust your thoughts to remember God in His greatness and generous love.

God, I love that You want to spend time with me!
Help me forget You not. Amen.

Light

For you were once darkness, but now you are light in the Lord. Live
as children of light (for the fruit of the light consists in all goodness,
righteousness, and truth) and find out what pleases the Lord.
EPHESIANS 5:8–10 NIV

Genesis 1 tells us that God created the heavens and the earth. But all of that was without form—empty and dark. So the Spirit of God, hovering over the waters, decided to make light—and from that, built the entire world. And He saw that that light was good.

Our God is one who transforms people as well as worlds. The apostle Paul, in his letter to the Ephesians, tells his readers that they were all once in darkness. But now they are "light in the Lord." And God sees that as good. Very good.

The transformation that changed you from darkness to light is no less dramatic than what your Creator God did in transforming this world. You are a new creature. Live like a new creature. Give up any ties with the dark, and please God instead. For He is your source of abundant life, joy, peace, and love.

Determine to live each day in the light. Seek God in scripture and in prayer. Thank Him for His gifts. Praise Him for being a great God who transforms. Enjoy life in the light.

God, help me live as a child of light and be drawn
to the best of what is good, right, and true. Amen.

Standing Strong

Finally, be strong in the Lord and in his mighty power. Put on the full armor of God, so that you can take your stand against the devil's schemes.
EPHESIANS 6:10–11 NIV

Are you a member of the Fraidy Cat Club, one who cringes over dark places, loud noises, or hostile environments? Most people are. But the truth is that God is the One who fights for you (see Exodus 14:14; Deuteronomy 1:30; 3:22; 20:4). Trusting in Him, you can stand strong behind His armor and in His strength. Put on all that God has provided to defend against the devil's attempts to confuse, manipulate, and scare you.

What schemes does the enemy use against you? Satan loves to batter you with shame that you haven't done enough or the idea that God can't possibly forgive you again. The enemy takes pleasure in making you doubt your salvation or in making you think that God could never love someone like you. The enemy wants to trick you into losing the peace and joy of abundance in Christ.

No worries. Your God-given armor has you covered. It's your task to put each piece on with focus, understanding that the battle has already been won. Stand strong. God's power looks mighty good on you.

God, I'm thankful for Your mighty power and protective armor.
Now help me stand firm, exchanging your truth for the enemy's lies,
confident in the knowledge that You are the one who fights for me. Amen

Life Jewels

*Choose my instruction instead of silver, knowledge rather
than choice gold, for wisdom is more precious than rubies,
and nothing you desire can compare with her.*
PROVERBS 8:10–11 NIV

Imagine a treasure chest full of sparkling red rubies, radiant gold coins, and gleaming silver candlesticks. Could anything be more spectacular?

Well, yes. Far more spectacular are these:

- instruction—learning;
- knowledge—understanding what you have learned;
- and wisdom—practicing that understanding in your life.

Wisdom will add a special radiance and beauty to all the daily dilemmas it touches. So sprinkle God's wisdom into each aspect of your life and watch for blooms to appear where once there was barrenness. For wisdom directs you to make the best financial choices, strengthens your relationships, and helps you find balance and peace in a fast-paced life.

Wisdom is the real jewel of life, and God is the abundant supplier. Yet how do you gain wisdom? You can download it into your brain via wise counsel, Christian messages, and spiritual songs. But the best method is to consume God's Word like a slice of pie, taking small bites and slowly savoring and swallowing. Then pondering how those small pieces of truth might be applied to your personal circumstances.

Choose instruction, knowledge, and wisdom—and you will have all the treasure you can imagine.

*God, I love the richness of Your Word. Show me
how to apply Your wisdom to my life. Amen.*

Be For Each Other

Let each of you look out not only for his own interests, but also for the interests of others. Let this mind be in you which was also in Christ Jesus.
PHILIPPIANS 2:4–5 NKJV

The word for, by itself, seems to be somewhat meek and mild. But to be for someone is a powerful act. And it's the key to beautiful and meaningful relationships.

Looking for opportunities to be for someone else can come in a variety of packages. Encourage her strength or applaud her talent. Remember an important event in her life. Believe the best when faults are obvious.

Notice the understated balance in the relationship equation outlined in the verses above. It's acceptable (and expected!) for you to look after your own interests as well as those of others. So remember to be for yourself. Celebrate an event important to you, be kind to yourself, notice your strengths, and follow your dreams.

And remember, above all, that God is for you. In fact, with Him for you, who can be against you? (see Romans 8:31). He demonstrates His forness daily in a thousand ways. He listens to you. Applauds your good works. Supports you when you are standing alone. He is so perfectly and personally for you that He gave His Son's life so that you could live, love, walk—and think—as He did. Your job? Go for it, as He intended.

Thank You for being for me, God! Amen.

God's Trademarks

GOD's Message: "Don't let the wise brag of their wisdom. Don't let heroes brag of their exploits. Don't let the rich brag of their riches. If you brag, brag only of this and this only: That you understand and know me. I'm GOD, and I act in loyal love. I do what's right and set things right and fair, and delight in those who do the same things. These are my trademarks." GOD's Decree.
JEREMIAH 9:23–24 MSG

Roses are known for their scent. Trains are known by their distinctive whistle. Crickets are known for their nighttime chirping. What is your defining characteristic? God says His trademarks are love, righteousness, and fairness.

God sees deep inside your heart. His desire is that out of your relationship with Him, love, righteousness, and fairness will overflow onto others, leaving small puddles that become your delightful trademark.

Busyness, volunteering, and achievements can be added to the list of things that are outer signs of worth. And you may tend to rely on those exterior things to demonstrate your worthiness. Yet your heart will be happiest when you find your worth in God.

As you understand and know Him, you will bask in His loyal love, and all those insecurities that cause you to find significance elsewhere will fade away.

Thank You, Lord, that Your heart desires the best of relationships with me. Help me know and understand You! Amen.

Wise Ways

"Leave your simple ways and you will live; walk in the way of insight."
PROVERBS 9:6 NIV

Wisdom, as quoted in Proverbs 9:6, invites you to turn from the confusion of a hectic lifestyle to walk a different path. She compels you to live the life of abundance that you are designed for. You are invited into her home where she has set a banquet feast specially prepared for you. She asks you to dine with her, to "leave your simple ways."

The "simple ways" from which Wisdom wants you to detour are a life lived without insight, thought, or understanding. Such a life is like a house with its windows shuttered, doors boarded up, and furniture covered. When the shutters are thrown aside, doors opened, and furnishings exposed by Wisdom, light, air, and color flood throughout the house. Dark corners are illuminated. Purposes become clearer. Priorities are set in order. Confusion is replaced with meaning.

So explore God's truths through His Word. Pause throughout your day to think about Him. Walk with Wisdom and she will help you to understand. In so doing, you will discover your great worth in God, comprehend life's meaning and richness, and realize that God has a plan for you to know Him and abide in Him. These truths will bring peace of mind and insight to everyday problems.

God, give me wisdom to leave any simple
ways and open my life to You. Amen.

Protective Peace

Do not be anxious about anything, but in every situation,
by prayer and petition, with thanksgiving, present your requests
to God. And the peace of God, which transcends all understanding,
will guard your hearts and your minds in Christ Jesus.
PHILIPPIANS 4:6–7 NIV

Anxiety is a fierce opponent with which you may often wrestle, and sometimes you may find that it has pinned you to the mat. To loose yourself from anxiety's hold—or avoid the battle all together—you need the Holy Coach's help. That means, in every situation, you are to go to God in prayer, tell Him what's happening and what you need, then thank Him for what He has done, is doing, and will do.

Once you enlist His aid and leave the results in His hands, God will send an unfathomable peace to stand guard over your mind where your thoughts originate and over your heart where your emotions live.

So when anxiety begins to push at your thoughts, when a problem is on the horizon, immediately run to God, then pray, petition, and thank. The situation may not be resolved as you had imagined, but you will know you received the result God was looking for—and be left with God's shield of peace, a transcendent gift beyond all understanding.

God, thank You for providing peace today right when and
where I need it. I trust You to reign in every detail. Amen.

Gathered Up

So spacious is he, so roomy, that everything of God finds its proper
place in him without crowding. Not only that, but all the broken and
dislocated pieces of the universe—people and things, animals and atoms—
get properly fixed and fit together in vibrant harmonies, all because
of his death, his blood that poured down from the cross.
COLOSSIANS 1:19–20 MSG

The vastness of all of the earth's oceans could not compare with the fullness of God. Yet all of His fullness was pleased (not frustrated or disappointed) to dwell in the person of Jesus Christ. And God's purpose in dwelling in Christ was to reconcile all the pieces of creation that had been torn apart by sin.

So no matter how broken up or beat down you may feel, you are—in reality—gathered up, contained in Jesus. You are restored, all in one piece, all in one place in the absolute fullness of God.

When you comprehend that the scattered pieces of yourself are gathered up and redeemed, the fissures that have left you painfully cracked can heal. You can look at yourself with the word "reconciled" scripted around you in flowing circles. You are complete.

God, help me walk today as one who is
gathered up, redeemed, and healed. Amen.

An Honest Approach

Honesty lives confident and carefree, but Shifty is sure to be exposed.
PROVERBS 10:9 MSG

Wouldn't you love to walk through life confident and carefree? You'd spend your days walking down the street, whistling a happy tune. Or driving along the coast in a convertible, your hair flying in the breeze.

Although life isn't always that simple, you can live confident and carefree.

Value honesty. Avoid what's false or duplicitous. Then your heart will be free of the worry of being found deceitful. And although you will still make mistakes, they will be honest ones, with a chance of being happily resolved.

Confidence comes from knowing you have done your best to be trustworthy and truthful in your dealings with others. And although being honest and upfront is sometimes difficult, especially when it means others might be displeased or you might get in trouble, the effort is worth it.

Being truthful with yourself is just as important as being honest with others. And while you are being honest with others and yourself, be honest with God as well. Tell Him just what is going on, how you feel, what you are thinking. He knows the whole truth anyway, so you might as well come clean from the start. You will both feel better about it—and about each other.

Lord, help me have an honest approach. Remind me when I slip into anything less. Thank You for helping me walk in Truth. Amen.

Simply Shadows

*So don't put up with anyone pressuring you in details of diet,
worship services, or holy days. All those things are mere shadows
cast before what was to come; the substance is Christ.*
COLOSSIANS 2:16–17 MSG

Small things cast large shadows. If you have ever been frightened by something insignificant, you know this is true. In the same way, rigid man-made rules are little things that cast large shadows, ones that would steal your sunlight and joy. But Christ is your beautiful reality.

Christ is the solid substance of life. He is your sure footing and your rock. He doesn't change or falter. When you keep your eyes directed at Him and not the shadows, you focus on what is real. Allowing His truth to seep in deeply will allow your mind to be "confident and at rest" (Colossians 2:2–4 MSG).

Looking at the real thing, knowing and being in touch with who Christ really is, helps you pick out what's false, enabling you to eliminate it from your life. So pay no attention to the worldly rules of others, their hollow philosophies, human traditions—"men's ideas of the material rather than the spiritual world" (Colossians 2:8 AMPC)—that have no basis in God or His Word. Instead, live, breathe, and abide in Christ. He is your reality. He will keep you out of the shadows and lead you into His Sonlight!

*There's no one like You, God! Help me
keep my eyes focused on You. Amen.*

Beloved Sheep

"I myself will gather the remnant of my flock out of all the countries
where I have driven them and will bring them back to their pasture,
where they will be fruitful and increase in number. I will place
shepherds over them who will tend them, and they will no longer
be afraid or terrified, nor will any be missing."
JEREMIAH 23:3–4 NIV

If you ever have an identity crisis, here is a beautiful reality to fall back on. You are God's beloved sheep. This truth is enough to outshine everything the world tells you, you are not. You can be confident that God has set you securely in His fold. He has elaborate plans to care for you, make you successful, and eradicate your fear and dismay.

Because your trustworthy Shepherd loves each member of His flock, you can trust Him to care for those you love as well as yourself.

Being God's sheep means that you (or ewe) can reside in a peaceful pasture, green with peace and gladness at any time or place. When you feel a little beat up by life outside the pasture, you can remember that your Good Shepherd understands. He promises not to lose even one of His fold. He keeps a careful headcount and goes in search of those who wander off.

Thank You, Good Shepherd, for providing what I need
in a pasture. I trust You to care for us all. Amen.

Wholeheartedness

*"For I will set My eyes on them for good, and I will bring them back
to this land; I will build them and not pull them down, and I will plant
them and not pluck them up. Then I will give them a heart to know Me,
that I am the Lord; and they shall be My people, and I will be their
God, for they shall return to Me with their whole heart."*

Jeremiah 24:6–7 NKJV

God is wholehearted. He is present in the moment. He does not love
partially but completely. God loves enthusiastically with all His passion,
and that is how He desires you to love Him.

Life may have left your heart bruised and broken, but God can
do what no one else can. He can give you a new heart—one that
comprehends His greatness.

Who else but God can rescue you from your wanderings? Who
else can build you up, layer upon layer of strength and courage? Only
God can plant your roots deeply in a place that becomes a lasting home.

Your heart is safe with your faithful God. It can expand and dream.

Return to Him now. Discover the freedom of hoping in a future
that is good. Find your ease in loving God with your whole heart. Grasp
the deep and abiding love with which He first loved you.

God, help me grasp Your wholehearted love for me. Amen.

Finding the Right Way

Without good direction, people lose their way;
the more wise counsel you follow, the better your chances.
PROVERBS 11:14 MSG

Hikers have been known to freeze, go hungry, or get lost when they don't pay attention to necessary details. Sometimes search parties are required to rescue them. So before setting off on a hike in the wilderness, careful planning needs to take place.

Most of life can be set on course or fine-tuned with good directions. Relationships, parenting, and finances are all areas where wise counsel can make a difference. Sensible suggestions from a knowledgeable person are like gold coins in your pocket. They are a treasure trove for life.

Being humble enough to ask for help doesn't make you appear ignorant. On the contrary, only motivated people seek assistance. Be one of those who has a pocketful of solid advice to draw from on your journey to wherever it is you are going. You will get there sooner and have an easier time along the way with help.

Everyone has made wrong turns before. So if you find yourself off track, consider your options. If you have lost your way, now is a great time to seek advice. God loves to set you on the path to success. And He will put people in your life to do just that!

Father God, help me seek the best advice possible and direct
my steps today. I trust You to be at work in my life. Amen.

Hope

*"I will come to you and fulfill my good promise. . . . For I know the plans
I have for you," declares the Lord, "plans to give you hope and a future."*
Jeremiah 29:10–11 niv

Hope is beautiful. At times you see it, shining and bright, dancing
ahead of you, making your steps lighter and forming a smile on your
lips. These are the times when a new home, tiny new baby, or a new
job fill you with expectation.

Other times, although hope may not seem apparent, it is still
present. This is when you may be chilled deeply by grief, having lost a
relationship, parent, or long-held dream. This is when the warmth of
hope, like a well-worn quilt made by loving hands, God's hands, can
be pulled around your shoulders, and you can rest under its comforting
weight, snuggling up to the knowledge that one day you will again "see
the goodness of the Lord in the land of the living" (Psalm 27:13 niv).

God declares hope over, around, and through you. He has prepared
a future for you and has plans for your well-being. A powerful as well
as personal being, God doesn't give you someone else's future. He has
made one just for you. Allow your heart to hope in Him and whatever
future He has planned.

*Father God, I thank and trust You for the future You have planned for me.
Please make my hope a constant, in good times and bad. Amen.*

Green Garden

A life devoted to things is a dead life, a stump;
a God-shaped life is a flourishing tree.
PROVERBS 11:28 MSG

When God tends your garden, you are guaranteed vibrant growth and lush foliage. You will be like a healthy and fruitful tree, giving shade to all those around you.

Allowing God to shape your life after His own heart produces breathtaking results. He gently prunes away unwanted branches, like interests and relationships that won't produce growth for you or Him. He promotes the dreams and desires He has planted in you so that you will thrive and bear fruit after fruit. He nourishes your soul with His truths so that your roots are grounded securely against storms and conflicts. Because He longs to walk and talk with you, your meeting with God, the Master Gardener, each morning hastens your transformation process.

A God-shaped life glistens inside and out. But spending time on things that don't bring enthusiasm to your spirit will leave you feeling dead inside. Excessive TV watching or Internet surfing can cause numbness. Watch out for and avoid things that dry up your sap and stunt your growth! Instead, pursue flourishing life provided by the Father, striving to spend less time in the world's shadows and more time in the Son's light.

Father God, I want all You have to offer!
Help me embrace a God-shaped life. Amen.

Beautiful Changes

*If you love learning, you love the discipline that goes with it—
how shortsighted to refuse correction!*
PROVERBS 12:1 MSG

Although the old and familiar are comforting, being willing to allow change within is important. For God, the only One who never changes, would like to transform you from the inside out as you move through life. This will happen, sometimes slowly, sometimes quickly, but always in a way that moves you from glory to glory.

Change occurs in you as you spend time with God, learning about Him from His Word. His truths go into the dark places of your heart and let in light. As you understand how completely you are loved and accepted, you will find the courage to let go of the ideal, of perfection. You will let go of fear and worry as you grow to trust God more and more. You will become satisfied, even overjoyed, with what God says about you, and stop seeking approval from others. Yes, woman, change can be beautiful.

When you believe deeply that God will never, ever abandon or reject you, you can let go of old habits and thought patterns that have kept you frozen in place. As you begin loving, learning, and thriving on correction, you will be find more and more pleasure in your inner beauty.

God, thank You for working out Your beautiful salvation in me.

Hidden Things

"This is GOD's Message, the God who made earth, made it livable
and lasting, known everywhere as GOD: 'Call to me and I will
answer you. I'll tell you marvelous and wondrous things
that you could never figure out on your own.'"
JEREMIAH 33:2–3 MSG

Are you the type of woman who appreciates a surprising plot twist? Your life is like a well-told story full of unanswered dilemmas. But here's the good news: God holds the key to the mysteries of life and desires to share them in sweet fellowship with you.

God's answers are sometimes long in coming, other times they're quick, but He always hears when you call Him and is not slow to speak. He unravels every single mystery as you patiently listen for, then follow His promptings. The beauty is in your relationship with Him. The almighty Father God whispers into the ear of you, His beloved daughter, telling you the wondrous things only He can impart. Listen and attend carefully. For at times He speaks softly to your spirit. At other times He will gently nudge your soul.

Need to know how to reach a troubled heart? Perplexed about relationships? Want to feel whole and safe amid transition? Call to God. He will answer, advise, and amaze you.

Father God, I trust You to show me marvelous and wondrous things.
Help me know when You are speaking. Quiet my soul to listen. Amen.

Quiet Please

Prudent people don't flaunt their knowledge;
talkative fools broadcast their silliness.
PROVERBS 12:23 MSG

Listening before speaking is a smart way to live. That's difficult when you feel like you could just pop with something to say. But God says to wait patiently instead of letting it all go in one big breath. That's because your tongue can get you into trouble quicker than anything else. So, if you want your words to count, you will hold them until the right time and place. Following are some ways to communicate powerfully.

Seeking to understand before being understood brings lots of reward. Doing so requires careful discipline, but it is worth the extra effort. Ask questions to clarify the other's viewpoint before expressing your own.

Active listening promotes healthy relationships. Lean forward and focus on what is being said instead of what you will say next. Your looking into someone's eyes instead of multitasking lets that person know she or he is valued.

Listen calmly and absorb the new information coming your way and you will appear wise. Others will respect your quiet demeanor.

Once you have listened well, it will be your time to speak. By then your understanding will have incubated and hatched some authentic wisdom on the situation.

Father God, please help me remember to pause before speaking.
I want my words to count in Your kingdom.

Aiming for Love

Now the purpose of the commandment is love from a pure heart,
from a good conscience, and from sincere faith.
1 Timothy 1:5 NKJV

To be able to hit a bull's-eye on an archery target takes careful focus on the circle in the center. So it is with love. If you want to shoot straight, to hit your target for the Lord, you must keep your concentration on Him, the God of all grace and love. Your arrows will stray off course if you are distracted by the rules. Even though the rules are good and reveal your need for redemption, they are not to be your focus. God is. Because God is love.

To shoot straight, love from a pure heart—without a hidden agenda. Only honest love is profound and will fly straight to the heart of the intended.

Pure love looks like intentional listening and seeking to understand. It believes the best despite another's mistakes. It helps quietly.

When you desire to love others exceptionally, God will direct your heart—and theirs. Be ready to set aside lesser things to fulfill your mission. And know that God, who is constantly guiding your steps by pure love, will keep your aim true.

Father God, thank You for Your heart of love poured out over me.
Show me one way to touch someone with that same love today. Amen.

Shining Brightly

The light of the righteous shines brightly,
but the lamp of the wicked is snuffed out.
PROVERBS 13:9 NIV

Great beauty is seen in the flame of a candle, the glow of a firefly, or a twinkling star. You are a light that shines brighter than these because of the righteousness of Christ. Steady and sure, your flame glows with the glory of Christ in you.

Your unquenchable light is made for eternity. This world will not satisfy your eternal soul. Focus on what is lasting—God's love, Word, and the spirits of His people. Take time for each in your day. When you focus your effort on what is lasting, you carry it with you into eternity.

Make time to hear your child's discovery. Hold the hand of an elderly neighbor. Seek out a quiet moment and listen to the secrets of someone's heart—maybe even your own. Ask God to reveal Himself in His Word. These moments will make your heart happy.

You are transformed by trials, your rich golden light deepening with endurance. You are stronger than you think and more vivid than you can imagine. Never be intimidated by the darkness around you. It's no match for you. You were made to shine forever, so don't hide your glory.

Father God, thank You for intending me to live eternally with You.
Help me focus on the things that last forever. Amen.

Your Heart's Desire

Souls who follow their hearts thrive;
fools bent on evil despise matters of soul.
PROVERBS 13:19 MSG

What does your heart desire? If you are walking with God, you should be paying attention to your heart's yearnings. That may be the very thing God has already gone ahead and prepared for you to do or be.

You were created with talents, preferences, and a personality unique to you. And God will direct your plans to follow where those things lead. Listen to what your heart hopes for. Test it and determine how and where God is using your heart messages to direct you.

Sometimes you may be unsure of what you want. You have been so busy taking care of others that you haven't stopped to consider what you desire. No worries. God knows the longings of your heart. Ask Him to clarify any dormant dreams or uncertainties.

Scripture promises that if you delight in the Lord, He will give you the desires of your heart (see Psalm 37:4 NIV). Trusting God to do so might not seem reasonable or safe if you have had disappointments in the past. Yet God alone is worthy of your total confidence. Because He loves you like no other, you can trust Him. Have confidence in all He is doing in your life, as well as what He plans to do.

God, thank You for the delights You bring to my life.
I trust You to bring good things in my future.

Life Together

Don't let anyone think less of you because you are young.
Be an example to all believers in what you say, in the way
you live, in your love, your faith, and your purity.
1 TIImOTHY 4:12 NLT

Living life together in community tumbles a mass of people together, much like a giant bowl of tossed salad. In the case of believers—all brought together in one faith as one body—there are all sorts of people: young and old, rich and poor, able and challenged, male and female, married and single. These contrasts make the body of Christ strong and rich in diversity.

Living life with newer believers gives the opportunity to be a pattern for others to follow. New believers look to your behavior to learn self-control or patience. Youth observe your choices in entertainment and understand purity. Noticing your own hard-earned faith, those who are suffering experience increased trust in the heavenly Father's care for them. Loving intentionally encourages others to do the same.

A life well-lived in fellowship with other believers will be an example for them to follow, one that they can absorb through observing. Be open about trials and temptations, successes as well as failures. In the process, you will demonstrate God's transformational power, ready forgiveness, and best of all, the true you in Christ.

God, let my life reflect the grace and love that
You pour in and through me so graciously. Amen.

Building with Love

The wise woman builds her house, but with
her own hands the foolish one tears hers down.
Proverbs 14:1 NIV

"Building a house" does not refer to how clean the floor or sink might be. There is no need to stock the fridge, fold the laundry, or unload the dishwasher before one is considered a wise woman. A clean home is pleasant, but a loving one is even better.

Loving herself well and her family well is the skill the wise woman uses to build her house. Considering God's command to "Love your neighbor as yourself" (Mark 12:31 NIV) helps you focus on that which is important in your home and let go of the unimportant. It's not having the prettiest clothes or the cleanest carpet. It's not having children with perfect report cards. It's not even about home-cooked meals.

What does a home built with love look like? It looks like connection, acceptance, forgiveness, and honest conversations. The wise woman builds her home with a balance of healthy boundaries and kindness. She builds with hugs and smiles and laughter. She constructs a home for herself and those she loves with creativity and courage and cuddling.

Loving well is not easy, and mistakes will happen. Sometimes the walls may need patching or the floors recarpeted. No problem. God is the best of home renovators and takes great pleasure in moving right in! After all, God is love.

God, let love reign here. Amen.

God's Gift: Power, Love, and a Sound Mind

For God has not given us a spirit of fear,
but of power and of love and of a sound mind.
2 TIMOTHY 1:7 NKJV

Have you ever been completely surprised and delighted by a present? God the Father has given each believer the amazing gift of His Spirit. This gift is too immense to wrap yet lives inside you so that you are never without it.

God has gifted you a spirit of power, for He knows you will have many battles to fight. You will need to endure hard times. You may need to defend yourself against those who would want you to think you are less than you are. Using your spirit of power for good will only confirm your courage.

God has given you a spirit of love. This gift whispers of endurance, grace, and even boldness. To love boldly despite past hurts isn't easy. But God's love triumphs over all obstacles. So don't be afraid to love others and yourself with abandonment.

A sound mind is a gift that is well balanced and keeps all things in calm perspective. When the chaos of the day begins to swirl around you, breathe deeply and remember you have the sound mind of Christ. It's steady and able to accurately prioritize the steps needed to flourish.

Father God, I'm in awe of Your Spirit within me.
Thank You for Your amazing gift! Let power, love,
and a sound mind be my watchwords every day.

Trail of Tears

*"Walking and weeping, they'll seek me, their GOD. They'll ask directions
to Zion and set their faces toward Zion. They'll come and hold tight
to GOD, bound in a covenant eternal they'll never forget."*
JEREMIAH 50:4–5 MSG

God had driven the Israelites from the Promised Land. They cried from grief and shock every step of the way to Babylon, just like the Native American tribes cried their own Trail of Tears when driven from their homelands. Seventy years after the Israelites' exile, they returned, again walking and weeping—this time in shame and repentance.

With each step, each tear, they sought God. No longer sure of the way, they had to ask for directions. Despite their uncertainty of their reception, they set their faces toward Zion.

When the Israelites arrived in Jerusalem, they sought God and jumped into true worship. They hugged the invisible God with all their heart, mind, soul, and strength; and God tied them to Him with a new covenant (see Jeremiah 31:31). This covenant was eternal, unbreakable—unforgettable—and one that later, with Jesus, was extended to Gentiles as well.

Whatever your personal trail of tears, God waits for you to return, to hug Him tight. Through Christ's death on the cross, you are bound to God in a covenant of love that will never end.

*Oh Lord my guide, when I've gone astray, bring me back as I seek
Your guidance step by step. Thank You for Your eternal embrace.*

How Slow Can You Go?

He who is slow to anger has great understanding,
but he who is hasty of spirit exposes and exalts his folly.
PROVERBS 14:29 AMPC

Only one person handles anger perfectly: "The LORD is merciful and gracious, slow to anger, and abounding in mercy" (Psalm 103:8 NKJV).

Humans struggle with handling anger. You have heard the advice to count to ten, but you may have days when you don't make it past one before you lose your temper. At other times, you may count to a hundred before your anger dissipates.

If that describes you, you are not alone. Almost 10 percent of Americans struggle with anger issues. Reality TV draws viewers as much by the way it exposes and exalts nasty confrontations between contestants as by the competition itself.

Those slow to respond in anger will pass the hasty of spirit in life's race. When the hasty of spirit meet a problem, they respond in a knee-jerk reaction that stops their forward progress.

The difference between the two responses resembles the fable of the tortoise and the hare. The tortoise who is slow to anger will pass the rabbit who races from the starting line but explodes in anger before he reaches the end.

The prize for winning the race? A greater understanding of who God is and what He wants. The hasty rabbit only exposes his own folly.

Father God, make me as slow to anger as You are, that I
may mine the ores of Your understanding and compassion.

The Avenger

This is what the LORD says: "See, I will defend your cause and avenge you; I will dry up her sea and make her springs dry."
JEREMIAH 51:36 NIV

Israel was fed up. God may have given Babylon permission to take Judah, but her captors abused the privilege. "Nebuchadnezzar king of Babylon has devoured us, he has thrown us into confusion, he has made us an empty jar. Like a serpent he has swallowed us and filled his stomach with our delicacies, and then has spewed us out" (Jeremiah 51:34 NIV).

Such is part and parcel of the human experience. You or someone you care for has been or will be wronged, slandered, hurt.

Few are like Job, who said, "The LORD gives and the LORD has taken away; may the name of the LORD be praised" (Job 1:21 NIV). They are more likely to be like the Jews in Babylon, eager to claim their pound of flesh from their captors.

Yes, the Bible tells us to forgive our enemies. But here's the rest of the story: God doesn't let the wrong done to us go unpunished.

You are in Christ. He bore the burden of God's wrath for all sin—including sins committed against you.

You are in Christ, under the protection of the God of the angel armies at His command. Revenge isn't up to you. It's up to God, and He has taken up your cause.

Almighty Defender, I release my hurts to You.
Fill me with Your love and peace.

A Balanced Life

A simple life in the Fear-of-GOD is better
than a rich life with a ton of headaches.
Proverbs 15:16 MSG

If we all could choose between a simple life or one rich with treasure, who wouldn't choose the latter? Who wouldn't prefer to work for a Fortune 500 company than to subsist as part of the working poor?

Solomon, the writer of Proverbs, must be mistaken. Headaches and inner turmoil should characterize the poor, not the rich. Whereas the poor search for their next meal or a place to sleep, the rich enjoy the peace that comes from stability.

Except money doesn't buy happiness. As Jonathan Swift said, "A wise man should have money in his head, but not in his heart."

Solomon isn't comparing wealth and poverty but using them as illustrations. Possessions may ease headaches, but the better way—the more effective, excellent way—to ease inner confusion and pain is the fear of the Lord. It's your life blood as a Christian, pumping from your new heart throughout your body. It activates the mind of Christ in you and moves your hands and feet as a member of Christ's body. The Holy Spirit serves as the generator, replacing the headaches of the old life with simple trust and the fear of the Lord.

Righteous God, You are all I need, whatever the balance
in my bank account. Let me live in Your shadow,
my fear of You making me unafraid of anything else.

Waiting for Hope

When life is heavy and hard to take, go off by yourself. Enter the silence.
Bow in prayer. Don't ask questions: Wait for hope to appear. Don't run
from trouble. Take it full-face. The "worst" is never the worst.
LAMENTATIONS 3:28–30 MSG

Jeremiah wrote today's verses when he was mourning the fall of Jerusalem. The prophecies he had preached for years had come to pass, and his heart was broken. We'd all be wise to listen to his response.

When disaster strikes, do you go into fight or flight mode? Perhaps you respond somewhere in between.

Jeremiah suggests both responses. When life is "heavy and hard," he lists six steps to prepare you to "take it full-face."

To get ready to fight, you must first retreat. That means to (1) go off by yourself, (2) get quiet, (3) pray, (4) be still, and (5) listen for God's voice. Let His promises sink in. And (6) wait for hope to fill your tank.

Only after your retreat are you equipped to face the problem. You won't run from it, ask questions, or try to make sense of it. You just take it head on—and realize the worst is never the worst. It can't be. God is by your side.

Heavenly Father, right now life seems heavy and hard.
Let me retreat into You and wait for Your hope to
appear so that I will be ready to face what lies ahead.

Heart Weights

The heart of the righteous weighs its answers,
but the mouth of the wicked gushes evil. The LORD is far
from the wicked, but he hears the prayer of the righteous.
PROVERBS 15:28–29 NIV

Evil isn't pretty. You may laugh at the Wicked Witch of the West who melts at the touch of water, but imagine evil gushing out of someone's mouth like vomit. Wickedness is an illness that causes the person afflicted with it to overflow with immorality.

No wonder the Lord says to stay far away from the wicked. They choose wickedness by rejecting God, breaking His covenant, and chasing after false gods. Their behavior makes them magnets that repel God.

But the righteous—you who are made right by being made new creations in Christ—attract God. He is close to you. When you pray, the Holy Spirit takes the whispers of your heartstrings and brings them to the Father. The Lord hears your prayers, the prayers of His child. The only thing that interrupts heavenly cell service is sin, and forgiveness is only a prayer away.

The Lord is far from the wicked but near the righteous. Learn it. Live it.

King of kings and Lord of lords, as I head to the election booth today,
may I weigh my decisions. May I recognize the candidates You seek and
that seek You. Thank You that You hear me whatever my needs are.

Making Plans

We can make our own plans, but the LORD gives the right answer. People
may be pure in their own eyes, but the LORD examines their motives.
Commit your actions to the LORD, and your plans will succeed.
PROVERBS 16:1–3 NLT

People plan in two basic ways. To borrow phrases from writing par-
lance, you are either a pantser or a plotter.

A pantser starts writing with a basic idea and continues until the
story reaches its finish. You may approach life like that, living each day
as it comes without planning for the future.

Or you may resemble a plotter, who makes detailed plans about
characters, plot, and motives and writes confidently about what comes
next. Perhaps you are a life plotter, planning your days in fifteen-minute
intervals, creating five-year plans, and putting money in your bank for
retirement.

Whatever your approach to planning, today's passage applies. If
you plan without consulting God, you are building on shaky ground.
You may settle for what looks good and sounds good without checking
the building material.

God probes deep, looks at your blueprints, and determines what's
right. He looks for what's good about your plans—and, more importantly,
who is in charge of those plans.

Plans made without God will have a fatal design flaw. All plans
committed to the Lord will succeed.

Lord, let me invite You into my plans before I start. Without You,
I will fail. I name You my life project manager and designer-in-chief.

Working Out

It pays to take life seriously; things work out when you trust in GOD.
PROVERBS 16:20 MSG

Today's verse reads like a contradiction:

The first part says, take life seriously. Concentrate without frills or fun.

The second, it will all work out. Don't worry, be happy. What goes around comes around.

Although the two statements seem to collide, God's Word is true and does not lie. Things work out for those who take life seriously.

Taking life seriously doesn't mean it depends on you. You are strongest when you are weak. The outcome is up to Christ.

It doesn't involve working harder, twenty-five hours out of every twenty-four. If you are focused on work only, your life is out of balance.

A serious life may include working hard, being concerned about the future, and maintaining a savings account, but only because your life is balanced, centered on God's will. As the second part of the verse states, "trust in GOD." Or as other translations put it, heed God's Word and listen to His instructions.

Live deliberately. Live consistently. Listen for God's instructions before you act.

When you live as God directs, both vertically and horizontally, things will work out for you. You can count on it.

Eternal, wise God, I trust everything will work out when
I live according to Your plan as revealed in Your Word.

Crown of Glory

Gray hair is a crown of glory; it is gained by living a godly life.
PROVERBS 16:31 NLT

It's refreshing to read that the long life gray hair imputes to its owner suggests that the person has lived a godly life. When you add "a crown of glory"—translated as "splendor," "honor," and "dignity" in other Bible versions—on top of that gray head, the goal becomes desirable.

You don't earn a crown of glory overnight. Your godly life began the day you were born again in Christ and has continued, consistently though not perfectly, to the present day. The Amplified Bible, Classic Edition, describes the lifestyle as one of "moral and spiritual rectitude"; that is, you have lived a balanced life, horizontally and vertically, in right relation with your fellow humans and with God.

One adage says "Only the good die young." Proverbs turns that on its head by saying some of the godly live to old age. Matthew Henry wrote, "Old age, as such, is honourable, and commands respect, but if it be found in the way of wickedness, its honour is forfeited, its crown laid in the dust."

If you have gray hair, picture that crown on top of your head. Continue the good fight that has earned the tiara. Rule your kingdom by teaching those who come after you to follow in your footsteps.

God Almighty, You have given me a crown of glory.
May I one day place it at Your feet in glorious worship.

God's Treasure Hunt

*The refining pot is for silver and the furnace
for gold, but the Lord tries the hearts.*
PROVERBS 17:3 AMPC

Gold. Its allure is undeniable. San Francisco grew into a bustling metropolis of twenty-five thousand people within a year of the discovery of gold in 1849. A long list of gold strikes followed over the next eighty years or so in places such as Colorado, Alaska, and South Dakota's Black Hills.

Silver comes a close second—ask Molly Brown, whose husband made their fortune in Leadville, Colorado.

God placed those rare metals in the earth. Yet when God digs for treasure, He ignores the rare metals. Instead, He digs for those who love and trust in Him.

Just as the metals removed from the mine are useless until they are refined and become the beautiful elements humans crave, your heart requires a similar testing. In Christ you are holy and righteous. But to reach that reality here and now, God sends tests to remove any impurities. His standard doesn't change between you and another of His children. His holiness is absolute. His scales reveal your exact spiritual weight, and He prescribes a training regimen customized just for you.

When God is finished, you will be the rarest treasure on earth—a child of God, holy and dearly loved.

*Holy God and Judge, may I pay attention when You try my heart.
Try me and change me until I'm pure as snow.*

Heaven's Art Gallery

A present is a precious stone in the eyes of its possessor;
wherever he turns, he prospers.
PROVERBS 17:8 NKJV

Use it or lose it. If you don't take advantage of vacation days, you lose them at the end of the year. If you don't exercise, your muscles will atrophy.

Today's verse makes the same analogy. View God's gifts as precious stones. Use them and you will prosper, physically and spiritually. Ignore them to your peril.

Consider Jesus' parable of the talents in Matthew 25:14–30. The man who had five talents made five more; the one who had two talents also doubled his gift. They both prospered.

As for the one who hid the one talent he had, God took it away and gave it to the first two, ones who knew how to use His gifts.

When God gives you a gift, He expects you to use it. Like parents who treasure their children's schoolwork, He awaits your efforts. If human parents give each picture, essay, and test a place of honor on the refrigerator, what will God do with your work?

When you delight in the gifts God gives to you, returning them to His use, He treats them as precious. He showers more gifts on you. He wants to fill His art gallery with your works.

Loving Father, may I treasure Your gifts to me, polishing them,
sharing them in praise to You. May any increase flow
back to You and Your kingdom.

Extreme Living

We who have run for our very lives to God have every reason to grab the promised hope with both hands and never let go. It's an unbreakable spiritual lifeline, reaching past all appearances right to the very presence of God.
HEBREWS 6:18–19 MSG

The three big questions in life are: Who are you? Where are you going? What are you doing here?

Who you are depends on where you are. Who are you? You are someone running for your life. Where are you? Running to God.

And what are you here for? To grab hold of the promised hope with both hands and climb the spiritual lifeline to God's presence.

Your life in Christ is an extreme sport. You are running for your life, and God is your sanctuary. And your only way to God involves rope climbing. You have to grab the lifeline with both hands and never let go.

Imagine clinging to that lifeline, the rope burns you will develop. Winds will buffet you, seek to knock you off. You will climb so high, you will go past earth's atmosphere to the presence of God.

But the lifeline is unbreakable, the promised hope gives you every reason to go on, and when you reach the top, you are in God's presence.

Grab hold and start climbing. The promised hope is the glue that keeps you attached to the lifeline.

Clinging to my lifeline, inspired by my promised hope, I climb to You, Lord. Teach me to breathe in Your rarified spiritual air.

Wisdom's Hiding Place

The perceptive find wisdom in their own front yard;
fools look for it everywhere but right here.
PROVERBS 17:24 MSG

Wisdom is closer than you think.

Experience has taught you that you will find something in the place you least expect. Even so, you don't expect to overlook something in your own yard.

How do you happen to overlook the obvious? The problem may not lie in your search methods, but in your definition of wisdom. If it's derived from human experience, you will use physical methods to discover it.

You may use the scientific method to come up with a mathematical equation: if you do A plus B, you will be wise, for example.

Perhaps you think the answer lies in the past. What have the great minds of the ages said about the subject? You soon discover that human beings tend to repeat past failures rather than learn from them.

Perhaps you travel the world to discover what other cultures have learned about life's questions. Their answers, such as the popular *Art of War* by Sun Tzu, have much to teach but leave you short.

Any answers you have found have led to more questions. Eventually you come back home to your backyard.

But for those looking for wisdom with the magnifying glass of faith, you will find it in your own front lawn. God's Word is the compass that will lead to True North.

Lord God, correct my vision so I'll discover
the wisdom lying in my own backyard.

God with Us

"Me, my master? How and with what could I ever save Israel?"
JUDGES 6:15 MSG

It's often when you are faced with seemingly impossible tasks that you learn the most about yourself and God. At that moment when you feel you can't go another step, or will never make it through the schedule of intense meetings, or cannot dig out from under the laundry pile, you find out, in fact, you can. And you do. And in the doing you realize it's not just you—that it's never been just you. God has been with you all along.

Gideon was staring at an impossible task. The Midianites, a nasty enemy, had ravaged the land and oppressed the Israelites. Now an angel had come to tell Gideon he was the man for the job. Gideon was anything but sure—he certainly didn't *feel* like a mighty warrior.

But God is seldom wrong about these things (make that never). And the key was, Gideon just had to show up. That's all God wanted. "I'll be with you. Believe me, you will defeat Midian as one man" (Judges 6:16 MSG). Gideon didn't need to know how, and the "with what" part was answered—with God. Even with this assurance, though, Gideon's insecurity begged for a sign. But can you blame him? He was facing an army. That's almost as bad as the laundry pile.

*Dear Lord, help me recognize that I don't have to
tackle my challenges all on my own. Amen.*

Life, Full and True

"Imagine a person who lives well, treating others fairly,
keeping good relationships. . .lives by my statutes and faithfully
honors and obeys my laws. This person who lives upright and
well shall live a full and true life. Decree of GOD, the Master."
EZEKIEL 18:5, 9 MSG

If you live well, you will have a full and true life. God double stamps His promise by calling it a "Decree of God."

Living well isn't all that simple, of course. The two positive commands about getting along with others (see Ezekiel 18:5) are followed by prohibitions against destructive behavior as relevant now as they were in Ezekiel's day. The "don'ts" (vv. 6–7) range from casual sex to piling up debt.

God's standards have never changed. Yet today you have an advantage unavailable to the people in Ezekiel's day. God Himself dwells within you.

An upright existence, time lived the way God wants, will bring you the benefit of a full and true life—love, joy, peace, and all the fruit of the Spirit.

A true life frees you to be transparent, 100 percent single-minded in your loyalty to God, as you enjoy the continual presence of your all-knowing, all-powerful, loving Father.

Pretense ends. You are who you say you are. God fits you with a life custom-made for you.

Living God of truth, fill me with the knowledge and love
for Your Word so that I will have that full and true life.

Just a Storyteller

Then I said, "Sovereign LORD, they are saying of me,
'Isn't he just telling parables?'"
EZEKIEL 20:49 NIV

Poor Ezekiel didn't just tell parables. He had to act them out.

God told Ezekiel to build a scale model of Jerusalem and then lie on his side "the same number of days as the years of their sin" (Ezekiel 4:5 NIV)—390 days on one side for Israel; 40 days on the other for Judah.

Ezekiel not only performed live parables, he also received dramatic visions that inspired songs like the modern "Ezekiel Saw the Wheel" and the classic "Dem Dry Bones."

His audience enjoyed the entertainment he provided. They didn't care about the message, taunting him when he got serious. "He just tells parables." They didn't get the point. So Ezekiel complained to God about it.

Frustratingly enough, God didn't answer Ezekiel's complaint! The very next verse says, "The word of the LORD came to me: 'Son of man, set your face against Jerusalem and preach against the sanctuary'" (Ezekiel 21:1–2).

You might not understand everything God has asked you to do. Other people might mock. God might not explain Himself. But, like Ezekiel, you can choose faithfully to obey what God calls you to do. As in Ezekiel's case, time will prove the truth of God's message.

Lord, whether I am an actor in my own life parable or involved in some other ministry, may I be faithful to You even when people misunderstand.

God's Reward System

So do not throw away this confident trust in the Lord.
Remember the great reward it brings you! Patient endurance
is what you need now, so that you will continue to do God's
will. Then you will receive all that he has promised.
HEBREWS 10:35–36 NLT

Let's be honest: pie in the sky by and by—the promises of God's eternal kingdom when all wrongs will be made right—may not satisfy today's empty stomach.

Maybe you doubt you will ever receive all God's promises, or maybe you want them now.

The "great reward" is worth the wait because it consists of "better and lasting possessions" (Hebrews 10:34 NIV). They are of finer quality, diamond and not cubic zirconium, and they will last, never decay. The promises waiting for you will never lose their finish.

All you need is patient endurance. If you hold on when it's no longer convenient and you fear you won't survive, you will receive all the promises of God—all three thousand plus of them. Patient endurance may not be what you want, but it's what you need.

Remember the words of Leo the Great: "If we are steadfast in our faith and in our love for [God], we win the victory that He has won, we receive what He has promised."

Eternal God, fill my heart and mind with Your promises when I am
tempted to give up. I can count on You to fulfill each and every one.

Faith Goes to Court

*Now faith is the assurance (the confirmation, the title deed) of the things
[we] hope for, being the proof of things [we] do not see and the conviction of
their reality [faith perceiving as real fact what is not revealed to the senses].*
Hebrews 11:1 AMPC

The tension between faith and what can be proven has always existed,
but it exploded exponentially with Darwin's theory of evolution, which
was tested in the 1925 Scopes trial. Today's culture rarely would expect
faith to win a court battle based on evidence alone.

Hebrews 11:1 describes the nature of faith in legal terms. It's a
"title deed. . .proof" that leads to a conviction in the courtroom of life.
In this introduction to the Faith Hall of Fame, those analogies are used
to define faith.

Faith is like a spiritual ESP, a sixth sense available only to believers.
It meets the burden of proof of things we cannot see. A jury using faith
alone will accept as real fact what isn't revealed to the five physical senses.

Faith looks beyond what all the eyeglasses, hearing aids, and nasal
drips in the world can experience. It allows you to see God Himself.
Once you take up this faith, your virtual reality shifts to God's perception
of the world.

*Unseen God, thank You for revealing Yourself in Your Son Jesus. Thank
You for the gift of faith that enables me to live in light of Your reality.*

Your Last Day on Earth

"Son of man, with one blow I will take away your dearest treasure.
Yet you must not show any sorrow at her death. Do not weep; let there
be no tears. . . ." So I proclaimed this to the people the next morning,
and in the evening my wife died. The next morning I did
everything I had been told to do.
Ezekiel 24:16, 18 nlt

What would you do if you knew today was your last day on earth?

For Ezekiel, it took an all too real form when God told him his wife would die soon. The morning after he received the news, he told his congregation. That night his wife died.

Ezekiel doesn't record how he wrestled with the events. His description is almost cold. "I told the people. My wife died. I did what God told me to do, which meant I avoided all the socially acceptable forms of expressing grief."

Oh, Ezekiel. Your wife, your dearest treasure. Did you tell her? If so, how did you tell her? What did you say to your children? Did you weep in the privacy of your home? Where did you turn for comfort?

Ezekiel didn't understand, but he knew God and trusted Him. When God puts you in an impossible situation, He will give you the strength to endure, one day at a time.

Father God, sometimes Your will seems harsh.
But like Ezekiel, may I obey and trust.

God's Training Plan

Strip down, start running—and never quit! No extra spiritual fat,
no parasitic sins. Keep your eyes on Jesus, who both began
and finished this race we're in. Study how he did it.
HEBREWS 12:1–2 MSG

You are in a race this very minute. It started the moment you believed in Christ, and you won't cross the finish line until you get to heaven. Previous contenders—believers from before Abraham to the last soul who died seconds ago—fill the stadium.

Jesus Christ, your Lord and Savior, is the race's MVP. He began the race before the creation of the world and finished it first. He set the standard and guaranteed your finish. You follow in His footsteps. So study His race well in the Gospels.

In addition to Jesus' race, dig into the lives of the heroes in the Faith Hall of Fame (Hebrews 11). Devour the Bible. The Pentateuch teaches you the rules of the competition. The books of history and prophecy demonstrate the race in real life, including what mistakes to avoid. The Epistles expand the original rulebook, applying them to the rule of grace. Revelation celebrates the end of the race for every believer.

God will reveal your unique training regimen through your study. Get ready, get set—go. See you at the finish line.

Wonderful Counselor and Coach, strip me of everything
that hinders my race. Lead me in Jesus' steps and be
the wind at my back until I finish the race.

God the Dragon

*Do you see what we've got? An unshakable kingdom! And do you
see how thankful we must be? Not only thankful, but brimming with
worship, deeply reverent before God. For God is not an indifferent
bystander. He's actively cleaning house, torching all that needs
to burn, and he won't quit until it's all cleansed.*
HEBREWS 12:28–29 MSG

An "unshakable kingdom," completely clean and pure, reminds one of
the mythical Camelot, the one described in song as "there's simply not
a more congenial spot for happily-ever-aftering."

It also resembles the majestic Rocky Mountains, a natural wonder
that causes one to overflow with worship in deep reverence of the Creator.

Although Camelot is prone to destruction from the worm of
disloyalty, God's kingdom can never be shaken. For His indestructible
power not only creates His kingdom but always brings home His pure,
virginal bride—the Church. He burns away the filth of your past and
makes you anew, clothed in the righteousness of Christ, your sinful
past gone.

God invests Himself completely in you, His child. He's not an
indifferent bystander. Like a dragon, He purifies and protects His
treasure with fire.

When God turns up the heat of trials in your life, rejoice that He
is making you perfect, holy, His work complete.

*Lord, thank You for burning away what needs to be cleansed. I trust the
transformation process to You as I hide under the shelter of Your wings.*

Sacrifice of Praise

Through Jesus, therefore, let us continually offer to God a sacrifice
of praise—the fruit of lips that openly profess his name.
HEBREWS 13:15 NIV

On this day of Thanksgiving, your prayers—for your family, friends, health, blessings, bounteous food—may echo those across the country. Yet this day is important. Because God commands you to remember what He has done and to share with your children His great works.

But as important as Thanksgiving is, it's redundant in some ways, because you are commanded to praise God continually. In Ephesians 5:20, God tells you to give thanks in everything. Hebrews 13:15 pushes it one step further, suggesting you continually offer a sacrifice of praise. There's never a time when praise shouldn't be offered. In fact, it must be offered.

Thanksgiving is more than a holiday. It is a nonstop event, 24/7, 365 days of the year. It's a sacrifice of praise because you are outside the camp with Christ, unwelcome in the city you left behind, not yet arrived at the eternal city (see Hebrews 13:13–14).

When the food is consumed today, the guests gone, the holiday at an end, may your thoughts fly to God in an attitude of praise. And as you quietly stand with Christ outside the camp, you will learn the value of this sacrifice.

To know God is to praise Him.

Loving Father, today and every minute of the next year,
teach me the delightful sacrifice of praise.

Wave-to-Trough Wisdom

If any of you lacks wisdom, you should ask God, who gives generously
to all without finding fault, and it will be given to you. But when
you ask, you must believe and not doubt, because the one who doubts
is like a wave of the sea, blown and tossed by the wind.

JAMES 1:5–6 NIV

James's words on wisdom remind one of the ads that say, "Got milk?"
God gives wisdom generously to all who ask. It leaves its stamp on you
as clearly as a milk mustache.

God will give you wisdom without hesitation. The gift is yours
without conditions. Only one thing can ruin it: doubt.

Doubt expresses itself by making God's wisdom one of multiple
options. You must ask for wisdom with the intention of following it. If
you choose a different path, your life will twist and shift about, plunging
from wave to trough like a boat in a hurricane.

How do you distinguish God's wisdom from other sources? How do
you recognize His voice? Practice. Use the helpful advice your mother
taught you when you crossed the street: "Stop, look, and listen." Take
one small step, stop, look, and wait for God to speak again.

When you reach a fork in your life's road, tune into God's GPS—He
will always take you by the best route.

Wonderful Counselor, I need Your wisdom today. Remove my
doubts and open my eyes to Your direction. In Jesus name, amen.

Perils of Pretenders

"Son of man, your people. . .say to each other, 'Come on, let's go hear the prophet tell us what the LORD is saying!' So my people come pretending to be sincere and sit before you. They listen to your words, but they have no intention of doing what you say."

EZEKIEL 33:30–31 NLT

At this point in his life, Ezekiel was more popular than ever. People sought him out, listening to his latest "messages from the Lord"—while they made fun of him behind his back, having no intention of doing what he said.

God warned Ezekiel of their hypocrisy while addressing Ezekiel as the "son of man," a title reserved for Jesus and this prophet. He saw visions of heaven few prophets entertained, but he was still only a "son of man." Humble. Weak.

Perhaps God calling Ezekiel "son of man" here is a subtle reminder to you, as it was to Ezekiel in his day, that you have more in common with his listeners than you realize. God's words are more than country song lyrics. They will come to pass. They are not a fictional message to tickle your ears. They are meant to be believed, trusted, valued. If you ignore or mock them, you may find yourself falling into the perils of pretenders.

Believe God's words. Give them the weight due them.

Father, whenever I'm tempted to ignore Your Word, remind me that everything You say or have said is of undeniable value.

Dominoes

"My dwelling place will be with them; I will be their God, and they will be my people. Then the nations will know that I the LORD make Israel holy, when my sanctuary is among them forever."
EZEKIEL 37:27–28 NIV

When Moses asked for God's name, God answered, "I AM" (Exodus 3:13–14).

I AM. I always was. I always will be. A circle without beginning or end. I AM.

I AM created little "i ams," people born at a point in time with the potential to live forever with God (see Genesis 1–3).

God explores that circle with Ezekiel: I will live with them. I will dwell with them—in the flesh, in the incarnation of Jesus (see John 1:14). Because I live with them—I will be their God. Because I am their God—they will be My people. Because they are My people—the nations will know I AM the Lord.

The circle returns to I AM. The Lord is holy and makes you holy, His work complete when He sent His Son.

If God hadn't created, there would be no human beings. And He who dwelt among His children, made you an instrument to display His holiness.

You are His. He is yours. Reveal Him.

I AM, thank You for choosing me as one of Your people.
Through me may others see Your holiness.

Lesson Plan

Then shall they know, understand, and realize positively that I am the Lord their God, because I sent them into captivity and exile among the nations and then gathered them to their own land. I will leave none of them remaining among the nations any more [in the latter days].

Ezekiel 39:28 AMPC

One thing rings crystal clear in the Bible: God wants you to know Him. It echoes from the psalmist's prayer, "Let be and be still, and know (recognize and understand) that I am God" (Psalm 46:10 AMPC), to Paul's prayer that the Ephesians would be given a "spirit of wisdom and revelation [of insight into mysteries and secrets] in the [deep and intimate] knowledge of Him" (Ephesians 1:17 AMPC).

The knowledge isn't just a head knowledge, enough to pass an academic test, but a thorough understanding, recognition, and positive realization that God is your Lord. The knowledge you seek will change you from the inside out.

God wanted the same thing for the people of Israel. But they didn't come to that deep and intensely intimate knowledge of God until they went into both captivity and exile—and then when God brought them back to their homeland.

That's when they came to know God.

Whatever it takes, God will make you see Him as He is. Look for Him in all circumstances of your life, good and bad, beginning today.

Omniscient God, fill my heart with a hunger to know You more and more.

Emergency Preparedness

Nothing clever, nothing conceived, nothing contrived, can get the better of GOD. Do your best, prepare for the worst—then trust GOD to bring victory.
PROVERBS 21:30–31 MSG

Jacob the patriarch knew all about being clever and conniving. His name means "deceiver." In the end, at the river Jabbok, "he tried to get the best of GOD" (Hosea 12:4 MSG).

He didn't succeed. God got the best of him and made Himself known to Jacob. Armed by that experience, Jacob prepared to meet his twin, Esau, who had years ago vowed to kill Jacob. But the feared confrontation was a nonevent. God had changed Esau's heart, and the brothers parted peacefully.

Poet Robert Burns put it this way: "The best-laid plans of mice and men often go awry." A problem looms on your horizon. You face serious health problems. A child gets into trouble. You lose your job.

You do everything you can think of. You pull strings, consult doctors, exercise regularly, change how you eat, talk with counselors. None of those activities are wrong, but they won't decide the outcome. You have done your best and prepared for the worst.

When you have reached the end of your rope—the entire time you are making plans—one thing only will guarantee the best outcome: trusting God. It's as simple, and as difficult, as that.

Mighty God, let me trust You and not my own plans.
You will bring the victory.

Blindfold Faith

*Though you have not seen him, you love him; and even though
you do not see him now, you believe in him and are filled with
an inexpressible and glorious joy, for you are receiving the
end result of your faith, the salvation of your souls.*

1 PETER 1:8–9 NIV

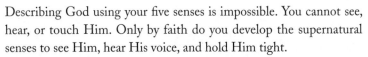

Describing God using your five senses is impossible. You cannot see, hear, or touch Him. Only by faith do you develop the supernatural senses to see Him, hear His voice, and hold Him tight.

Centuries before Peter wrote his letter, God gave Isaiah a bleak commission regarding the Israelites: "Make the heart of this people calloused; make their ears dull and close their eyes" (Isaiah 6:10). Perhaps God cut off their understanding so they could develop faith to see the unseen.

Today you live in between the seen and the unseen. A few hundred believers knew Jesus in the flesh. The day is coming when you will see Jesus as He is (see 1 John 3:2). But although today you can't see Jesus with your physical eyes, you offer the certainty of your faith. You love Jesus because He first loved you and died for you.

You believe and accept the rich gifts He showers on you, including your salvation.

By faith you see the joy beyond.

You don't trust because you know. You know because you trust.

*Invisible God, thank You for opening my eyes of
faith and enfolding me in Your loving embrace.*

Present and Future Hope

Therefore, with minds that are alert and fully sober, set your hope on the grace to be brought to you when Jesus Christ is revealed at his coming.
1 PETER 1:13 NIV

Your hope is both a present down payment and a future possession. Waiting for "the gift that's coming when Jesus arrives" (MSG), you act like a child at Christmas, quick to notice anything unusual in your surroundings, whether reindeer and jingle bells or a whisper of the Holy Spirit.

To fully appreciate this hope, you must remain sober, serious, and dedicated to the task at hand. You are holding your breath, not blinking.

Like an anchor, your hope goes deep and takes hold, grounded in grace that will come. Nothing can move you off course. When Christ returns, grace will complete your transformation into Christlikeness and you will be resurrected with an imperishable body (see 1 Corinthians 15:42).

You are able to grab ahold of that future hope of God's grace because of what it has already done. Your salvation is a completed act; you already have the eternal life that you will enter more fully when you reach heaven.

"Hope. . .can base our present reality on future grace" (Chris Tiegreen, *The One Year Walk with God Devotional*).

Eternal God, let me live in light of Your grace that sustains me in the present and gives me hope for the future.

Fools for Christ

It is God's will that by doing good, you might cure the ignorance of the fools who think you're a danger to society. Exercise your freedom by serving God, not by breaking the rules.
1 PETER 2:15–16 MSG

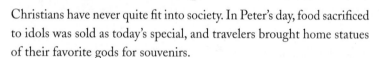

Christians have never quite fit into society. In Peter's day, food sacrificed to idols was sold as today's special, and travelers brought home statues of their favorite gods for souvenirs.

Today Christians are often perceived as fools for believing God's Word rather than the god of science. Even worse, we are sometimes seen as "a danger to society." Both then and now, people made new in the image of Christ who seek His holiness stand out as potentially dangerous.

The perception of Christians as countercultural doesn't catch God by surprise. In fact, He chose "foolish" people on purpose (see 1 Corinthians 1:27). He inserts you like a spy to confound the world around you.

That sounds good. But what does it look like? How do you make an impact on the world for good?

Peter offers simple advice. God made you free, but don't go wild with it. You start by doing good to your family, neighbors—everyone with whom you come in contact. You continue by exploring your vertical connection: serving God. Use your freedom as a force for good.

Dear Lord and Savior, let my life spread the news of the cure of Your salvation through people around me.

A Noble Calling

*For God is pleased when, conscious of his will, you patiently
endure unjust treatment. . . . But if you suffer for doing good
and endure it patiently, God is pleased with you.*
1 PETER 2:19–20 NLT

You might find it easy to recall a time when you have been treated
unjustly. Whether you have been wrongly accused of something or a
coworker has spread cruel rumors about you, your gut reaction could be
to lash out or host your own pity party. After all, you have done nothing
to deserve this treatment. It isn't fair.

However, Peter says it's a gracious and commendable thing to
patiently endure suffering at the hands of the unjust, even when that
unfair treatment occurs in the face of a good deed you have done. This
sort of radical, other-worldly endurance—which goes against your
instincts—is truly beautiful in the sight of God. And it will inevitably
bring God's blessing and favor on you.

This self-denying response isn't just a suggestion. It is a lifestyle
you are called to as a Christian. Thankfully, Jesus left you with a perfect
example. He underwent the ultimate injustice, loving those who reviled
Him, and all the while entrusting Himself to His Father who judges
justly. Whenever you are feeling wronged, remember, God is the overseer
of your soul, and He vindicates His children.

*God, give me the strength to patiently endure my sufferings,
for I know You will bless me in my efforts.*

A Holy Heritage

But Daniel resolved not to defile himself with the royal food and wine,
and he asked the chief official for permission not to defile himself this way.
DANIEL 1:8 NIV

You face an ever-present pressure in your life to bow before what's popular and powerful, to bend before what is socially acceptable. When you—as a Christian—try to stand tall for what you believe, it often feels as though you are fighting against a swirling current.

Daniel, who was specially selected to be educated in the Babylonian king's court, refused to assimilate into the pagan society. One of the ways he did this was by declining the king's food and wine. There are many different interpretations as to why he might have done this, but the strongest argument is that he was standing against the many temptations that come along with luxury. His restricted diet was a way of daily reminding himself of his Jewish heritage and that he was dependent on God—not the Babylonian king—for his sustenance and life.

The takeaway from this passage is not that you should go on a diet. It's a reminder of your heritage as God's child. You are set apart from the world and an heir of the kingdom. To keep your head above the raging current of social pressure, you need a daily reminder that you are not of this world.

Lord, give me the desire and the discipline to keep my eyes fixed on You.

An Anchor in the Sea

Humble yourselves, therefore, under God's mighty hand, that he may lift you up in due time. Cast all your anxiety on him because he cares for you.
1 PETER 5:6–7 NIV

Can you even fathom it? The almighty God of the universe cares about the ins and outs of your daily life. He is not an indifferent, uninvolved God, leaving you to fend for yourself. He is personal and present, desiring that you should cast your anxieties on Him. This truth should be soothing to your soul. It's a salve that you can apply whenever you are afraid or troubled.

The problem is that casting your burdens on the Lord is often easier said than done. You might be born with a tendency to cling stubbornly to your problems, believing you alone are capable of ironing out the wrinkles and restoring control. You may think having a white-knuckled grip on your worries will somehow solve them. But in reality, only God is in control. In the stormy seas of life, He is the only thing that remains steadfast and unshakable. Unless you are holding on to Him, you will be tossed unceasingly on the waves.

So how do you let go? You can begin by humbling yourself before God, acknowledging His might and ability to care for you. You can bask in the incredible knowledge that He eagerly desires to relieve you of your burdens.

Mighty God, thank You for being my anchor.

The Rightful King

*Now I, Nebuchadnezzar, praise and exalt and glorify the
King of heaven, because everything he does is right and all his
ways are just. And those who walk in pride he is able to humble.*
Daniel 4:37 niv

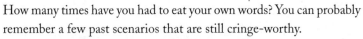

How many times have you had to eat your own words? You can probably remember a few past scenarios that are still cringe-worthy.

But in the bizarre case of the Babylonian king—Nebuchadnezzar— he not only had to eat his boastful words, but he was also forced to grovel on the ground, eating grass meant for oxen. In the blink of an eye, he was transformed from a mighty ruler, glorying in his kingdom from the palace rooftop, to a savage, living no better than an animal.

While Nebuchadnezzar's experience was unique, you may find you can relate to him in some way. It could be that you take a bit too much pride in surveying your accomplishments, believing your self-sufficiency is the sole origin of your success. But God doesn't want this attitude for you. After all, He's the ultimate provider and giver of gifts. Only He reserves the right to boast. God abhors pride, yet He looks kindly on the lowly. When Nebuchadnezzar's time of judgment had passed, he lifted his eyes to the heavens and acknowledged God's power in a spirit of humility. If you, too, bow your knee to the King, God will honor you.

Cultivate in me a spirit of true humility, my King.

Conquering Evil

Don't rejoice when your enemies fall;
don't be happy when they stumble.
PROVERBS 24:17 NLT

There's always that one person. She's the kind of person who makes you feel small, worthless, and inept. She is judgmental and impossible to please. You may find yourself struggling not to despise the very sight of her. So when this enemy fails or faces humiliation, there might be a part of you that thrills at the sight. A smug satisfaction unfolds in your spirit. After all, she's just getting what she deserves, right?

It might seem natural to revel in an enemy's downfall, but that is the complete opposite of how you are called to react as a Christian. In Romans 12:14, Paul says, "Bless those who persecute you. Don't curse them; pray that God will bless them" (NLT). For God, merely having a neutral, unaggressive stance toward your enemies isn't enough. He wants you to pray for them and bless them. Paul goes on to say that you are also to provide for your enemies if they are in need.

How in the world are you supposed to perform this radical task? By the power of the Holy Spirit. Call on His strength, and He will come to your aid. Take heart; the Lord will equip those who earnestly desire to do His will.

Help me delight in Your ways. You are a gracious, loving God.
Give me the strength to conquer evil by doing good.

The Author of Time

But do not forget this one thing, dear friends: With the Lord a day is like a thousand years, and a thousand years are like a day. The Lord is not slow in keeping his promise, as some understand slowness. Instead he is patient with you, not wanting anyone to perish, but everyone to come to repentance.

2 PETER 3:8–9 NIV

These days everything is fast. Instant information is available at your fingertips on the Internet. You have immediate communication with friends through text messages. In this modern age, you are accustomed to efficiency and quick answers.

But often your deepest concerns and problems are resolved at what seems to be a glacial pace. You pray and lay your needs before God. And then you wait for an answer. And wait. And wait some more. It may feel like God is occupied elsewhere, putting out bigger fires. Eventually, you might begin to think that God is indifferent to your daily struggles. But this couldn't be further from the truth. Remember, God isn't bound by time as you are.

His responses may seem painfully slow, but God is all-knowing and He sees the span of eternity in infinite detail—whereas all you can see is the moment before you. You can rest in the knowledge that His timing is perfect, even if it may not feel that way.

God, You are the author of time. I place my life in Your capable hands.

Abiding Forever

The world is passing away, and the lust of it;
but he who does the will of God abides forever.
1 John 2:17 NKJV

The world loves to fool you. It lulls you into complacency with its fleeting pleasures. It numbs and deadens and deafens. It distracts you with anything and everything—drawing you away from what truly matters. And it deceives you into believing that what it offers is permanent, even though the world and all the lusts it inspires are gradually passing away.

So what is there to cling to in a world of shifting sands and weak foundations? In his first letter, John says that the person "who does the will of God abides forever." In other translations, the word "abides" is sometimes translated "lives." While all humans are eternal beings, those who seek and follow God will have life abundant—the kind of life that is worth anticipating and rejoicing in. The kind of life that will give you hope and boldness to live out God's will. Because of Jesus' sacrifice, the promise of eternal life is within your grasp. Augustine wrote, "Hold fast to Christ. For you He became temporal, so that you might partake of eternity." You can cling to the permanency of this promise. It will not pass away.

God, in You alone I find true fulfillment and stability.
The treasures You offer will not rust or erode with time.
You are the one who satisfies my soul thirst.

High and Wide

*"The Lord our God is merciful and forgiving,
even though we have rebelled against him."*
DANIEL 9:9 NIV

In Daniel 9, Daniel comes before God in sackcloth and ashes, mourning his sin and the sins of Israel. With great humility, he confesses the nation's transgressions, pleading with God to turn away from His righteous anger. Daniel even fasted, depriving himself of food to show his devotion and sincerity.

Does this radical display of repentance make you squirm a little? When was the last time you approached God with a similar level of remorse for your sin and with the same drive for change and transformation in your life? In a society where sin is often downplayed or viewed as the norm, simply shrugging off your sin and shrinking it down to a speck in your mind's eye is easy.

But unfortunately, your view of sin directly affects your view of God's grace. If you believe your sins to be slight, then your perception of God's grace will also be small by comparison. However, if you acknowledge the magnitude and weight of your iniquities, you will come to realize just how high and wide God's grace stretches to wash it clean. As Daniel affirms, the Lord is merciful and forgiving, despite all your rebellion.

*Thank You, Lord God, for covering all of my sins, every last one.
Imprint this truth on my heart and make it fresh each morning.*

Otherworldly

*See how very much our Father loves us, for he calls us his children,
and that is what we are! But the people who belong to this world don't
recognize that we are God's children because they don't know him.*

1 JOHN 3:1 NLT

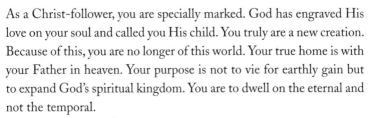

As a Christ-follower, you are specially marked. God has engraved His love on your soul and called you His child. You truly are a new creation. Because of this, you are no longer of this world. Your true home is with your Father in heaven. Your purpose is not to vie for earthly gain but to expand God's spiritual kingdom. You are to dwell on the eternal and not the temporal.

This mentality is foreign in a world where often the main focuses are self-promotion and gathering material wealth. Since many people do not know or understand your heavenly Father, chances are you will be misunderstood. Your customs and behavior will seem strange and otherworldly. In one of his letters, Peter addresses Christians as sojourners and exiles. How true this is! He calls you this because you are seeking a better country to call your own. You know that your stay here is fleeting.

When the pressures of this world are overwhelming, remember that your Father has lavished His love on you. He is your refuge. He is your home.

*Father, when I feel misplaced and alone, remind me that my hope
rests in the promise of abundant, eternal life in a better country.*

Forever Bride

"I will betroth you to me forever; I will betroth you in righteousness
and justice, in love and compassion. I will betroth you in
faithfulness, and you will acknowledge the LORD."
HOSEA 2:19–20 NIV

Throughout the book of Hosea, God speaks to Israel, His chosen people, who have fallen away and worshipped other gods. They were unfaithful, breaking the covenant God made with them. The Lord continually compares Israel to a straying wife committing adultery against Him. But despite Israel's rebellion, God still promises to restore her.

These verses may seem distant and irrelevant in the modern world. But as a Christian, you have been adopted into God's nation. You are one of His people, a citizen in His kingdom. When you bow before idols—which can be anything from money to relationships—it grieves the Lord. He is a jealous God, desiring your undivided attention.

But the most astonishing thing is that you are also betrothed to Him to be His bride—beautiful, pure, honored, and cherished. God offers to purify those who enter into a covenant with Him. His wedding gift to you is righteousness, justice, love, compassion, and faithfulness. In all of these things, He never fails or falters.

Rejoice! For you are God's forever-bride.

Lord, You are the ultimate lover of my soul. Even when I am unfaithful,
You remain faithful. Thank You for pursuing me.

Perfect Love

There is no fear in love. But perfect love drives out fear, because fear has to do with punishment. The one who fears is not made perfect in love.

1 JOHN 4:18 NIV

In this fallen world, love can be a dangerous game. You will face rejection and betrayal. You might place your hopes and trust in someone who isn't worthy of them. Eventually the people you love will let you down. All too often, the love that others exhibit is fickle and selfish. But love wasn't meant to break hearts.

God designed you to experience perfect love. This kind of love fortifies and sustains. It places you on solid ground. It surrounds you and fills you up. And it sets you free from fear. Can you fathom a love so whole, so pure? It might be difficult for you to imagine such a perfect love because no one has ever offered it to you—except for the One who laid down His life for yours, who shouldered God's wrath in order to spare you. His love is perfect and utterly selfless. In it there is no fear of condemnation. No fear of unfaithfulness. No fear of separation. Death's sting has been erased.

The power of Christ's perfect love has broken your chains. You are free.

Jesus, how exquisite and deep Your love is for me. Give me the eyes to see it. Turn my heart toward it daily. With You, I have nothing to fear.

A Deep Well

Love means doing what God has commanded us, and he has commanded
us to love one another, just as you heard from the beginning.
2 JOHN 1:6 NLT

Trying to discover how best to serve and love God can sometimes be a struggle. The list of Christian duties can appear overwhelming: daily quiet time, prayer, church services, serving the community, evangelizing. And the list goes on. There might be times in your life when the most you can do is get out of bed in the morning and survive the day, let alone attempt these other tasks.

Thankfully, John boils it down for you in his second letter. In its simplest terms, loving God means doing as He commands. And He has commanded you to love others with longsuffering and selflessness.

But isn't this just another item on the list of duties? At first glance, it may seem like another burdensome task you will have to bear. However, you must never forget that the first step to truly fulfilling this command is accepting God's great love for you. Then you can take His hand and love Him right back. By drawing from this deep well of love, you will find that you are able to pour it into the lives of those around you. Because God first loved you, you now have the power to love others radically.

Let Your love fill my heart and spill over onto others, God.
Thank You for first loving me.

The Best Plan

Do not boast about tomorrow, for you do not know what a day may bring.
PROVERBS 27:1 NIV

Planning ahead can be good. It's wise to ready yourself for the days to come. A runner trains before a race. An aspiring engineer invests in a good education. A mother-to-be paints the nursery and sets up the crib. Looking forward is necessary for a healthy, successful life.

So when does planning become boasting? When does it become harmful? It might be that you have a very specific idea of how your future should unfold. You may believe you alone are in control of the course of your life and the type of person you will become. While it's important to have dreams and goals, sometimes you can get so locked into what you think is best that you won't be receptive to God's movement or calling for your life. It could be that God's plans for you are quite different from what you would have chosen. Perhaps you already feel a pull in a new direction, but making the change scares you or it's not what you envisioned for yourself.

If you are having trouble handing over your future to God, remember that He knows you better than you know yourself. His plan will always be better. You may not know what tomorrow will bring, but God does, and He's in control.

Lord, You know what I need more than I do.
I trust You with all my tomorrows.

Even Now

"Even now," declares the Lord, "return to me with all your heart, with fasting and weeping and mourning." Rend your heart and not your garments. Return to the Lord your God, for he is gracious and compassionate, slow to anger and abounding in love, and he relents from sending calamity.

JOEL 2:12–13 NIV

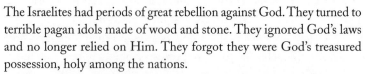

The Israelites had periods of great rebellion against God. They turned to terrible pagan idols made of wood and stone. They ignored God's laws and no longer relied on Him. They forgot they were God's treasured possession, holy among the nations.

Like Israel, you have probably rebelled against the Lord at some point in your life. You have strayed far from home. And when you look over your shoulder to see how far you have gone, you tell yourself that it's too late to turn back. You have done too much. Wandered too far. Surely if you went home, God's gates would be firmly shut, barring your reentrance.

But God says, "Even now return to me." Even after all you have done—after all the idols you have pursued, and all the commandments you have broken—come back home. All He requires is your whole heart, brimming with repentance. A heart that has been torn by the remembrance of the depth of your depravity and your deep, deep need for a Savior.

Like Israel, you also are God's treasured possession, His precious child. His gates remain open, anticipating your return.

Lord, truly You are gracious and compassionate, abounding in love. Thank You.

The Shadow of Fear

*When I saw him, I fell at his feet as if I were dead. But he laid
his right hand on me and said, "Don't be afraid! I am the First
and the Last. I am the living one. I died, but look—I am alive
forever and ever! And I hold the keys of death and the grave."*

REVELATION 1:17–18 NLT

Fear can cling to you like a shadow. It is always lurking, following
at your heels. Your daily life may be filled with fears both great and
small—some suppressed and some rising to the surface to churn in your
stomach. You may experience the fear of never belonging, of failure, of
loss, of the unknown, or of death. These can be debilitating, stealing
your joy and hope.

But when John saw the Lord and collapsed at His feet, Jesus placed
His hand on His servant and told him not to fear. For though Jesus
endured the wrath of God and death, He now lives forever and ever.
It's impossible to fathom the breadth of eternity, but Christ will fill it.
And He holds the keys of death and the grave. He has mastered them,
and He promises that neither of them shall take you captive. He has
rescued you.

Although there are many fearful things on this forsaken earth,
remember that nothing can usurp Christ's rightful rule.

In You, Christ, I am safe. You are my King and protector.

The Way of Integrity

Better is the poor who walks in his integrity
than one perverse in his ways, though he be rich.
PROVERBS 28:6 NKJV

You may be tempted to climb to the top of the pecking order—whether it's at work, within a group of friends, or in your community. A pesky voice tells you that you need to push ahead and think of yourself first. It urges you to gain recognition and approval and insists that your worth is dependent on the impact you make in the world. And the more you give in to this voice, the more you will find yourself clinging to the temporal and harming others.

Although trying to get ahead may feel like your basic instinct, it's actually a perversion—a sick twisting—of how God meant for you to live. He prizes integrity above fleeting riches. He desires a humble, selfless, honest lifestyle, one that doesn't seek applause or gain. Those who pursue integrity will receive rewards in heaven—rewards too precious and grand to imagine. And these gifts will be eternal. They will not fade or rust with time—like trophies, fame, promotions, or possessions.

Walking in the way of integrity may lack the sort of sparkle that is so desired here on earth. But on that path are all things worthwhile, lasting, and beautiful.

Lord, give me the strength and courage to
walk in a way that is pleasing to You.

A Choice of Wisdom

Those whom I love I rebuke and discipline.
So be earnest and repent.
REVELATION 3:19 NIV

A child—your child—breaks away from your protective grip and runs out into a busy street. A car screeches to a halt right in front of her, just missing her by several feet.

Your heart stops. It's one of those moments every parent fears. And then all that cherishing and unfathomable love you feel for her comes down on that precious child in the form of a rebuke. She may not think it's a wonderful moment. In fact, she may wail, pout, and stomp, but your correction is necessary.

God loves you even more than you love your own child—imagine!— so you can be assured that if you need discipline of any kind, it will be essential. His Word says that when those times of rebuke come, you should be earnest and repent. The wailing, pouting, and stomping will only prolong your misery, keeping you in harm's way and from living your life with all the victory God intended for you.

The next time you receive discipline from God, embrace that unfathomable love by accepting, with an attitude of remorse and a heart for sincere change, the insight He brings. It will never be a decision full of regret, but a choice of wisdom and a source of future joy!

Spirit, when I've gone astray, give me a sincere
heart for repentance and change. Amen.

A Joy in Faithfulness

A faithful person will be richly blessed.
PROVERBS 28:20 NIV

You are guaranteed the delivery of important documents, but the packet never arrives. Your spouse said, "My darling, I will love you forever," but then five years later you are shocked when served with divorce papers. And what about all those folks who volunteer but rarely show up. All the people who even make solemn vows to the Lord but forget all they declared. Their word comes to mean nothing.

They are the unfaithful ones.

So when loyal and dependable people show up on the scene, they are a breath of fresh air. There is a joy and peace to faithfulness—even a winsomeness. You listen to what those people have to say. When they give you their word, it means something. Those kinds of people are the faithful ones, the ones you want on your side, in your meetings, on your team. As a spouse, a friend, or employer.

God says those faithful people will be blessed. Of course, blessings from God may not mean wealth, but any gift from God is never a disappointment. It will be something you can look forward to with great anticipation.

How can you learn to be faithful in word and deed? Hold fast to the scriptures. Stay near the Lord. And ask for the supernatural ability to be that person of integrity.

Lord, let all the days of my life find me faithful in ways that please You! Amen.

Deep Water

But Jonah ran away from the LORD and headed for Tarshish.
JONAH 1:3 NIV

You are human. You may be caught doing, saying, and thinking things that are utterly ridiculous. Some of those moments are worth chuckling over. Some belong in the grieving category.

But one of the most shamefully ridiculous things you may find yourself doing is trying to run from God. As if you can actually hide from the Creator of the universe—the very Being who created you. Not possible. God is omnipresent—everywhere all the time. Yes, that concept is hard to fathom, but if you believe God's Word, then you must also accept the fact that God is ever around you, no matter where you are or what you are doing or saying or thinking. This truth can be comforting, but it can also be disconcerting if you are doing things you know are contrary to God's will.

When God told Jonah to preach to the people of Nineveh, he refused. Then Jonah decided that fleeing the scene would fix the problem. But it only got Jonah in deep water.

But there's good news. As He did Jonah, God will take you back, restore you, place you just where you need to be. And that will bring you not to a place of fear but to a place of freedom and joy.

Lord, help me know the best place to
run is into Your loving arms. Amen.

One Rotten Apple

Mockers stir up a city, but the wise turn away anger.
PROVERBS 29:8 NIV

Have you ever wondered if one bad apple really can ruin a whole bowl of apples? Wonder no more! It's true! It's because of a gas called ethylene. And so it goes with humans, too—the one bad-apple scenario (not the ethylene emission).

Have you ever known people at work, home, or even church who seem to derive pleasure out of mocking those around them? You know, generally stirring up trouble? You probably know quite a few. They love saying things like, "Did you see the way she snubbed you?" Or "Bless her heart. She is a beautiful woman, but she just doesn't know when to stop eating." Or "I'd help them out in their financial crisis, but I heard they did it to themselves, living too high on the hog."

Yes, those folks may not be full of ethylene, but they are certainly full of gas! And that gas has a putrid smell to it, causing discord, ruining the atmosphere of goodwill, and making peaceful coexistence next to impossible. But a wise woman turns away anger. She'll speak the truth in love but won't stir up trouble for sport.

Lord, please help me be a person of high standards and not full of mocking ridicule and discord. Help me not be the rotten apple in a lovely bowl of Granny Smiths but instead a beautiful delicious one everyone enjoys! Amen.

The Only Way to Live

*Leadership gains authority and respect
when the voiceless poor are treated fairly.*
PROVERBS 29:14 MSG

A man holds a cardboard sign reading NEED CASH at the traffic light. A woman evicted from her home camps out in her car. A huddling cluster of schoolchildren wolf down their cafeteria food, a telltale sign they aren't being fed at home.

These scenarios are only a tiny sampling of the face of poverty in this world. How can you help them all? It seems impossible. And yet the Bible says over and over that you are to watch out for the poor. How do you live? What do you do?

The enemy would like you to try to run here and there frantically trying to help everyone. And after a short time, you would undoubtedly be overcome with exhaustion. You might even give up entirely, which would be Satan's strategy all along.

So, how can you have a good conscience in a poverty-stricken world? Allow the Holy Spirit to guide you every day in knowing who you are to help and those who are to receive help from other generous hearts. It's the only way to live—not by your own wisdom and wits but by abiding in God and living out His perfect plan.

Lord Jesus, give me a compassionate heart for the poor and give me the discernment to know which sojourners I am to help along the path. Amen.

Joy to Your Soul!

The LORD is good, a refuge in times of trouble.
He cares for those who trust in him.
NAHUM 1:7 NIV

The Lord is indeed good and slow to anger, and He is your refuge.

But when you read on about the city of Nineveh in the book of Nahum, you will see that the Lord's patience doesn't last forever when people are bent on living a wicked life. Many parallels to today's world can be seen in these warnings to Nineveh. The sins once considered wrong in society just a few decades ago are now considered acceptable behavior, perhaps even celebrated. Good is now called evil, and evil good.

So how can you live to please the Almighty when all the fallen earth seems once again determined to disobey God's laws? Pray with a humble heart. Listen to the Lord and His still, small voice. Read His Word. Stay in fellowship with Christians who believe the Bible is truly the holy Word of God, not just a book of general guidelines. Come before God with a willingness to say, "I've wronged you, Lord. I'm sorry." And mean it.

The good news is that when you do repent, the Lord is gracious to forgive and put you back in intimate fellowship with Him. Repentance isn't a burden. It will lighten your load and bring joy to your soul!

Jesus, give me a meek heart. Show me my sins, then give me the courage to confess them and receive the peace of Your forgiveness. Amen.

When All the World Falls Apart

*The Sovereign LORD is my strength; he makes my feet like
the feet of a deer, he enables me to tread on the heights.*
HABAKKUK 3:19 NIV

Ever feel like the moment you get one part of your life put together and looking good, another part falls into bits?

That's the bitter effects of living in a fallen world. And the way of all humanity. Yes, some people seem to have an easier time of it than others. Yet if they live long enough, trouble will come. Whether it's a bad report from the doctor, a beloved friendship broken off, a financial crisis, a prodigal child, an unforgiving spouse, a stress-filled work environment, a flooded home, or a betrayal within the church. Trouble seems to hound humanity relentlessly.

But thank God there is hope amid your many trials. In Habakkuk you can see that even though the hour of trouble may come, the Lord is your strength. He will not only lift you up but give you a lightness of spirit. Just like the deer. If you have ever watched a deer leap through the woods, you know that amazing nimbleness, that graceful soaring in action.

And that strength and lightness is what God offers you. Rest in that knowledge. Call on the Lord, knowing His promise is meant not only for the whole world but for you.

*Holy Spirit, dwell in me fully so when trouble comes,
I might know Your strength. Amen.*

Beauty in Truth

"Every word of God is flawless."
PROVERBS 30:5 NIV

You are strolling along a footpath, and just inside the garden gate you spot a rosebush bearing a red rose in full bloom, flawless and fragrant. Perhaps on its petals are a few dewdrops, shimmering in the morning sunlight. Or maybe a hummingbird hovers over it, sipping its nectar. Then the intoxicating aroma of that lovely rose pulls you in closer. Such an exquisite sight—enough to make your heart ache with joy.

The book of Isaiah says, "The grass withers and the flowers fall, but the word of our God endures forever" (40:8). Even though God's creation is glorious, there is even more beauty in His Word, the flawless truth of God's living Word—the Bible. It has power to guide you. To comfort you. To challenge, illuminate, and convict you. To tell you of the mercy and grace of Christ who has the power to set you free for all time.

It's the greatest book ever written, and yet the Word of God goes far beyond mere literature. It's supernatural, living, and ever whispering His truths.

Along the footpath of daily life, this flawless beauty awaits you—if only you will enter the garden.

And listen to His voice.

Holy Spirit, please illuminate my path with the beauty of Your truth and give me the courage to live it out in my daily life. Amen.

The Most Beautiful Gift

"Those who are pure in their own eyes
and yet are not cleansed of their filth."
PROVERBS 30:12 NIV

It's hard to find balance in life. With just the tiniest nugget of anything, one can tip the scales in the other direction.

Such as in the matter of confidence. You should have plenty of confidence in what God can do through you. So much so, that you can go out into the world with hope and courage to make a real difference in His name. Otherwise, without that assurance, you are left in a state of timidity, unable to accomplish what God has called you to do.

Proverbs warns that someone thinking she is a perfect specimen of humanity is displeasing to the Lord. She might think, I'm quite glorious as is, and I don't need any tweaks in my character, thank you very much! This is especially painful to see when that same person—who thinks she is bathed in a pure white light—is really covered in the mire of an unwholesome life.

But humans have been offered the gift of grace through the sacrifice of Christ. A gift to open if one chooses to. That precious hope for all humanity arrived on such a day as this. It's called Christmas.

Lord Jesus, please search my heart. Let me be open to correction.
And give me the supernatural ability to make the necessary
changes in my life on this special day and every day. Amen.

Jesus Will Return

"Shout and be glad, Daughter Zion. For I am coming,
and I will live among you," declares the Lord.
ZECHARIAH 2:10 NIV

If you have grown up in the church, you have heard sermons on the Lord's return. And yet it's easy to fall into complacency concerning this glorious truth. So caught up in the minutiae of everyday strife, you forget that there is an epic battle for your soul raging all around you and that one day Christ will return and put an end to this fierce struggle.

When you are told in Revelation 3:11, "I am coming soon. Hold on to what you have, so that no one will take your crown" (NIV), it is, of course, not referring to anything in the material world but the condition of your spiritual being. The most important question for you to ask yourself is, "Will the Lord find me forgetful of His holy precepts, or will He find me full of His purpose?"

Your heart should cry, "Come, Lord Jesus, come," but your daily walk should be one of godly purpose, passion for sharing His salvation message as well as His return, and a genuine love for others as He has loved you. Then when you meet Him face-to-face, the Lord will say, "Well done, thou good and faithful servant!"

Lord God, help me always be prepared for Your glorious return. Amen.

A Cup of Compassion

"This is what the LORD Almighty said: 'Administer true justice; show mercy and compassion to one another. Do not oppress the widow or the fatherless, the foreigner or the poor. Do not plot evil against each other.'"
ZECHARIAH 7:8–10 NIV

Your kids missed the bus. Again. The dog chewed up your brand-new designer blouse. And your boss yelled at you for something that wasn't your fault. When you finally meet with a friend over a cup of coffee, her hug and listening ear make you burst into tears. Why? Not because it causes you more unhappiness but because your friend has offered you a cup of compassion.

The Bible offers excellent principles on how we are to live and act in this world, such as these verses in Zechariah, in which compassion seems to be the overall theme. Do you offer compassion instead of criticism? Concern instead of uninvited counsel? A listening ear rather than complaint?

Zechariah goes on to say, "But they refused to pay attention; stubbornly they turned their backs and covered their ears" (7:11). These people obviously didn't want to have a heart of compassion, and their defiant and merciless attitude was very displeasing to God.

But the good news is, you can be just the opposite. You can choose kindness and know the joy of being a blessing to others.

Lord, help me offer a cup of compassion to all those in need of it. Amen.

When You Walk into a Room

*"For as churning cream produces butter, and as twisting
the nose produces blood, so stirring up anger produces strife."*
PROVERBS 30:33 NIV

You are at a party. You see someone you know enter from across the room, and deep inside you groan. Why? Because you know what she'll do. She'll stir up trouble. After she picks up a plate of hors d'oeuvres, she'll flit her way around the room, dropping a juicy morsel of gossip here and a bomb of bad news there. A backhanded compliment here and a dainty piece of flirtation—directed at someone else's husband—there. And in her wake there will be nothing left but anger and strife.

What a painful way to go through life for her and for everyone around her.

Jesus, in His Sermon on the Mount, says, "Blessed are the peacemakers, for they will be called children of God" (Matthew 5:9 NIV).

When a woman holds this verse close to her heart and walks into a party, she will get a totally different reaction. People will smile back at her and give her a hug. They will be genuinely glad she's there. Why? Because they know she comes in a spirit of peace and love. How can that be accomplished? By staying in the Lord's presence day by day by day.

*O Lord, help me be that woman who enters a room with
love in her heart and words of peace on her lips. Amen.*

I'm Just One Voice

Speak up for those who cannot speak for themselves.
PROVERBS 31:8 NIV

Knowing when to speak up on someone else's behalf and knowing when to be silent can get pretty complicated, because when it comes to people and their multitude of problems, nothing is ever cookie-cutter easy. When this Proverb was written, advice to a king, the ancient culture was very different from today's, and yet the biblical concept of what is considered good and right is still very much the same. Large numbers of people continue to be poor and powerless—and they still need your help.

There are many examples of what you can do, but one idea might be to vote for those in authority who would be willing to create legislation that supports this scripture. To help people who are vulnerable, needy and powerless, to help themselves.

Sometimes you can feel overwhelmed by all the world's needs. You may ask, "What can I do? I'm just one voice." But with God's help, even that one voice can change the world.

Ask the Lord for direction. Show Him your heart—that you would like to speak up for those who cannot speak for themselves.

Dear God, please guide me today. Tell me what we can do together to fulfill this scripture. Amen.

Who Do You Worship?

Then the angel said to me. . ."These are the true words of God."
At this I fell at his feet to worship him. But he said to me,
"Don't do that! I am a fellow servant with you and with
your brothers and sisters who hold to the testimony of Jesus."
REVELATION 19:9–10 NIV

In this passage from Revelation 19, readers are warned not to worship angels. The moment John falls at the angel's feet in reverent adulation, the heavenly being stops John with a rebuke, telling John that he also is a servant of Christ, and that John is to worship God.

Perhaps you are not at all surprised by the angel's response. True, you may be faithful in church and don't openly worship anyone but God, but do you choose to entertain a private idol or two when you think no one is looking?

Or do you deify "things," such as recognition, money, or time? Do you rush off in the morning, stay at a breakneck speed all day, then drop into a comatose-like sleep on the couch? Perhaps you use the same modus operandi the next day. And the next. And then the weeks and months melt away without your thinking about what really matters. Would that same angel like to have a few words with you about your worship habits?

Lord Jesus, may I always worship You alone,
using all I have and am for Your glory. Amen.

Laugh at the Days to Come

She is clothed with strength and dignity;
she can laugh at the days to come.
PROVERBS 31:25 NIV

The only way a woman can be clothed in strength and dignity and laugh at the future is to know the One who longs to hold her future in His hands.

The Lord is the only One who can provide the Proverbs 31 promises mentioned. He is the only One who deserves your faith. Trusting in the Lord with all your heart is the only right way to live. So what does that kind of passionate faith look like? It turns your wringing hands into praising hands—not because you naturally rise every morning feeling perky and carefree, but because deep down you choose to believe worry is worthless and praise is priceless.

If you trust in God, He will indeed work all things for your good (see Romans 8:28). You can count on it. As a Christian, you should count on it! That kind of trust—which is so very counter to what the world preaches—releases you from a life without hope. And it gives you the freedom to know joy—even amid earthly sorrows.

Lord, please lift my head from the mire of my worries to a greater faith in You. Let me be clothed in strength and dignity, and let me so trust in You so I can laugh at the future. Amen.

Contributors

Emily Biggers is a Tennessee native living in Bedford, Texas. She teaches gifted and talented students in first through fifth grades. She loves to travel, write, spend time with family and friends, and decorate. She is currently in the process of adopting a little girl from Honduras. Emily's devotions appear in the months of May and October.

Bestselling author **Darlene Franklin**'s greatest claim to fame is that she writes full-time from a nursing home. She lives in Oklahoma, near her son and his family, and continues her interests in piano and singing, books, good fellowship, and reality TV in addition to writing. She is an active member of Oklahoma City Christian Fiction Writers, American Christian Fiction Writers, and the Christian Authors Network. She has written more than fifty books and more than 250 devotionals. Her historical fiction ranges from the Revolutionary War to World War II, from Texas to Vermont. You can find Darlene online at www.darlenefranklinwrites.com. Darlene's devotions appear in the month of November.

As an author, speaker, mentor to authors, ghostwriter, editor, and product developer, **Shanna D. Gregor** has served various ministries and publishers for more than twenty years to develop more than eighty books that express God's voice for today. Through her company, Gregor Connections, she offers editorial services and author mentorship and helps others create, write and develop products. She and her husband, Blaine, are empty nesters, enjoying thirty plus years of marriage. Shanna's devotions appear in the months of January and September.

Bestselling and award-winning author **Anita Higman** has more than forty books published. She's been a Barnes & Noble "Author of the Month" for Houston and has a BA in the combined fields of speech communication, psychology, and art. Feel free to drop by Anita's website at www.anitahigman.com or connect with her on her Facebook reader page at www.facebook.com/AuthorAnitaHigman. Anita's devotions appear in the month of December.

Marian Leslie is a writer and freelance editor. She has lived in southwestern Ohio most of her days but has ventured far and wide through the pages of many good books. Marian's devotions appear in the months of April and August.

Donna K. Maltese is a freelance writer, editor, and writing coach. Mother of two grown children and grandmother of a three-year old, she resides in Bucks County, Pennsylvania, with her husband. Donna is active in her local church and is the publicist for a local Mennonite project that works to feed the hungry here and abroad. Feel free to email her at donna@writefullyconfident.com. Donna's devotions appear in the month of March.

Hillary McMullen received an English degree from Sam Houston State University. She has published a variety of works—including a middle-grade novel—and has contributed to several devotional books. Hillary lives in the charming town of Navasota, Texas, with her husband and two cats. Hillary's devotions appear in the month of December.

Karin Dahl Silver lives in Colorado Springs, Colorado, with her husband, Scott. When she is not writing or editing, she loves to hike, bake, and have long talks about art. Karin's devotions appear in the month of June.

An author, speaker, mom, and wife, **Stacey Thureen** desires to help women stay grounded in their faith so that they can find stability on the seesaws of life. Connect with her at www.StaceyThureen.com. Stacey's devotions appear in the month of February.

Amy Trent has lived in beautiful Northern California for fourteen years. She enjoys hiking in the mountains with her husband of twenty-eight years. They have two young adult daughters and a teenaged son. Amy is an RN and is passionate about living a healthy lifestyle. Writing is a new interest for her. Amy's devotions appear in the month of July.

Scripture Index

Bible Reading Plan
Read Thru the Bible in a Year

1-Jan	Gen. 1–2	Matt. 1	Ps. 1
2-Jan	Gen. 3–4	Matt. 2	Ps. 2
3-Jan	Gen. 5–7	Matt. 3	Ps. 3
4-Jan	Gen. 8–10	Matt. 4	Ps. 4
5-Jan	Gen. 11–13	Matt. 5:1–20	Ps. 5
6-Jan	Gen. 14–16	Matt. 5:21–48	Ps. 6
7-Jan	Gen. 17–18	Matt. 6:1–18	Ps. 7
8-Jan	Gen. 19–20	Matt. 6:19–34	Ps. 8
9-Jan	Gen. 21–23	Matt. 7:1–11	Ps. 9:1–8
10-Jan	Gen. 24	Matt. 7:12–29	Ps. 9:9–20
11-Jan	Gen. 25–26	Matt. 8:1–17	Ps. 10:1–11
12-Jan	Gen. 27:1–28:9	Matt. 8:18–34	Ps. 10:12–18
13-Jan	Gen. 28:10–29:35	Matt. 9	Ps. 11
14-Jan	Gen. 30:1–31:21	Matt. 10:1–15	Ps. 12
15-Jan	Gen. 31:22–32:21	Matt. 10:16–36	Ps. 13
16-Jan	Gen. 32:22–34:31	Matt. 10:37–11:6	Ps. 14
17-Jan	Gen. 35–36	Matt. 11:7–24	Ps. 15
18-Jan	Gen. 37–38	Matt. 11:25–30	Ps. 16
19-Jan	Gen. 39–40	Matt. 12:1–29	Ps. 17
20-Jan	Gen. 41	Matt. 12:30–50	Ps. 18:1–15
21-Jan	Gen. 42–43	Matt. 13:1–9	Ps. 18:16–29
22-Jan	Gen. 44–45	Matt. 13:10–23	Ps. 18:30–50
23-Jan	Gen. 46:1–47:26	Matt. 13:24–43	Ps. 19
24-Jan	Gen. 47:27–49:28	Matt. 13:44–58	Ps. 20
25-Jan	Gen. 49:29–Exod. 1:22	Matt. 14	Ps. 21
26-Jan	Exod. 2–3	Matt. 15:1–28	Ps. 22:1–21
27-Jan	Exod. 4:1–5:21	Matt. 15:29–16:12	Ps. 22:22–31
28-Jan	Exod. 5:22–7:24	Matt. 16:13–28	Ps. 23
29-Jan	Exod. 7:25–9:35	Matt. 17:1–9	Ps. 24
30-Jan	Exod. 10–11	Matt. 17:10–27	Ps. 25
31-Jan	Exod. 12	Matt. 18:1–20	Ps. 26
1-Feb	Exod. 13–14	Matt. 18:21–35	Ps. 27
2-Feb	Exod. 15–16	Matt. 19:1–15	Ps. 28
3-Feb	Exod. 17–19	Matt. 19:16–30	Ps. 29
4-Feb	Exod. 20–21	Matt. 20:1–19	Ps. 30
5-Feb	Exod. 22–23	Matt. 20:20–34	Ps. 31:1–8
6-Feb	Exod. 24–25	Matt. 21:1–27	Ps. 31:9–18
7-Feb	Exod. 26–27	Matt. 21:28–46	Ps. 31:19–24
8-Feb	Exod. 28	Matt. 22	Ps. 32
9-Feb	Exod. 29	Matt. 23:1–36	Ps. 33:1–12
10-Feb	Exod. 30–31	Matt. 23:37–24:28	Ps. 33:13–22
11-Feb	Exod. 32–33	Matt. 24:29–51	Ps. 34:1–7
12-Feb	Exod. 34:1–35:29	Matt. 25:1–13	Ps. 34:8–22
13-Feb	Exod. 35:30–37:29	Matt. 25:14–30	Ps. 35:1–8
14-Feb	Exod. 38–39	Matt. 25:31–46	Ps. 35:9–17
15-Feb	Exod. 40	Matt. 26:1–35	Ps. 35:18–28
16-Feb	Lev. 1–3	Matt. 26:36–68	Ps. 36:1–6
17-Feb	Lev. 4:1–5:13	Matt. 26:69–27:26	Ps. 36:7–12
18-Feb	Lev. 5:14–7:21	Matt. 27:27–50	Ps. 37:1–6
19-Feb	Lev. 7:22–8:36	Matt. 27:51–66	Ps. 37:7–26
20-Feb	Lev. 9–10	Matt. 28	Ps. 37:27–40
21-Feb	Lev. 11–12	Mark 1:1–28	Ps. 38
22-Feb	Lev. 13	Mark 1:29–39	Ps. 39
23-Feb	Lev. 14	Mark 1:40–2:12	Ps. 40:1–8
24-Feb	Lev. 15	Mark 2:13–3:35	Ps. 40:9–17

25-Feb	Lev. 16–17	Mark 4:1–20	Ps. 41:1–4
26-Feb	Lev. 18–19	Mark 4:21–41	Ps. 41:5–13
27-Feb	Lev. 20	Mark 5	Ps. 42–43
28-Feb	Lev. 21–22	Mark 6:1–13	Ps. 44
1-Mar	Lev. 23–24	Mark 6:14–29	Ps. 45:1–5
2-Mar	Lev. 25	Mark 6:30–56	Ps. 45:6–12
3-Mar	Lev. 26	Mark 7	Ps. 45:13–17
4-Mar	Lev. 27	Mark 8	Ps. 46
5-Mar	Num. 1–2	Mark 9:1–13	Ps. 47
6-Mar	Num. 3	Mark 9:14–50	Ps. 48:1–8
7-Mar	Num. 4	Mark 10:1–34	Ps. 48:9–14
8-Mar	Num. 5:1–6:21	Mark 10:35–52	Ps. 49:1–9
9-Mar	Num. 6:22–7:47	Mark 11	Ps. 49:10–20
10-Mar	Num. 7:48–8:4	Mark 12:1–27	Ps. 50:1–15
11-Mar	Num. 8:5–9:23	Mark 12:28–44	Ps. 50:16–23
12-Mar	Num. 10–11	Mark 13:1–8	Ps. 51:1–9
13-Mar	Num. 12–13	Mark 13:9–37	Ps. 51:10–19
14-Mar	Num. 14	Mark 14:1–31	Ps. 52
15-Mar	Num. 15	Mark 14:32–72	Ps. 53
16-Mar	Num. 16	Mark 15:1–32	Ps. 54
17-Mar	Num. 17–18	Mark 15:33–47	Ps. 55
18-Mar	Num. 19–20	Mark 16	Ps. 56:1–7
19-Mar	Num. 21:1–22:20	Luke 1:1–25	Ps. 56:8–13
20-Mar	Num. 22:21–23:30	Luke 1:26–56	Ps. 57
21-Mar	Num. 24–25	Luke 1:57–2:20	Ps. 58
22-Mar	Num. 26:1–27:11	Luke 2:21–38	Ps. 59:1–8
23-Mar	Num. 27:12–29:11	Luke 2:39–52	Ps. 59:9–17
24-Mar	Num. 29:12–30:16	Luke 3	Ps. 60:1–5
25-Mar	Num. 31	Luke 4	Ps. 60:6–12
26-Mar	Num. 32–33	Luke 5:1–16	Ps. 61
27-Mar	Num. 34–36	Luke 5:17–32	Ps. 62:1–6
28-Mar	Deut. 1:1–2:25	Luke 5:33–6:11	Ps. 62:7–12
29-Mar	Deut. 2:26–4:14	Luke 6:12–35	Ps. 63:1–5
30-Mar	Deut. 4:15–5:22	Luke 6:36–49	Ps. 63:6–11
31-Mar	Deut. 5:23–7:26	Luke 7:1–17	Ps. 64:1–5
1-Apr	Deut. 8–9	Luke 7:18–35	Ps. 64:6–10
2-Apr	Deut. 10–11	Luke 7:36–8:3	Ps. 65:1–8
3-Apr	Deut. 12–13	Luke 8:4–21	Ps. 65:9–13
4-Apr	Deut. 14:1–16:8	Luke 8:22–39	Ps. 66:1–7
5-Apr	Deut. 16:9–18:22	Luke 8:40–56	Ps. 66:8–15
6-Apr	Deut. 19:1–21:9	Luke 9:1–22	Ps. 66:16–20
7-Apr	Deut. 21:10–23:8	Luke 9:23–42	Ps. 67
8-Apr	Deut. 23:9–25:19	Luke 9:43–62	Ps. 68:1–6
9-Apr	Deut. 26:1–28:14	Luke 10:1–20	Ps. 68:7–14
10-Apr	Deut. 28:15–68	Luke 10:21–37	Ps. 68:15–19
11-Apr	Deut. 29–30	Luke 10:38–11:23	Ps. 68:20–27
12-Apr	Deut. 31:1–32:22	Luke 11:24–36	Ps. 68:28–35
13-Apr	Deut. 32:23–33:29	Luke 11:37–54	Ps. 69:1–9
14-Apr	Deut. 34–Josh. 2	Luke 12:1–15	Ps. 69:10–17
15-Apr	Josh. 3:1–5:12	Luke 12:16–40	Ps. 69:18–28
16-Apr	Josh. 5:13–7:26	Luke 12:41–48	Ps. 69:29–36
17-Apr	Josh. 8–9	Luke 12:49–59	Ps. 70
18-Apr	Josh. 10:1–11:15	Luke 13:1–21	Ps. 71:1–6
19-Apr	Josh. 11:16–13:33	Luke 13:22–35	Ps. 71:7–16
20-Apr	Josh. 14–16	Luke 14:1–15	Ps. 71:17–21
21-Apr	Josh. 17:1–19:16	Luke 14:16–35	Ps. 71:22–24
22-Apr	Josh. 19:17–21:42	Luke 15:1–10	Ps. 72:1–11
23-Apr	Josh. 21:43–22:34	Luke 15:11–32	Ps. 72:12–20
24-Apr	Josh. 23–24	Luke 16:1–18	Ps. 73:1–9
25-Apr	Judg. 1–2	Luke 16:19–17:10	Ps. 73:10–20
26-Apr	Judg. 3–4	Luke 17:11–37	Ps. 73:21–28
27-Apr	Judg. 5:1–6:24	Luke 18:1–17	Ps. 74:1–3

30-Oct	Jer. 45–47	1 Tim. 5:17–6:21	Prov. 14:1–6
31-Oct	Jer. 48:1–49:6	2 Tim. 1	Prov. 14:7–22
1-Nov	Jer. 49:7–50:16	2 Tim. 2	Prov. 14:23–27
2-Nov	Jer. 50:17–51:14	2 Tim. 3	Prov. 14:28–35
3-Nov	Jer. 51:15–64	2 Tim. 4	Prov. 15:1–9
4-Nov	Jer. 52–Lam. 1	Titus 1:1–9	Prov. 15:10–17
5-Nov	Lam. 2:1–3:38	Titus 1:10–2:15	Prov. 15:18–26
6-Nov	Lam. 3:39–5:22	Titus 3	Prov. 15:27–33
7-Nov	Ezek. 1:1–3:21	Philemon 1	Prov. 16:1–9
8-Nov	Ezek. 3:22–5:17	Heb. 1:1–2:4	Prov. 16:10–21
9-Nov	Ezek. 6–7	Heb. 2:5–18	Prov. 16:22–33
10-Nov	Ezek. 8–10	Heb. 3:1–4:3	Prov. 17:1–5
11-Nov	Ezek. 11–12	Heb. 4:4–5:10	Prov. 17:6–12
12-Nov	Ezek. 13–14	Heb. 5:11–6:20	Prov. 17:13–22
13-Nov	Ezek. 15:1–16:43	Heb. 7:1–28	Prov. 17:23–28
14-Nov	Ezek. 16:44–17:24	Heb. 8:1–9:10	Prov. 18:1–7
15-Nov	Ezek. 18–19	Heb. 9:11–28	Prov. 18:8–17
16-Nov	Ezek. 20	Heb. 10:1–25	Prov. 18:18–24
17-Nov	Ezek. 21–22	Heb. 10:26–39	Prov. 19:1–8
18-Nov	Ezek. 23	Heb. 11:1–31	Prov. 19:9–14
19-Nov	Ezek. 24–26	Heb. 11:32–40	Prov. 19:15–21
20-Nov	Ezek. 27–28	Heb. 12:1–13	Prov. 19:22–29
21-Nov	Ezek. 29–30	Heb. 12:14–29	Prov. 20:1–18
22-Nov	Ezek. 31–32	Heb. 13	Prov. 20:19–24
23-Nov	Ezek. 33:1–34:10	James 1	Prov. 20:25–30
24-Nov	Ezek. 34:11–36:15	James 2	Prov. 21:1–8
25-Nov	Ezek. 36:16–37:28	James 3	Prov. 21:9–18
26-Nov	Ezek. 38–39	James 4:1–5:6	Prov. 21:19–24
27-Nov	Ezek. 40	James 5:7–20	Prov. 21:25–31
28-Nov	Ezek. 41:1–43:12	1 Pet. 1:1–12	Prov. 22:1–9
29-Nov	Ezek. 43:13–44:31	1 Pet. 1:13–2:3	Prov. 22:10–23
30-Nov	Ezek. 45–46	1 Pet. 2:4–17	Prov. 22:24–29
1-Dec	Ezek. 47–48	1 Pet. 2:18–3:7	Prov. 23:1–9
2-Dec	Dan. 1:1–2:23	1 Pet. 3:8–4:19	Prov. 23:10–16
3-Dec	Dan. 2:24–3:30	1 Pet. 5	Prov. 23:17–25
4-Dec	Dan. 4	2 Pet. 1	Prov. 23:26–35
5-Dec	Dan. 5	2 Pet. 2	Prov. 24:1–18
6-Dec	Dan. 6:1–7:14	2 Pet. 3	Prov. 24:19–27
7-Dec	Dan. 7:15–8:27	1 John 1:1–2:17	Prov. 24:28–34
8-Dec	Dan. 9–10	1 John 2:18–29	Prov. 25:1–12
9-Dec	Dan. 11–12	1 John 3:1–12	Prov. 25:13–17
10-Dec	Hos. 1–3	1 John 3:13–4:16	Prov. 25:18–28
11-Dec	Hos. 4–6	1 John 4:17–5:21	Prov. 26:1–16
12-Dec	Hos. 7–10	2 John	Prov. 26:17–21
13-Dec	Hos. 11–14	3 John	Prov. 26:22–27:9
14-Dec	Joel 1:1–2:17	Jude	Prov. 27:10–17
15-Dec	Joel 2:18–3:21	Rev. 1:1–2:11	Prov. 27:18–27
16-Dec	Amos 1:1–4:5	Rev. 2:12–29	Prov. 28:1–8
17-Dec	Amos 4:6–6:14	Rev. 3	Prov. 28:9–16
18-Dec	Amos 7–9	Rev. 4:1–5:5	Prov. 28:17–24
19-Dec	Obad.–Jonah	Rev. 5:6–14	Prov. 28:25–28
20-Dec	Mic. 1:1–4:5	Rev. 6:1–7:8	Prov. 29:1–8
21-Dec	Mic. 4:6–7:20	Rev. 7:9–8:13	Prov. 29:9–14
22-Dec	Nah. 1–3	Rev. 9–10	Prov. 29:15–23
23-Dec	Hab. 1–3	Rev. 11	Prov. 29:24–27
24-Dec	Zeph. 1–3	Rev. 12	Prov. 30:1–6
25-Dec	Hag. 1–2	Rev. 13:1–14:13	Prov. 30:7–16
26-Dec	Zech. 1–4	Rev. 14:14–16:3	Prov. 30:17–20
27-Dec	Zech. 5–8	Rev. 16:4–21	Prov. 30:21–28
28-Dec	Zech. 9–11	Rev. 17:1–18:8	Prov. 30:29–33
29-Dec	Zech. 12–14	Rev. 18:9–24	Prov. 31:1–9
30-Dec	Mal. 1–2	Rev. 19–20	Prov. 31:10–17
31-Dec	Mal. 3–4	Rev. 21–22	Prov. 31:18–31

SPECIAL EDITIONS OF THE BIBLE PROMISE BOOK®
FOR EVERYDAY ENCOURAGEMENT

The Bible Promise Book® for the Overwhelmed Heart

In *The Bible Promise Book® for the Overwhelmed Heart* edition, you'll find dozens of timely topics—including Comfort, Faith, Trust, God's Love, Grace, and dozens more—you'll encounter hundreds of verses from God's Word guaranteed to speak to your daily needs. *The Bible Promise Book® for the Overwhelmed Heart* is ideal for personal use and for ministries.

DiCarta / 978-1-63409-223-4 / $15.99

The Bible Promise Book® for Women

A beautiful gift edition for women features more than 60 relevant topics—including Adversity, Duty, Friendship, Modesty, Protection, Sincerity, Strength, and Zeal—you'll find nearly 1,000 total verses included. Each topic includes a brief introductory comment to put the verses into a 21st-century context. Handsomely designed and packaged, *The Bible Promise Book® for Women* makes an ideal gift for any occasion.

DiCarta / 978-1-61626-358-4 / $9.99